The
Education of
Harriet Hatfield

Books by May Sarton

POETRY

Encounter in April
Inner Landscape
The Lion and the Rose
The Land of Silence
In Time Like Air
Cloud, Stone, Sun, Vine
A Private Mythology
As Does New Hampshire
A Grain of Mustard Seed
A Durable Fire
Collected Poems, 1930–1973
Selected Poems of May Sarton
(edited by Serena Sue Hilsinger and Lois Brynes)
Halfway to Silence
Letters from Maine
The Silence Now

NOVELS

The Single Hound
The Bridge of Years
Shadow of a Man
A Shower of Summer Days
Faithful Are the Wounds
The Birth of a Grandfather
The Fur Person
The Small Room
Joanna and Ulysses
Mrs. Stevens Hears the Mermaids Singing
Miss Pickthorn and Mr. Hare
The Poet and the Donkey
Kinds of Love

As We Are Now
Crucial Conversations
A Reckoning
Anger
The Magnificent Spinster

NONFICTION

I Knew a Phoenix
Plant Dreaming Deep
Journal of a Solitude
A World of Light
The House by the Sea
Recovering: A Journal
At Seventy: A Journal
Writings on Writing
May Sarton—A Self-Portrait
After the Stroke

FOR CHILDREN

Punch's Secret
A Walk Through the Woods

The
Education of
Harriet Hatfield

A novel by
MAY SARTON

W · W · NORTON & COMPANY
New York   London

The text of this book is composed in Gael, with display type set in Baskerville.
Composition and manufacturing by The Haddon Craftsmen, Inc.

First Edition

Library of Congress Cataloging-in-Publication Data
Sarton, May, 1912-
The education of Harriet Hatfield: a novel / by May Sarton.—
1st ed.
p. cm.
I. Title.
PS3537.A832E38 1989
813'.52—dc19   88–38042

ISBN 0-393-02695-7

W. W. Norton & Company, Inc., 500 Fifth Avenue, New York, N. Y. 10110
W. W. Norton & Company Ltd., 37 Great Russell Street, London WC1B 3NU

1 2 3 4 5 6 7 8 9 0

The
Education of
Harriet Hatfield

1

How rarely is it possible for anyone to begin a new life at sixty! When Vicky died our friends took it for granted that I would simply go on living, gardening, and reading for pleasure in our house; that I would go on unchanged by her death, as though I were not recovering from an earthquake, and persuaded that I must recreate a self I can live with for the rest of my life. Vicky had always been a power, and I suppose until now I was simply an adjunct to that power, doing volunteer work to keep busy, and managing the household for her. We were closely united, I see now, partly because I accepted early on that she had to be in control and so did everything I could to follow her lead.

I have been living since her death in a strange empty silence, wondering who I am now, and perhaps also who I was while she lived. In some ways it was rather like living with a thunderstorm, you see. Is a good marriage always founded on one of the partners willingly abdicating for the sake of peace?

I loved Vicky because she was such a fountain of energy and conviction, such a giver to life in her profession as editor and owner of a small publishing house, and, frankly, so devoted to me that I was carried along on her tides. We had a truly happy life together for thirty years. Who could ask for more?

But now that I have inherited money (she left me comfortably off) and a huge space around me and inside me, the question is what shall I do with them? I even thought of joining the Peace Corps; more than one woman my age has done so. But I knew really that the Peace Corps did not fit my needs or capacities and would be a temporary escape. So, what then?

It came to me one night that it had to be something useful, needed, and close to home, something I could invest in and make grow, something I could control for a change. That night I began to dream of a women's bookstore, a bookstore which would be not only a place for buying books, but a meeting place, a welcoming refuge where people could browse and talk. Maybe there could be a fireplace and a table with comfortable chairs around it. As soon as I began to imagine this I realized it was exactly what I must do and I did not sleep a wink, my head was so absorbed in thinking and planning.

I had to laugh at myself for thinking I could embark on such a venture with no business experience whatever, but it felt like an instinct as powerful as a cow's instinct to eat grass. That is what made me laugh, the certainty that I was at the same time a little crazy, no doubt, and absolutely right that this was the adventure for me, godsent, in fact. Hatfield House: A Bookstore for Women was the name that came to me at dawn.

More than once in our peregrinations, Vicky and I had stopped in at this sort of bookstore. There is one in Andover, for instance. Vicky liked to drop in at bookstores and talk with the owners. "You have to keep your hand on the pulse of what people want," she often said. And of course the small bookstores were the great support of the sort of thing she published. "I can talk them into taking things they would never have thought of," she also said. And I, tagging along, was amused to see what effect she did have. A stout woman as she grew older, she had, I suppose, what is called "presence," a flashing blue eye, a hearty laugh, a vivid sense of who she was, and if no one there knew it, they soon would.

"Victoria Chilton," she would announce and wait for an appropriate response. If none was forthcoming, for sometimes she had addressed a young part-time person, she would add, "May I speak to the owner, please?"

"Where is *Fairfield?*" she would ask, having glanced around the new-books table and not found her last success.

"We had it, we had it, Miss Chilton," the owner might say, "but it's sold out."

"You mean you ordered two copies and they have sold?" She was laughing by then at herself as well as at the unfortunate owner of the bookstore. Vicky was aggressive, I have to admit, but not in a mean-spirited way. People liked her. "No reason why you should order more but people are crazy about English houses these days and this is really a remarkable evocation of what country house life was like fifty years ago. I'll make a deal with you. Take twenty more and if they don't sell we'll take them back."

And by then I had been introduced, we were drinking coffee, and it was all quite friendly and cozy.

The trouble is that evoking Vicky is dangerous for me because even six months after her death, it brings on a wave of acute loneliness. And at the same time, a wave of self-doubt. I am still the prisoner of the past, still overshadowed by my powerful and loving friend. Shall I ever discover who I am alone? And feel free to be that hidden person, whoever she may be?

The middle one in a family of three children, two boys and me, I have had to learn to be most of my life what other people expected of me. My brothers are awful teases and I learned early on to hide whatever was precious to me so it would not be laughed at. Vicky, on the other hand, an only child brought up

11

like a boy, never doubted that what she most wanted she could have, and went about happily seeing that she got it. Her parents adored her, showing only faint surprise that they had produced such a determined character, and by their standards at least, such a maverick. So she decided against anything as usual as Barnard or Radcliffe and instead enrolled in the Sorbonne and spent two years in Paris. She made her way into the publishing business first as an adviser on foreign books to a university press, translated *avant-garde* works from the French, and had made a niche for herself in literary circles before she was thirty. We met at an Alliance Française luncheon in Boston where she introduced a French poet. I remember envying her evident enjoyment of being herself and doing what she did so well, but I was a little put off by her laugh that day. It did not occur to me that she had noticed me and when she came over to introduce herself and invited me to dinner that night at her parents' house in Chestnut Hill, I was amazed.

"You don't even know my name," I remember saying.

"No, but I like your face."

"My name is Harriet Hatfield."

"Please come to dinner, Harriet Hatfield."

Oh dear me, how long ago that was! Thirty years.

The trouble with overpowering people is that they tend to take over. I am a rather shy and private person and at first Vicky's pursuit of me was alarming. I was not ready to enter into any such relationship. I had, I suppose, always been drawn to women rather than men but I had never even imagined what Henry James called a Boston Marriage. At twenty I had been in love once with a young man when I was a student at Smith but by the time we graduated I had come to see that I was not deeply in love, only dazzled, and I did not see myself as a doctor's wife. I am really a rather selfish person and at that time as intact as a clam in a shell. I had a stopgap job at the Museum of

Fine Arts in the order department of their shop, took a course or two there in history of art and watercolor painting, but I had no illusions about my gifts. Marriage was what I thought I wanted and there were various young men who "liked my face" as Vicky had said she did, and took me out to dinner. My brothers introduced me to their friends always hoping, and then teased me unmercifully because I did not fall in love.

"Harriet is immune," Fred used to say.

By then he was married, which did not help. Only Andrew, the youngest, took my side. And my dear father, who sometimes intervened with a twinkle in his eye, said more than once that he liked me just the way I was and did not look forward to the day when I might leave home.

Meanwhile Victoria Chilton had erupted like a volcano on the domestic scene, making me feel more uncomfortable than I had been before, more on the defensive, more vulnerable than ever to family pressures. At the same time I was experiencing a strong undertow of feeling, and quite unable to see my way, in fact terrified of drowning. It was a year of battling Victoria, myself, and my family; a painful year which I would rather forget. But of course in the end she won and carried me off to Venice and the Italian Alps where I had never been.

How strange life is! With all the talk and analysis that goes on these days it astonishes me to think how little we talked about ourselves, how much we simply took for granted, for we were deeply in love. What we did was make plans, to find a house somewhere near Boston where Vicky could embark on publishing, for she knew exactly what she wanted to do, of course. She said things like, "You'll cook and I'll garden," and sometimes I laughed at her because she seemed so sure about everything.

"What if I don't want to cook?"

"Then you won't, that's all. We'll hire someone."

We were having a picnic in an olive grove, I remember, and it seemed to me that we were making a map of a new world, ours, and I knew I was committed to it. It was an extraordinary elation and sense of adventure that possessed me, and also, looking out over that peaceful landscape and its eternal images of olives and white oxen plowing in the distance, a sense of safety as though I had arrived at my destination after a long journey.

We are like the philopena in a double almond, I thought.

And now I have the same feeling, that Hatfield House will be the second great adventure for me, and that again I am arriving at my destination after the long journey through grief. And I am ready for whatever comes.

2

Today I have found the right place, I think, after weeks of searching first in Brookline, then in Wellesley, then in Somerville . . . looking for the right neighborhood as well as a house I can afford. I am sure I want to be in a neighborhood of diverse kinds of people but they must be readers, after all. I had been looking for a Victorian house, if possible with a mansard roof, large enough for at least two rooms for the bookshop and where I could myself live upstairs. Everything that seemed possible was too expensive, or so said my lawyer, Jonathan Fremont, an old Bostonian WASP who is Vicky's executor and perhaps fears I may squander my inheritance. "You will lose money on this venture for some years before you can establish yourself, so you must be wary, Miss Hatfield."

Nevertheless, all caution to the winds, I knew when I saw the house in Somerville that this was it. Many academic people taking refuge from Cambridge prices have settled there recently and there is as well a large "working" community of what Vicky called "ordinary people": black, white, and Puerto Rican, Italian, Irish—a good mixture. When I saw the house I knew I had found the right nest. Downstairs there are three large rooms and a kitchen which I shall close off and use as a storeroom eventually. Upstairs, two big rooms plus a delightful old-fashioned bathroom with a copper tub in it, and a back room I shall convert into a small kitchen. There is a small barn where I can garage my car. What persuaded me was an atmosphere, a kind of distinction and charm that reached me at once, even though the place is rather run-down, needs paint and a lot of bringing back from years of neglect. In the front room there is a fireplace, I am glad to say, and that will be the center of the shop, with a round table perhaps and three or four comfortable chairs around it where customers can sit and browse.

I have been writing this late at night because I am too excited to sleep. I suppose I am a crazy old woman, but what fun it is to be free to be just that!

Fred, my older brother, who has now retired, has been unexpectedly quite a help. He volunteered to come and see the house, thought it a good investment much to my astonishment, and persuaded Mr. Fremont, who seems to regard me as some kind of incompetent old woman, that we should buy quickly. Somerville is changing rapidly, and all its real estate values are rising as a result of the influx of academic people.

"But is the business itself a good investment?" Mr. Fremont asked, his nose trembling slightly like a rabbit's, his right hand twiddling his watch chain.

"Of course not," Fred said. Oh how delighted I was! "Harriet is not going into this for money, but as a public service, what? And," he said pointedly, "surely Miss Chilton must have had some idea how her fortune would be spent, not on first-class round-the-world trips on the QE II, for instance!"

"I wonder what she did envisage," John Fremont murmured. "She was such a definite woman herself."

"Vicky never felt more at home than in a bookstore, you

know," I ventured, "and actually our library will be an asset as I start building up an inventory . . . if that is the word."

"You are not intending to sell the library?" Mr. Fremont was acutely upset and red in the face.

"Oh not the important first editions, not the books we loved, but there might be five thousand or more accumulated over the years and all in good condition."

"I can see that you have very clear ideas about all this," Mr. Fremont admitted grudgingly, "but you have no business experience, after all."

"I intend to hire an accountant, a business manager, whatever it is called."

"Very good, but you can expect, from what I hear, to lose money for at least five years."

"Where did you hear that?" Fred asked.

"I have made it my business to look into things."

At this I glanced over at Fred, who had taken out his pipe and was busy filling it. "It's going to take months to get work done in the house and it's my intention to make a survey of women's bookstores in various cities, talk to the managers, get some idea what the special problems and assets are. Do that while workmen are busy . . ."

"It's to be a women's bookstore, is it?"

"Yes."

It was Fred who had asked the question, puffing a cloud of delicious sweet hay smell from his pipe, but I sensed at once a certain chill in the air emanating from both these men.

"What in hell is a women's bookstore? Books have no gender, do they?"

"Oh Fred," I winced, remembering all the times he had put me down when I wanted to ride a boy's bicycle, when I played Hamlet in a school production—always, it seemed, when I wanted to do something women were not supposed to do. He is

17

five years older than I and his power always has been in his ability to make me feel ridiculous in some way. But at the same instant I realized with a sense of triumph that I had gone beyond his ironies now because I had money. I had real power to do what I wanted to do, regardless of what anyone might say.

And I plunged in forcefully. "The women's bookstores are the equivalent these days of men's clubs, I suppose. Places where women can talk to each other, find sustenance, and come to some idea of who they really are."

"And complain about how insensitive and brutal men like your brother are, I presume." Fred blew out a cloud of smoke.

There they were, already, I thought, two men who have no idea what I am up to and already resent whatever it may be. "Sorry, but my mind is made up. I know what I want to do and I am going to do it."

"Thanks to Victoria's money," said Mr. Fremont.

"Let me tell you something, Mr. Fremont. For thirty years I helped Vicky run her business. I kept the household going. I made the garden. I ran her errands. I considered myself, and I was, an active helpmeet. I have earned that money, and Vicky, I feel sure, would be the first to back this adventure of the bookstore."

"Are you so sure?" Fred asked, putting on now that familiar mask of knowing it all. "I did not get the impression that Vicky was a feminist."

That was, and he knew it, a body blow, for Vicky had been rather violently antifeminist. Like many powerful women with successful careers she was apt to identify with men rather than women and felt a little superior, perhaps, to women. "Any woman who proves that she can do successfully what men do, in her case running a publishing house, is by her action rather than her belief, a feminist." It was said vehemently out of my own convictions, but once said, I saw the humor of it, and laughed.

18

"No feminist she, but don't you see she taught me to be one by being what she was?"

"My little sister is growing up," Fred said then.

"Yes, Fred, she is," and I looked him straight in the eye.

"It is going to be an interesting experiment, Harriet, and I wish you well, wish you what your heart desires."

That was my first confrontation about the bookstore. And I felt that I had won, won at least my own self-respect. How long would it be before I could put my dream to the test?

It soon became clear to me that I am not a practical person, so at times in the next year I was in a state of panic because of a whole lot of business affairs that had to be concluded. Here I have to admit that Mr. Fremont was a helpful watchdog. The hardest thing was breaking up our house, selling furniture, for instance. But I kept Vicky's big desk for myself, a kind of anchor for me in the bookstore part of the house, and was able to furnish my apartment upstairs very comfortably.

Angelica Lamb stepped in with an excellent suggestion of a young architect to draw up plans for the bookstore. Most of our friends were supportive even though most of them had no real sympathy with what I wanted to do. Angelica really behaved like a sister and without insisting made several other good suggestions. One was to draw people in with something other than books—cheese and wine, for instance. But I disagreed with her on that. I felt sure that once the shop existed and could be seen it would draw women in little by little. I also balked at her idea that I might have poetry readings, for I am not very interested in poetry. Vicky was, and I always felt ashamed that I just could not react as she did. In college at Smith I had majored in history and I had been fascinated for years by all that was coming out about "herstory," how much had been buried about women's lives in the past and was now being discovered.

Slowly my rather vague ideas were coming into focus. There

must be a table or set of shelves devoted to what has become a kind of canon in the women's study programs. There must be a large selection of paperbacks, of course.

But even Angelica raised doubts about the emphasis on women. "Why does it have to be limited at all? A good bookstore should be open to all literature," she felt.

But here I was adamant. In the women's bookstores I visited in Philadelphia, Washington, and New York I always had the sense not of limitation but of a door that had been opened and always I saw a great variety of customers.

I suppose the hardest day was when Vicky's and my house in Chestnut Hill was emptied. It had sold for a very handsome price but I had not somehow faced the actual uprooting and every time a piece of furniture was carted off, I felt a sharp pang, as though it had become a piece of my own flesh. Then there was the garden. There would be no garden in the new house, no seed catalogs and plant catalogs; only book catalogs would come to me from now on. Would the new owners care for the garden? the tree peonies? the old-fashioned roses?

"Oh Angelica," I cried out, "what am I doing?"

"You simply must close it off," she said, "you can't look back now. You can't afford to, Harriet." And she had dragged me off at five for a drink and supper at her house where I would find dear old Patapouf, our ancient Labrador retriever, waiting for me. Angelica had offered to take her in until I could have her back. And I hugged her and sat down beside her for she was really all that was left of my life with Vicky now. Patapouf licked my face and licked off the tears.

When we had settled down with a drink, Angelica looked across at me and raised her glass, "To the *vita nuova,*" she said, "and a brave woman."

"Not brave, just driven," I said, taking a good gulp of scotch.

"I see that, and I sometimes wonder what it is that drives you.

You have chosen not to mourn. You have given yourself no time for that."

This surprised me. Had I not mourned? I had to admit to myself that there was some truth in her remark. "I don't know. I guess I have been fighting for a life of my own. I know it sounds odd, but really for years I have been living Vicky's life."

"You seemed an exemplary couple, you know. I often envied you." Angelica had not married, was involved in innumerable charities and good works, and took off on long travels until very recently. She was now over seventy, and although she often said she did not feel her age, I had noticed and so had Vicky that she was no longer embarking on journeys to Tibet or Timbuktu.

"I loved Vicky, you know, and when one loves someone living their life does not feel limiting. I enjoyed Vicky's powerful life and all that it drew into the house. But when she died, Angelica—this will shock you—I did not feel extreme grief."

"Weren't you lonely? Didn't you feel cut in two?"

"Don't laugh at me, but I think I felt very much as I did when I graduated from Smith, lots of woe at the loss of all that those four years had held and which was gone forever, but also a wild excitement. Now I can begin to live!"

"It is rather odd," Angelica granted. Her large pale gray eyes opened wide. She had never been a beauty but her unwavering eyes made her rather plain face arresting. "I miss Vicky. She was such a life-giver. When she walked into a room the atmosphere became electric at once."

"She took over."

"Yes, I suppose she did." And she got up. "I must see what Alice is up to in the kitchen. Excuse me for a moment."

For the rest of the evening we talked about the bookstore. Angelica was looking around for someone who could help me with the business side.

"An efficient mouse is what I need."

"One who will not take you over?"

"Exactly. One who does not displace very much atmosphere."

"Joan Hampstead might do . . ."

"And who is that?"

"Oh, someone I have been on a committee with, the committee for the library, actually. She is a divorcée, needs a job, I think, and most important you would feel at ease with her. A very intelligent mouse."

And that is exactly what she turned out to be.

But after dinner I was suddenly exhausted and got a taxi to take me to the hotel where I was stowed until I could move into the new place. There I lay in bed, unable to sleep for hours. I missed Patapouf's warmth beside me though she had become awfully heavy to lift onto the bed. And I wondered in a kind of anguish how I was going to manage this new life, what a lot I still had to prove to myself and the skeptical Mr. Fremont.

3

After all the frustrations and exhilarations of getting ready I sent out invitations to the opening of Hatfield House in early September for September tenth from three to six. Of course my list had had to be chiefly mutual friends of mine and Victoria's, for whom else did I know? But I had posters stuck up at the Coop and a few other bookstores or shops that would accept one. Joan Hampstead was invaluable in helping do this as I was too shy to ask for myself.

By now we had established an easygoing working relationship and had some good laughs as we unpacked boxes and boxes and filled and arranged the shelves.

"Should I shelve M. F. K. Fisher with cooking, women, or lit.?" Joan asked, and we pondered and agreed that she really included too much else to be placed with Julia Child, the queen of the cooking shelf. I did succeed in my idea of a table filled with the classics of the feminist movement and a dazzling table of art books, biographies, and the newest poetry in Vicky's honor. This table would be referred to as "Harriet's Choice."

I decided on champagne as the easiest and most festive drink, with orange juice in reserve for nondrinkers. Angelica insisted on having a huge cake catered for me, and that meant plates which we dashed out to get, paper napkins, of course, and plastic forks. Since the new owners of the house had not moved in I plundered the garden of chrysanthemums and asters, a glorious bunch in the middle of the round table in front of the fireplace. It was, as I had dreamed, surrounded by four small round leather armchairs where people could sit and read comfortably. I had placed my desk at the back where I could see what was going on but not obtrusively, and at half-past two I am saying a little prayer to Sylvia Beach, my heroine among women booksellers, to hover over us and give us her blessing. But when at three no one has showed, I begin to feel horribly nervous.

"What if no one comes, Joan?"

Patapouf, lying under my desk, gives a growl. No doubt she is dreaming. I had imagined that she would help put people at their ease, be the welcomer, waving her great black plume of a tail, but what if she thinks I am being invaded by hostile strangers? For the moment every single thing so carefully prepared seems to be in peril.

But at this moment a chauffeured limousine stops at the door and, of all people I dread to see, Vivyan Powers emerges and walks in and shakes my hand and turns to Joan, whom I quickly introduce. She is dressed, I note with some surprise, in expensive stone-washed jeans and jacket and purple Reeboks.

"I didn't know how to dress," she announces. "After all, what in hell is a women's bookstore about? What are you up to, Harriet? You look awfully tame in that old tweed suit, I must say."

"Did you expect a clown of some sort?"

But Vivyan is already wandering around, picking up Adrienne Rich and laying her down like a hot cake. "Am I the first victim?" she asks.

"The first customer so far."

Patapouf now emerges and goes right over to Vivyan and smells her shoes. "So you're still alive," she says, bending down to pat her huge black head.

"Champagne?" Joan brings a glass on a tray.

"Never say no," Vivyan says, and then, "You must join me so we can have a toast."

I do not intend to drink so early in the day and am relieved to see two old friends, Professor and Mrs. House, looking in the windows. "Welcome, friends!"

Helen comes in the door first and gives me a hug. "It's so exciting," she says, and Harold follows and kisses me on the cheek.

"What an achievement!" he says after I introduce them to Joan and Vivyan. "You really are an amazing woman to have managed all this in less than a year!"

"We've worked like dogs," I say, including Joan.

"Mr. House is brave to dare enter this sanctuary," Vivyan says.

"Really? But I am much too curious to be held at bay," he answers, laughing his short bark of a laugh. "Who knows? I might get converted."

It is really a thrill when at last three young women in very long skirts, peasant blouses, and high boots troop in shyly. "We saw the sign," one says, "in the Coop."

"Oh, look at the biography," another goes right to the table. "It's a treasure house! Masson . . . I've looked and looked for that. De Beauvoir . . . I was told it was out of print."

My head is beginning to hum with pleasure and relief. This is the scene I have dreamed of for so many months. Champagne is passed just as Angelica appears bearing the fabulous cake and lays it on the table.

25

"You'll have to cut it, Harold, I'm much too nervous!" and then I hug Angelica. Now she is here all will be well. "Without Angelica," I announce, "none of this would have been possible."

"Nonsense!" she says.

Quite a buzz of people have arrived, last an elderly woman who looks a little lost for a moment, then stands at the table marked "Harriet's Choice" and becomes absorbed in the books. She shakes her head. "Never knew all this existed!"

"I'm Harriet Hatfield," I say, going over to her, "please feel welcome."

"Oh, so you are the owner," she says, giving me a penetrating glance behind rather thick glasses. "Well, I'm Sue Bagley. I live right around the corner and I expect you'll see a lot of me." She smiles at me with what seems like delight. "What fun I shall have. What a lot I shall learn."

Harold, who has cut the cake, now proposes a toast, "To Harriet and Hatfield House—may they flourish!"

And quickly I get a glass of champagne for Sue—what is her name?

At four or so my brother Fred, with Andrew in tow, turns up and I am happy that they have to make their way through a crowd to reach me, sitting on my desk in absorbed conversation with two middle-aged nuns in mufti, the small cross at each throat the only sign of their way of life. It is the first real conversation I have had so far and I hate to be interrupted. We are discussing the recently published collected *Flannery O'Connor.* They tell me they are Sisters of Loretto. I feel at home with them right away, the dark one with hair pulled back in a pony tail and very bright dark eyes and the other, a little older, in a simple dark blue jumper and open shirt—a face crisscrossed with lines but full of character.

"Damn," I murmur to them, "these are my brothers," and

then, "Hello, Fred. Hi, Andrew. I didn't expect to see you here."

"It's clear you don't need help," Fred says. "We imagined we might fill vacant space."

"It's a subway crowd. How can I get to the champagne?" Andrew asks. "I must say you're doing very well."

"We haven't sold a book yet."

At this point Joan emerges looking flustered. "We've forgotten to have the guest book signed," she whispers. It had been her idea that a guest book would be one way to build up a mailing list.

"Oh dear. What a dunce I am!"

The older sister offers to mind the book and carry it around for signatures and addresses. How amazing, already I have new friends who offer to help!

Fred comes back with a glass in his hand and offers it to me, but I don't dare and so he lifts it to me and drinks it as we talk. "Andrew is impressed," he says. "He came to laugh, I suspect, and is staying in a rather different state of mind. See, he's over there apparently deep in a study of your shelves."

And so he is, I can see, tall Andrew towering over the crowd. "I wonder what he thinks he will find."

"Gunpowder." This brings on the giggles and suddenly we are both laughing. Fred's voice evidently wakes Patapouf for she emerges from under the desk, wagging her tail furiously. "Pretty noisy here for an old dog," he says, bending down to rub her back and head. "Who are all these people anyway? The only ones I know are Angelica and Vivyan. Of all people, what is she doing here in blue jeans, for God's sake!"

"Showing off in her own inimitable way, I suspect." I look around. There really are quite an assortment of people of all ages milling about, some with books in their hands. I see a stunning young black woman just coming in with a green bag over her shoulder. Harvard, no doubt. "Who are they? I haven't any idea. That is what is so exciting."

Joan is now sitting at the cash register on the high stool our architect had provided behind a high counter, so whoever sits there can see what is going on, though I objected to a mirror behind it that would show up a thief. She is busily making out invoices and a small line of people with books in their hands is forming. The head of the line holds a heavy pile of art books, Georgia O'Keeffe among them, in the new paperback. She is very thin and dressed in black leotards with a long tunic over them, an intriguing silhouette, though I cannot see her face or guess her age.

Four women have taken over the armchairs round the table and are immersed in books, the cake plates piling up around them, I see, and go over quickly, abandoning Fred, to make some order. Andrew kindly helps me take a tray to the tiny kitchen.

"Hey, you can open another bottle of champagne," I tell him, "as long as you're being useful."

For a few seconds we are alone and hidden from the throng. He is smiling at me and I know making up some joke or thrust. "All I can think of is a salt lick for deer. You are obviously providing something the deer need," and at that I can't help laughing.

"So far the deer seem rather tame, I must say."

By five, Angelica, Vivyan, and the Houses have left, Fred and Andrew too, and the complexion of the party is beginning to change.

"I got forty names and addresses for you," the elder sister says, handing over the book. "What fun!" And then they too are off, assuring me that they will be back. So all my supports seem to be abandoning me and for a second I panic. How long will this go on? How shall I handle all these folk? Several white-haired women come in alone and I am happy to see two of them start talking as they pick up books on the biography table. Have they known each other before? The third makes her way over to where I am standing alone surveying the scene. "Are you Harriet Hatfield?" she asks.

I like her face, thin and brown like weathered wood. "Yes, I am. How did you know?"

"Somehow you look in command of the ship standing there."

"Totally ignorant and at sea, but I suppose I am in command, with the help of Joan Hampstead over there at the counter."

"It's a brave venture, but what I want to know frankly is why a women's bookshop? Why separate the sexes?" I find her penetrating look disturbing. It does not seem the time or place to be grilled.

"Ask me that question in six months. I might have the right answer."

"Oh I'll come back, and meanwhile I do wish you every success."

I look at my watch, feeling suddenly exhausted. It is half-past five, only a half-hour more and then Joan and I can go somewhere for dinner. But suddenly a host of young women pile in, talking excitedly and laughing, two of them clearly paired, all a little terrifying in their wild mops of loose hair and either very long skirts and leather jackets or very short skirts and high boots. Are these my people, I wonder? Will I ever be able to connect?

Patapouf suddenly emerges barking loudly and I realize that one of the young women has a terrier on a leash. "Maybe you had better take your dog out," I venture. "Patapouf is almost too good a defender. Lie down, Patapouf!" Now the terrier is growling and Patapouf, her tail wagging, advances towards her. I suppose when a dog sees another dog under circumstances like this it must be a little like a human seeing another human in some foreign place.

"I'm sorry. I'll take Teddy out," the girl says. "She can stay in the car," and she goes. Three of the others have settled into the comfortable chairs around the table as if indeed this were a club and they were already members. I bring out a tray of champagne and sit down with them.

"I'm glad to see you," I said. "Are you students?"

"M.I.T.," says the wildest-looking one. "I'm going for engineering."

What does one say next? But I am spared some fumbling response by the return of Teddy's mistress.

"She's my lover," says the engineer; "has a job with an architect's office."

"How did you find out about the store?" I ask.

"Oh, Erica saw a poster somewhere and we decided to come and see. Thanks for the champagne."

They are looking me over, I think.

"We live a few blocks away," Erica explains. "It will be nice to come and browse."

"That's what this shop is all about," I say as warmly as I can, "browsing and talking."

"A joint," one who has not yet spoken says. "What made you decide on Somerville?"

"The house. It was exactly what I wanted."

"You don't come from around here?"

"Well, not exactly. Until last year I lived with a friend in Chestnut Hill. When she died—she was a publisher and very successful at it . . ."

"And what did you do?" Erica asks. I am slightly troubled by their close attention. They are genuinely interested, I feel, but do I want my life probed just today? Right now?

"What did I do?" I laugh. "Just about everything from proofreading to gardening, to God knows what. I kept things as peaceful and efficient as possible so Vicky could work." I turn to Erica's friend, "What is you name, by the way?"

"Veronica," she says. "I hate my name."

"I am Harriet Hatfield."

"That must have been hard, your friend dying," says another young woman, who has been silent till now and had come alone. A narrow face with a bush of reddish hair dominating the rather small intent hazel eyes. She is wearing jeans and a red turtleneck. "How long did you live together?"

"Thirty years."

They all react to this at once, leaning forward.

"That's amazing," Erica says. "Thirty years . . ." She drinks some champagne.

"What made you decide to have a bookstore like this?" Veronica asks.

"I don't know how to say it, but I wanted to create something on my own. Now and then Vicky and I had been into women's bookstores here or there when she went out to drum up trade. I liked the atmosphere. I felt at home in it. People like us—I mean Vicky and me—don't have that many places where they feel at home. She hated any feminist talk herself, but somehow she did connect with the women we met in the bookstores. It seemed logical to me—an adventure—a *vita nuova*—a challenge."

"It took some guts, I'll say," the one with red hair smiles. "You are some brave lesbian."

That word always makes me wince and somehow cuts me off now. And I look over to Joan, still busy at the counter. Help. I do not utter it but I feel desperate.

"You don't like that open word, do you?" Red Hair pursues me. "Why not?"

"Vicky hated it. But anyway, apart from that, do people have

31

to be labeled? It seems to create distance rather than intimacy. It sets one apart."

"Oh," Veronica ponders this, "it's a way out for you, but you see, it's not for us. It's a matter of honor."

"You have to remember that I'm old enough to be your mother, or even your grandmother."

"You don't seem old," says Erica.

"Well, you must come back and educate me. It's time now that we close up."

"Oh we haven't had time to look around and buy books," says Red Hair, whose name I still do not know.

"All right, we'll wait fifteen minutes. How's that?" I go over to Joan to explain. "You must be dead, but you've certainly been adding like crazy."

"We've done well," Joan says.

I lean against the high counter, watching the girls fluttering around from tables to bookcases and cannot help smiling. Will they come back? They do buy, each one paperback, and dash away like birds in flight, all suddenly gone. I can hear Erica's terrier barking.

I lock the door. Joan begins to collect champagne glasses and what is left of the cake to stow it in the small downstairs fridge. "Come on, Joan. I'll do that later, for God's sake. You must be ready to leave this place and relax. I'll just take Patapouf out for a short walk while you sit down and rest. Won't be a minute."

But when we come back she is at the counter and announces, "One thousand dollars in the till, Harriet."

"Not bad for the first day." Tired I am, but this vast sum creates a spurt of adrenaline. "Patapouf will be quite all right here," I say. "Let's go." We go out by the back door, the door that leads right up to my quarters, leaving Patapouf to guard the shop. "Let's try that little French place down the street. My party, of course."

"Not 'of course.' That is kind of you."

Seated at a window table in the corner, we look across at each other and I, at least, feel the relief of not being among strangers and so visible. "Nice here," says Joan.

We decide on coq au vin and I order a bottle of Beaujolais Villages. "Ah, now we can relax."

I am looking around at the clientele, delighting to see that it could not have been a restaurant anywhere near Chestnut Hill. There are mostly students, as far as I can tell, several men sitting together, several older women sitting alone. Then I come back to Joan, who does look rather white and exhausted. "Are you regretting that you ever came into this crazy business? You must be exhausted."

"Exhausted, maybe. Regretting it, no."

"It's wonderful to be with someone a little more mature than those girls. But you know, Joan, you are the most discreet person I have ever known. I realized the other day when we were shelving the books that I know almost nothing about you, except that you are on a committee with Angelica."

"Just as well." She frowns now and unfolds her napkin.

"You are married, are you?"

"Was married."

I wait for more, but it does not come. Instead the wine comes and is uncorked for us. I take a sip and when our glasses have been filled, raise mine to her and meet her eyes, perhaps for the first time, and see how dark they are, and how somber. "Did your husband die?"

"No, we divorced last year, my fortieth year."

"It sounds like a tough year for a separation. Do you have children?"

"No." Joan drinks half her glass of wine. The atmosphere after all our jolly work together becomes strained.

"I guess I'm asking questions you really don't want to answer.

Forget it. Only I have grown to admire you, Joan, and want to be a friend, that's all."

"I find it very hard to talk about Martin," she says, "or about myself. I envy you that you can."

"Well, I was taken aback, I must confess, when those girls near the end began asking personal questions."

"I was too busy to be aware of that, but you looked quite at ease. And I imagined that this is the atmosphere you have said you want."

"True. I'm in for it. But, Joan, when one of them, Veronica by name, introduced the one who brought her dog in by saying 'This is my lover, Erica,' I can't describe how bothered I was. And later the word 'lesbian' was bandied about."

"Dear Harriet, you are an innocent, aren't you?" This fact seems to delight Joan and for the first time she smiles.

"I don't know. Vicky and I never talked about those things. But you have to remember that I am a grandmother in relation to people of nineteen or twenty. Can one close the generation gap? I wonder." For I feel suddenly old and abandoned, way off somewhere on an island of time, untouchable. "They seemed amazed that Vicky and I had lived together for thirty years. Is that so odd?"

"No. But perhaps rare even among heterosexual marriages. What are the figures now? Half of all marriages end in divorce?"

"Why?"

"At around fifty men fall in love with young women," she says coolly but it is clear to me that she is speaking of her own experience.

"I suppose the first fine careless rapture goes out of any intimate relationship quite early on. But isn't it possible to have been building some kind of foundation meanwhile—shared interests, responsibilities?"

"Yes, but it is strange what an earthquake a passionate encounter may make; the foundations simply break down."

How lucky I am, I think, because Vicky and I were so settled in together that a passionate encounter was not in the cards—or only once and briefly.

There is a silence. One of the things I like about Joan is that I can be silent with her and she with me. Out of the silence she speaks with unusual intensity.

"There is a huge emphasis these days on happiness, on being fulfilled—I believe that is the word—whatever the cost to anyone else. People are greedier about sex than even about money, as I see it. Enjoyment, taking what you want, has become a kind of imperative." This is a lot for Joan to utter and I ponder it for a moment.

"Excess and then what?" I ask. "It looks from my side of things like a deliberate self-indulgence and then the punishment that implies, wild swings . . ."

"Some people don't get punished," Joan says bitterly.

"They manage to 'adjust,' if that is the word, to their own needs."

"They love themselves as they are," Joan says.

"You do sound bitter." It pops out, for I had not meant to expose her at all.

"Well," her eyes open wide, "I am. Martin got what he wanted and in the process left me nearly penniless."

"It was a no-fault divorce?"

"Yes. How women have been conned by that statute, or whatever it is. After twenty years of marriage, being the housekeeper, cook, cleaning woman, and chauffeur for Martin, I got half of what our house was worth and that was all."

"How unfair!" I am really shocked.

"It's fine for men. They don't have to pay alimony these days. They get off more or less free."

"Oh Joan, I hope I can raise your salary by the end of the

year." But as soon as I say that I know it is the wrong response. She does not want pity.

"You'd better wait till you know what all this adds up to. It will be interesting to see whether the next week brings in more people. After all, the first day had to be exceptional."

And for the rest of the meal we talk about the store, both a little relieved at this point to move out of personal matters into what we share.

It is after nine when I get home. I did not dare hug Joan goodbye though I wanted to. Such a stalwart aid! In bed at last, with Patapouf beside me breathing deeply and giving an occasional muffled bark, I lie awake a long time. Warm September air blows the white curtains at the window gently in and out and I can see the ash tree lit up by a streetlamp, the only tree in my domain and already precious.

I do not need to look at Vicky's photograph set up on the night table, I feel her presence so keenly. It seems strange to have no one with whom I can share all that is taking place. Of course she would have sneered at those girls and shut them up at once had she been I. Why hadn't I?

Because being open is the foundation I am building all alone. I realize how vulnerable that makes me. But I need to enlarge the place of my tents, and this afternoon I saw how it would happen. I have to be prepared for shock and not turn away. But in spite of the slight panic these thoughts bring with them, deep down I feel happy. I feel ready for whatever may happen. I am glad I am sixty and more or less grown-up.

But before I fall asleep I wonder for a moment why Jonathan Fremont did not come to the opening.

4

We had agreed, Joan and I, that the shop hours would be from ten to six, and that she would come in the morning and I would be on hand in the afternoon. I would be there from 2 P.M. on. But there were problems. For one, the salesmen from publishing houses were apt to turn up in the late morning and it was up to me to do those interviews and decide what to buy. It is not a task I enjoy, although the salesperson is sometimes a woman. Candace Smith from Norton, for one, is congenial and quick to see what I am after. But how am I to know so soon what will be my needs in late fall and for Christmas and then in the early spring? The number and variety of books presented to me are immense, and sometimes I feel swamped and dulled into passivity by the weight of the decisions. The *leitmotif* becomes "Let me think this over."

Thanks to Joan we do have a system. She places a card in the last one to sell of any book, a card which is then removed and a reorder set in motion. At least that is the idea for the nucleus of books I mean to keep in stock, classics like *Out of Africa* and *The Autobiography of Alice B. Toklas.*

Joan rings me upstairs if a salesperson appears but if I am out he or she simply has to come back. I have it in mind to find someone to work on Saturday mornings so that Joan can have the weekend. I myself would like the weekends too, and perhaps eventually we can arrange for replacements for both of us. One problem is that I have to read so much. I am not going to sell books I know next to nothing about! And Vicky and I used to joke about booksellers, that they never read books, only sold them. It would be fine to stay in bed late on Saturdays and read.

The first week will be exciting, of course, because we can have no idea what will happen, whether a reasonable number of customers will drop in, whether my idea of tea in the afternoon and elevenses in the morning will take hold.

The day after the opening, I sit down at my desk with Patapouf lying beside me, feeling rather like a spider waiting for a fly. The first wanderer-in takes me aback because she looks at first like a bag lady, laden down with messy packages, a torn slip showing under an ancient long skirt.

"May I help you?" I ask, wondering whether to get up or not.

"I'd like to sit down," she says.

"You are welcome. That's what those chairs are for."

"Thanks. I do my shopping and then there is nowhere to sit while I wait for the bus."

I go back to listing some books I want to order.

"What kind of books do you sell?" she asks. "Women's books," she says with heavy irony. "I suppose that means those Gothic novels. All the same, that's what women read."

At this I wake out of my passive stance. "Ah, you are a different kind of reader then. As a matter of fact we don't have those novels you dislike. No market for them really in a store like this."

"Oh."

"Why don't you look around . . . when you have rested." And I add, "There'll be a cup of tea at four but I don't expect you'll want to stay that long."

"Oh no. Jackie—that's my cat—wouldn't stand it if I stayed away that long." Then she notices Patapouf. "You have a dog. Doesn't he get bored here?"

"It's a she and she is very old."

We are interrupted before I can ask what she does read by a very tall thin young woman bubbling over with curiosity. "What a splendid bookstore!" she announces. "Am I glad you are here! I just moved into the neighborhood with my husband—he's at Harvard—a month ago. I'm dying to get at some of the books. May I just wander around?"

She has on high black riding boots and a stunning black, broad-brimmed hat and wears heavy black-rimmed glasses. They add to her look of surprise and delight, I observe. "Where are you from?" I had guessed San Francisco, but I am wrong, of course.

"Lawrence, Kansas."

"So you are a long way from home."

"Oh it was never home," she answers. "David was a lowly instructor there. We were captured, you might say, like wild animals and put in the academic cage."

"Harvard is not a cage then?"

"It's a lot better now we can afford a car."

She has pulled out a book from a shelf of novels and begins to read. I wonder what she has chosen. It turns out to be Sylvia Townsend Warner, that new paperback with four of her novels in it, and I can't help being pleased by her choice.

When she asks me about Warner, I explain that when I first discovered her with *Lolly Willowes* I felt she was a true original. "You may have seen her stories in the *New Yorker.*" But of course she is too young. I have to laugh. "At sixty I forget that some things are ancient history to someone your age."

39

"I'm thirty. That's not young."

But now she is silent and sits down with the book. I go to the shelf of biography and letters and pull out Warner's *Selected Letters,* one of my favorites. "You might like to glance at this," I say, laying it on the table.

The old woman is saying goodbye at the door. "I'll be back," she says. "Thanks for letting me sit down."

I could not have been more amazed after the door closes than I am when I hear, "The big problem is whether we should have children. David wants to be a father but I . . . I'm not sure."

"What do you want of your life?" I venture to ask.

"I don't know. I'm a painter actually, a painter with no success."

It would be a fine sentence with which to open a novel, it occurs to me, as I sit down beside her. But what could make someone blurt out such a painful quandary to a total stranger? I had envisioned the store as a kind of haven, but I am not setting myself up as an amateur psychiatrist, although Joan has teased me that the big risk will be just that. People need to talk to someone . . . and why not be the listener after all?

"It's the pressure," she is saying. "At thirty I have to make up my mind, don't I?"

At this I smile. "You're asking me and I never married and never wanted children, so what can I say?"

"I don't feel maternal, you see. It's as though that had been left out of me. I never even played with dolls when I was little, but I always wanted to draw and was quite possessive about those things I did with crayons on paper bags, and once in a while my mother pinned one up on the refrigerator. When she threw several away while she was vacuuming I had a tantrum."

"It looks as though you had to go on painting, doesn't it? Success or not. And what is success anyway? From what I hear these days it's all a gamble."

Too bad that at this moment a gaggle of college girls pushes in. But I do manage to say, "Why don't you bring some of your work over? I'd like to see it." In the back of my mind the idea has come to me that a large stretch of wall on one side of the store might be used to hang works of art.

"That would be great. Thanks. And by the way, my name is Martha Blackstone."

"And mine is Harriet Hatfield." On that we shake hands and Martha leaves after paying for the Warner novels.

Suddenly, as it draws near to four, the place is filling up and I am kept too busy for a while, making change and selling books, even to put the kettle on in the kitchen. It is exciting to be in business really for the first time.

So I am pleased that Jonathan Fremont arrives when Hatfield House looks like a going concern. That is a piece of luck.

"Sit down, Jonathan. I'm about to make tea."

"I think I'll just look around."

I go back into the kitchen and set up a tray with cups and the big teapot Vicky and I used so often, a Chinese teapot with a bamboo handle. I set out some cookies and listen to the murmur of voices in the shop. When I come back the atmosphere has changed for, as I soon realize, Jonathan has decided to get into conversation with the girls and find out who they are.

"We're from Lesley," one of them is saying, but in a tone that suggests she thinks it is none of his damn business. He is the only man there and a lot older than anyone else.

I persuade him to sit down beside me and pet Patapouf, who has emerged from under my desk and is wagging her tail furiously. She has always been crazy about men. Vicky and I used to laugh about it. I feel shy as I pour out and try to behave like a lady on my own premises.

"It's quite an investment, isn't it?" he says with a smile. "Did the party go well?"

"Oh yes, old friends turned up, of course. We did a roaring business."

"You do seem to be in your element."

"I am," I say firmly. "I think Vicky would be pleased. After all, books were her passion."

"The books she published anyway."

"It's just a marvelous place," one of the girls says as she comes over to the table. "I didn't know a lot of these books existed. May I sit down and have a cup of tea?"

"Of course. Your friends too."

"Do take my seat," Jonathan says, getting up. There are three girls and only four chairs. What else can he do?

"Just bring the desk chair over, then we can all sit," I suggest.

Of course Jonathan's presence makes the whole tea party a little stiff and wary, so much so that after everyone has settled in with a cup and a cookie, I find myself trying to explain him as he sits there rubbing Patapouf's back. "Mr. Fremont is my financial adviser," I say. "He is afraid this is a crazy thing to invest in, and has come to see what is going on."

"Oh, we must all buy lots of books," one girl says, "though we are dead broke, of course." And the other two burst into laughter.

"But we are so happy that you have come," says the solemn one of the three.

"And we want to help in any way we can," the third chimes in.

What more can I ask? It has occurred to me before this occasion that the people I most want to reach will find buying even paperbacks expensive. Nevertheless it is an expansive moment and I am enjoying it and Jonathan's air of quizzical curiosity.

"Aren't there plenty of bookstores in Cambridge already?" he asks.

"Well, there's the Grolier, you can browse there," the solemn girl grants.

"But nobody really cares, you know. I mean, you can't sit down in most bookstores."

"And they don't carry what we want. I walked in here and was positively dazzled. My God, all I could think of was 'and the saints came marching in!' " That is the articulate one, the first one to speak.

"I don't quite understand," says Jonathan. "Who are the saints, then, so prevalent and accessible in this room?"

"Gertrude Stein, Adrienne Rich, Margaret Atwood, Susan Gubar . . ."

"Oh," says Jonathan.

"We want to learn about ourselves. We want to find role models."

"What are your names, by the way?"

Edna, Elizabeth, and Cynthia are their names. But now they are eager to look around in peace and do so while Jonathan helps me with the tea things.

"Good luck, Harriet," he says and shakes my hand. "I'll look in now and then."

The atmosphere changes as soon as he has left. Edna, the articulate one, comes over to my desk and says, "He's a creep."

"Gross," says Elizabeth.

"Oh, but harmless, I assure you. After all, this is rather wild and . . . Well, I inherited the money to do this and he is the executor of the will. It's all very odd to him. Old women are not supposed to go on wild goose chases, especially with recently acquired money." I suddenly begin to laugh at myself and the girls catch my mood and are laughing with me.

"You're not old, are you? Why call yourself old?" Cynthia, the solemn one, inquires. She has several books of poems in her arms.

"Old enough to know better in Jonathan Fremont's view, I guess."

"It's nearly five, we've got to run," Elizabeth says, looking at her watch, and with a flutter they are on their way, the books of poetry left on my desk, and not a single sale made.

"We'll be back!" is Edna's last word.

"Thanks for the tea!" Elizabeth adds.

I am alone for a few minutes and a little at loose ends, but now Angelica comes in, bringing me flowers from her garden—so like her—while Patapouf emerges again barking her delight. "There's my friend," says Angelica.

"Sit down. Oh, I am glad to see you!"

"You are surviving?"

"A lot of life has already come and gone, Angelica. It is fascinating!" And I tell her about Martha, the painter, and about the old woman who came to sit down and who despised women who read Gothic novels, and that Jonathan turned up.

"Did anyone buy a book?" she asks, teasing me.

"Well, yes, Sylvia Townsend Warner went out with Martha. Oh dear, a whole afternoon's sales, one book!" The balloon of excitement goes limp. "It looks as if I have an impecunious clientele so far. And that is going to be a problem."

"I wouldn't worry. It sounds to me as though word was going to get around, as though, dear Harriet, you have your finger on the pulse of a real need. And that, after all, is the important thing, isn't it?"

She has come, she announces, to take me to her house for dinner after I have closed up, and bring Patapouf with me.

In the final hour several customers turn up and actually buy books, including a couple of young men, much to my astonishment. And by six I am tuckered out but too keyed up to relax, so I quite enjoy the fairly long drive to Chestnut Hill through the traffic. It becomes a way of resting, with Patapouf's head on my knee. Driving has always been one of my ways of relaxing. When Vicky was alive I sometimes took off in the car by myself and called it playing hooky.

I pick up a bottle of Vouvray for Angelica and look forward to a peaceful evening's talk with her. A nourishing friend in every way. How rare that is! And when you come right down to it aren't friends what we need most, more even than lovers? Is Angelica such a rare friend because she has never been a lover? Never been obsessed by one person? Always managing to have a clear open space for anyone who needs it?

5

For some reason I am not able to define why Joan does not attract the confidences that pour in on me every afternoon. Perhaps shyness breeds shyness and her rather dour outlook on life may seem forbidding, especially to the very young. When I ask her what has happened that morning the answer is often "Nothing much. A few sales." She needs my advice about reordering. How are we to decide what must be reordered and what should not be? I simply trust a hunch in that case. Joan exerts subtle pressure to try to develop my business sense. There she is an optimist.

Our routine is working well, however, and I wake up in the morning eager to start the day. When I walk Patapouf the neighbors begin to be aware of my existence and say hello. A frazzled old woman walks her corgi at the same time, around half-past seven, and we greet each other, the dogs straining at their leashes. I like the neighborhood because it's such a mixture of people. At that time in the morning hard hats are off to work. There are more men than women on the street. The men congregate at a lunch counter which is jammed till eight or so and I wonder why they spend money on breakfast, such an easy meal, until it occurs to me that that counter is their club away from their wives and children. That kind of joint is what women often lack. Perhaps the bookstore around four can become that.

I find that the people I love best are those who come in to browse, the silent shy ones, who are hungry for books rather than for conversation. There are several whom I have already seen. Eventually perhaps we shall meet. But meanwhile I am busy at my desk and try to let them feel free, unpressured, to take it for granted that they are welcome.

Martha Blackstone has come back with a portfolio of strange imaginary landscapes—watercolors. I am simply not equipped to judge a work of art. I find them not exactly pleasing but interesting and original. She uses very somber colors, and towering distorted trees loom over black streams or are reflected in a still pond.

"What do you think?" she asks, for I am taking my time to look and try to see what she is after.

"They are strange," I say, "a little nightmarish. I don't know why."

"I guess they are dreams," she says. "I begin and then this landscape I have never seen takes over."

"The trees are so ominous," I say. "I am troubled by their root system." In two of the landscapes the roots are spread out under the earth but visible. "Why don't you hang two or three on that wall? Let's use the store as a gallery." I want to do it, yet I am a little troubled that I do not really cotton to her work.

"If only we could see people like that, with the roots visible," she says.

"I'm not sure I want to," and I laugh.

"Do you really want to hang them?" she asks, frowning.

"Yes. In a way they are happenings. That is what I want for the store." The landscapes are matted, not framed, but we agree to hang them first as they are. "What happens if someone wants to buy one?" I ask.

"That would be great. A hundred dollars apiece. Is that okay?"

The old woman who needs a place to sit has come in while the landscapes are spread out on the table. She eases herself into a chair with a sigh, her packages around her. "I guess I'm interrupting something," she says. "Is it all right if I sit for a little while?"

"Of course." Martha is packing up and says she will be back tomorrow with hangers.

"You never told me," I say to the old woman, "what you like to read; not Gothic novels, as I remember."

"Silly as all get-out. What I like to read is history, not made-up stories, but real things, how people lived in the olden days. It cheers me up," she chuckles. "It's a bad world, but it was worse in the sixteenth century, especially for women." She squints at me through her glasses as though she is bringing me into focus. "I can't afford to buy those books. Social Security leaves pretty little over, and my husband is sick, Parkinson's."

How I have misjudged her! "That's hard."

"It's the medicine," she confides. "That's what leaves us broke every month."

At this moment unfortunately the phone rings. "Excuse me," I say, "this won't take long."

It is my old friend Amelie, and it is a shock. She is calling to ask if I know that Caroline is dying of cancer. "It is a strangely wonderful death," Amelie says, "for she has no pain, knows it is incurable, and, how shall I say it? is simply seeing her friends one by one, lies with her old cat on her lap. Why I am calling is to ask you to make up a bundle of books she might like to have around, even if she can't read for long at a time. I'll pick them up tomorrow. Would you like to see her? I think she would be happy if you could drop by."

"I'm in shock," I answer. "Caroline seemed so well."

"She is eighty, you know. No one lives forever." It is so like Amelie to be quite matter-of-fact.

When I put the receiver down the old woman has left and I am sorry, for I had been going to offer to lend her a book.

I feel quite shaken. I had hoped that Caroline might come to the opening. Now I know why she didn't. What would the world be like without her? So alive, so aware of other people . . . At least I can put together some books for her. It is difficult to decide what. Nothing to waste reading time, something with style. Well, of course, the collected essays of Virginia Woolf for one. Only the first volume is out, but it is just the thing. Freya Stark, I think, and go upstairs to find a small book of selected essays by her. I am so absorbed in this task that I hardly notice that the store has filled up during my absence.

The white-haired woman who had objected to the idea of a women's bookstore is standing at my desk with a pile of books. "You are trusting," she says. "I might have just absconded with these."

"I'm sorry I kept you waiting."

"No problem. Will you accept a check? I don't carry cash any more. My purse has been stolen twice in the last year."

"Good heavens! Of course I'll accept a check. You live in the neighborhood, do you?"

"Not really. I live on Memorial Drive. Somerville is unknown territory."

It is satisfactory to tuck a check for sixty dollars into the drawer and of course I look at her name, Marian Tuckerworth. "Thank you, Miss Tuckerworth."

"Mrs.," she corrects me. "My husband died last year. I confess

I was quite fascinated by your opening, such a motley crew, and you yourself so unlikely."

At this I laugh. "I suppose I am. I'm a newcomer to Somerville myself, as you no doubt guessed."

"Then why here? How did it all happen? Or am I being disgracefully curious?"

What I sense in the penetrating way she looks at me and in something abrupt and defensive about her is that here is a person of primary intensity. That is a phrase of Vicky's. She used it about women in a pejorative sense. Men don't suffer from that affliction, she used to say.

"I suppose in a way I am a widow like you. I lost my friend and companion of many years, Victoria Chilton, last year and felt rather at loose ends until I thought of the bookstore. Then everything speeded up. I found this house. I want the store to seem like a home, to welcome the odd lonely person, to be a meeting place in a way." Am I talking too much? But why not, after all? And I really want to know how she is dealing with being alone herself. "Let's sit down," I say. "It's just about time to put the kettle on and take a break."

But two of the four chairs are occupied by silent browsers so she sits on the end of my desk. "I really must be getting home."

"Did you find it hard to be suddenly alone?" I ask.

"In some ways, but my husband died after a long illness, so in a way I chiefly felt relief. And now I am too busy trying to organize an association to relieve home caretakers; so often elderly women are slaves to a sick husband, helpless because a nursing home seems out of the question. Loyalty, you know, a sense of having to be responsible."

"What a splendid thing to be doing!"

"Maybe, but it is at present chiefly endless paperwork to try to get funding. Some of it is rather like Hospice, I suppose. One has to depend on volunteers a lot, and it's not easy to find them."

"I must have a bulletin board," I say at once. "Then you could advertise!"

"Where do you get all this energy?" She is smiling at me now, a warm smile illuminating her rather austere face.

"It's such an adventure, you see. I never know who or what will turn up."

We are interrupted now by a young girl who has picked out a book of Adrienne Rich's poems, and, while I go back to the cash register to make change, Marian Tuckerworth vanishes with her heavy pile of books. Of all the people who have come to the store so far I have not liked anyone quite as well. Maybe because I feel we could connect. There appear to be no barriers.

It is time to put the kettle on and when I sit down at the table fifteen minutes later, my companions turn out to be the two nuns who had been so helpful on the opening day. They seem like old friends and tell me their names, Sister Mary Smith and Sister Christopher Baker. After I pour the tea there is a moment of silence.

"There's nothing like tea, is there?" Mary says, drinking down half the cup in one swallow. "My mother couldn't have managed without her cup of tea at five every morning, and then in the afternoon when Dad came home from the machine shop. They were Irish, newcomers you know. Tea at five with a boiled egg or a bit of ham made it feel like home."

"Have you ever been in Ireland?"

"Well, I want to go." She looks over at Christopher. "But as Chris knows we are pulled southwards these days. So I've never been to Dublin or Cork, but I know Managua and a few remote villages in El Salvador very well."

"We are on leave after six rather grueling months working with prisoners in El Salvador," Chris explains.

"Oh." I am flooded with shame at my own ignorance. I ask myself, Whose prisoners?

"The prison camps are filled with rebels captured by Duarte's soldiers. We bring in medicine and clothing," says Christopher.

At this Mary suddenly laughs. "We improvise. Everything is needed there, so we can't go wrong."

"After six months we get two months at home. It takes a while to get rested. They stuff us with vitamins and treat us altogether far too well."

"What heroes you are!" I say. I feel quite awed.

"Oh no, the prisoners are the heroes." Chris is fingering a small cross brightly painted with flowers. "See this. It's carved out of a bone. An old man gave it to me. He had made it there in prison. Now we bring them paints when we can. They want color so badly. It is so deadly gray and brown in the shacks called prisons. They are starved for color as well as for food."

As they talk their eyes are shining. Theirs is a chosen life. They are doing what they want to do. And it is beautiful to see, to share in for a moment over a cup of tea. There is something I am burning to ask, but don't quite dare. Perhaps someday I shall if they come back.

We are joined at this moment by Sue Bagley, whom I recognize, luckily, and who accepts a cup of tea and sits down with us, gobbles a cookie, and peers at us with extreme interest through her thick glasses.

"Let me introduce Sister Mary and Sister Christopher—this is Sue Bagley." I hate to have the talk about El Salvador interrupted, but it is a game of musical chairs and what can I do? "If I remember, you are a neighbor, Miss Bagley."

"Right down the street in one of those dilapidated three-story apartment houses."

I leave them to take money from two customers who are waiting at the register, sure that Chris and Mary will know how

53

to talk with Miss Bagley, or rather, it turns out, listen to her, for she is voluble and is in the middle of an impassioned speech about how much she distrusts and even hates our present administration. Sentiments with which the sisters naturally are in perfect accord.

"Nuns," Sue Bagley announces, "are the most radical women in America these days. It's quite extraordinary. Did you know that?" she asks me as I sit down again. "Are you aware of that?"

"Oh dear, there is so much I don't know," and I cannot help laughing. "The bookstore is my higher education, I guess. But is what Miss Bagley says true?" I turn to Chris.

"There have been radical changes, certainly, since Pope John the Twenty-third opened the doors," she answers smoothly. "When we were permitted to take off the habit and look less like—what did we look like?—medieval ghosts, things began to happen very fast."

"But aren't you up against a rigid hierarchy just the same?" Sue Bagley is a little too aggressive, I decide. "Is that an indiscreet question?" She turns to me. "You look as though it were." But before I can answer she proceeds, "I am awfully curious. Can't help it. Have to use my mind somehow. Make discoveries, you know. This bookstore is a discovery."

"Do you have a job?" I ask.

"Now that," she says, "is an indiscreet question. Of course not. I was a public accountant, then I nursed my father till he died, then . . . well, it was too late. So I lead a rather placid life and am hungry for experiences like this."

I feel a certain dread because it is clear that Sue Bagley will be coming in often. For the first time I realize what I am getting myself into, but that is because I do not really like her, whereas I felt drawn to the two nuns at once.

There has been so much coming and going this first week that there is hardly time to finish any of the many conversations made possible by these four comfortable chairs. Now I see that a voluble constant customer could become a problem. Am I to be chained to Sue Bagley's aggressive questioning for life? I am in the middle of this reflection when her rather strident voice rises above the murmur in the room to ask, "For instance, you, Miss Hatfield. Whatever made you open a women's bookstore at your age?"

I am not about to give this time, and I answer in my own circuitous fashion. "People do what they want to do, don't they? I had always dreamed of doing this and last year it became possible—because of an inheritance."

"You're going to have a problem with all these lesbians trooping in," Sue says, rather obviously referring to a couple of women, not young this time, in pant suits, who are eagerly looking over what I think of as "my table." Have they heard? The elder of the two, with short-cut gray hair and wearing a bow tie, looks up. So I get up in case they have, go over to them, and introduce myself.

"She doesn't know what she's getting into," I hear Sue Bagley whispering loudly.

"She knows," says Chris. "And now I'm afraid we have to be off. Nice to meet you."

Do I dare? After the two women congratulate me on the choice of books and introduce themselves as Alice and Patience, I suggest they come over and sit down and have a cup of tea. Sue Bagley, observing this, has evidently decided to follow the nuns out and waves a goodbye to me at the door.

"Just about enough for two cups." I empty the teapot.

"Thirty years ago," says Patience, the younger of the two, her red hair not yet tinged with gray, "we used to hang out at Sylvia Beach's Shakespeare and Company in Paris. There has been nothing like it, around here anyway, but you do create an atmosphere . . ."

"In spite of that insulting woman who just left," says Alice. "I heard her warn you."

"Oh well, she's lonely and eccentric. I pay no attention." But I want to answer Patience's kind remark. "What do you mean about 'an atmosphere'?"

"Oh, I don't know. How does one define an atmosphere?" Patience looks over at Alice, inviting her to define it, I suppose.

"Intelligent, welcoming, and not commercial." Alice is clear-cut. "You won't make money, I'm afraid, but you'll make friends."

"Good. That is what I hope. Already in this first week so many strangers have dropped in and stayed to talk, I am amazed."

"But what do you do when someone drops in and stays and stays?" Patience asks.

It makes me laugh because I have been asking myself that very question. "God knows. I suppose one can pretend to be very busy filling out nonexistent orders."

"It must be fun," Alice says. "You look as though it is."

"I'm almost afraid of everything going too well," I answer. I feel these two are in tune with me and I am enjoying this rapport. "What is lurking in the background that will erupt later on?"

"Homophobia," says Alice. "You just had a taste of that when we came in."

"Oh well," I shrug, "who cares?"

They exchange a look and then Patience says, "Maybe you are not involved, immune as it were."

"Involved? Immune?" I am taken by surprise. Why not be frank? "I lived for thirty years with a woman you may have heard of, the publisher Victoria Chilton."

"Yes, of course. A distinguished imprint," Alice reacts at once.

"She died last year and I inherited a small fortune. So here I am!"

"I suppose money does give one a kind of immunity," Alice muses.

"We simply lived our lives in Chestnut Hill and took ourselves for granted." I am now on the defensive but do not understand why. "It was our life and we did not feel connected to other women couples or even know many."

"Didn't you ever meet slurs or raised eyebrows or something like that?" Patience asks.

"I'm not aware that we did," I answer. "Tell me something about you. Did you live in Paris long?" They have to be older than they look—at least seventy to have been in Paris before 1940.

"Patience was studying at the Sorbonne and I was working at the Bibliothèque Nationale and the Cluny on my doctorate. That is where we met."

"In front of the lady and the unicorn tapestries," Patience says, smiling with the happy memory of it.

"We ended up living in a small town in Ohio where I was teaching medieval history," Alice says.

"But you live here in New England now . . ." I am sewing it all together like a tapestry in my mind.

"Yes, I'm retired and Patience teaches at the Winsor School in the French department."

"Oh." I sense that we are on the border of some revelation, but once more a crucial conversation is interrupted while I add up several sales and greet two or three newcomers. Sometimes the business of being a bookseller provides me with an escape from a long-winded, lonely person like Bagley, but sometimes it is frustrating, and I hope Patience and Alice will come back.

For the moment I have other things on my mind. I invited Joan to have supper with me in my apartment upstairs and it is about time to rescue Patapouf and close up for the day. I had left her upstairs as she seemed to long to be left alone and to sleep, the dear old thing. By now, however, she will be feeling restless, so I lock up a little early for once.

We go out into the autumn dusk, walking together among all the people coming home from work or out to shop for their suppers, and I am happy to stop whenever Patapouf wants to for her endless sniffing of trees and hedges, for then I can stand and drink in the light, especially as the setting sun lights up a beech tree turning it a startling gold. At that moment I miss Chestnut Hill badly, our garden and our beautiful trees. But I remind myself that I have exchanged all that beauty for the human scene around me, for the friendliness of a city neighborhood where people do not shut other people out with high gates and fences. There are compensations.

"Will she bite if I pat her head?" a very dirty little boy asks me. Patapouf is wagging her tail very hard. I have been in a reverie and have not noticed the boy or his friend.

"First let her sniff your hand," I suggest, "then she'll know you are a friend." And pretty soon he is kneeling down and patting her head quite gently while Patapouf wags her tail. The other little boy meanwhile has decided to pat her back but does not know quite how.

"Patting is not hitting," I suggest. So he stops and gives me a disgusted frown.

"Come on Peter, this is boring," he says, and off they go, Peter looking back once to wave goodbye.

How can Martha not want a child, I ask myself. I have been thinking quite a lot about her and wonder when she will come back, and whether anyone will buy a painting.

Now it is time to hurry home and put the meat loaf in the oven. I look forward to a talk with Joan. She will be my first guest for a meal. Vicky and I had a cook, Emma, who mothered us and spoiled us. Cooking, too, is a new exercise for me. I have squash, the frozen kind, melting in the double boiler and shall add sour cream and brown sugar when it has melted. But as I set the table in a corner of the living room, I feel suddenly tired. Joan can open the wine, I decide. I made chocolate mousse yesterday, so I can sit down for five minutes, and I do, feeling the tension flow out of me as I stroke Patapouf's silky ears.

Joan sits by the fire, which she has lit for me, drinking her martini, and I sit opposite with my scotch. I realize how much I have wanted someone to talk with, someone I know and who is part of the enterprise.

"Do you get awfully tired?" I ask. "Today suddenly I feel done in."

"Actually, no. I find it fun," she says.

"So many people, so many lives."

"That's your side. I keep busy at the register."

"How are we going to find a Saturday person?"

"Maybe someone will turn up. I don't mind doing that for a while, though."

"Really? But you don't want the store to eat up your life."

"I don't have a life."

"What did you do before?"

"Brooded."

"I expect your friends asked you over for dinner, knowing you must be at loose ends."

At this Joan shakes her head, implying that I am a little crazy. "My friends were *our* friends, you see."

"I don't understand."

"A divorced woman, Harriet, is not a social asset."

I must look bewildered, as bewildered as I feel. It just seems to me unbelievable that friends would drop a friend who is suddenly single.

"Couples invite other couples . . . I suppose one becomes a threat."

It does occur to me now that some of our friends, Vicky's and mine, have not been very attentive since her death. But that, I decide, is because she was the attraction, not I. "Well," I lift my glass, "here's to a new life for you, too."

"I am not a people person like you," Joan says thoughtfully, "but I enjoy working here."

"We make a good team."

"I'm glad you think so."

"The only trouble is I feel I'm on a roller coaster—and way behind on reading all I should be reading. You know, Joan, the women who come in here know so much more than I do about feminism. They ask for books I have never heard of!"

"You don't have to cater to everyone's likes and dislikes."

"I'm humiliated by my ignorance," I say, as the timer rings to tell me it is time to take out the meat loaf and doctor the squash.

Joan follows me into the kitchen and opens the wine for me, a Chateau Neuf du Pape of which she appears to approve. "Has it occurred to you that you are going to be inundated with lesbian women, by the way?"

"How do you know they're lesbians?" But it is true that Alice and Patience had seemed to me obviously a couple. And I wonder why.

"I know by the books they buy," Joan answers.

"But I don't like this word 'they' as though lesbians were some breed apart from other human beings."

"I'm sorry," Joan says quickly. She is blushing. "I didn't think."

"I don't think of myself as labeled and stuck in a closet as someone outside the pale, you see." I feel quite hot, not with shame, but with my own blundering unconsciousness.

"You do not label yourself so no one labels you," says Joan.

"Someone who was in the shop today said money was a protection." I stop to think about this. Joan can take silence. That is one reason I feel at home with her.

"Good meat loaf," she says.

"Thanks." But I am upset and cannot come to terms yet with why that is. Maybe Joan's blush was because she had forgotten that I was one of the "they" we were discussing. Maybe I am upset by the idea that I have been sheltered and still am by Vicky's money. Or maybe by Bagley's obscene warning. Yes, it all ties together suddenly.

"Joan, when I dreamed up this bookstore I dreamed of it as a nourishing place where women of all kinds could come. It never occurred to me that the women were bound to be feminists, and some of them lesbians." And suddenly I laugh. "The obvious never occurred to me. That is the joke."

Joan smiles and lifts her glass. "Astonishing woman," she says.

"I'm not even a feminist, I suppose. Not a militant one anyway. So here I am, the founder of a club which I don't belong to myself."

"Hoist on your own petard," and Joan laughs now, an affectionate laugh.

"So what?" I ask her and myself. "I have avoided commitment for six decades of my life, but I'm in for it now, aren't I?"

"I guess you are," she says soberly.

"We'll ponder this dilemma, if it is one, over chocolate mousse. It was Vicky's favorite."

Over coffee we talk about the shop from the point of view of business. Only the paperbacks are selling in any quantity. Who can afford twenty bucks for a novel? We are losing money in part because of reordering. For each of us this shop talk is a rest. And after supper Joan offers to go with me for Patapouf's evening walk. I accept gladly. In the daytime the neighborhood is friendly and peaceful but after dark I sometimes feel a little afraid.

"I love looking at the lighted windows, don't you?" All through the neighborhood top floors of houses seem to be rented to students, or so I imagine, as I look up and wonder what they are studying.

"I suppose so. I confess I am nervous," says Joan.

"I'm nervous sometimes, but it is exciting, too. A whole new world after dark—a metamorphosis."

Joan has been thinking, meanwhile, about the shop and before we part she suggests that I try to reach my Chestnut Hill friends who would, after all, buy twenty-dollar novels.

"Well, they know where I am," I say. "Not many came to the opening."

"Your friend Miss Lamb has bought about two hundred dollars' worth, you know."

"She's a real friend," I say. "The others have dropped me, more or less. After all, I have literally moved out. Vicky was the drawing card."

"And it's a long way to go."

When I have washed the dishes I go to bed and lie awake a long time, watching the electric clock jerk from minute to minute. Bleeding time it looks like. I feel confused about myself and my life for the first time since Vicky died. I wish she were here beside me and I could ask her advice. Now whom can I ask? I have got myself into a job where I do not choose the people I see or talk with. They choose me. In the adventure of the first week I am far too involved to realize what that means. What I do realize is that to those who wander in I come through as friendly, someone to whom they want to tell their stories. Impersonal as I am, not involved as a family is, or even as friends are, I suppose it is quite natural that I have become such a target—and of course I am in most cases old enough to be their mother or even grandmother. Who is it who teased me about becoming an amateur psychologist? That certainly put the fear of God into me!

Yet a great deal in these first days has been illuminating and valuable, and whatever Joan may think, the confiding has not been chiefly by lesbians. No, I comfort myself. The store has brought in a wide range of women and a few of them, no doubt, will become friends as time goes on. Life itself has a way of sorting things out.

And finally I sleep with nothing solved. How can it be? But now I have a better sense of where things stand, less confusion and more hope.

6

It has been agreed that Caroline would like me to come at eleven this morning. I set out with a bag of five carefully chosen books, including Georgia O'Keeffe to look at, hoping one or the other will be the right one. I have not spoken with Caroline herself, so I know nothing yet about her state, but have promised the nurse to stay no longer than a half-hour.

There she is, on a chaise in the garden under a parasol, smiling and waving. Dressed in a flowery wrapper, covered by a white silk Chinese shawl, she is lying beside a small border of lilies and late roses, radiant in the autumn light. It all looks like an Impressionist painting, and I tell her so.

"A flowering moment of glory," she says. "Friends have been absolutely angelic about gardening for me." She has sat up to be kissed and to welcome me, but now she lies back on the pillows and I see that she has lost weight and looks wan, dark circles round her gray eyes, although they are as luminous as ever. "I hope I live long enough to see the gentians flower. I planted them last autumn."

"Dear Caroline, let us hope so."

She smiles at me then. "No one tells me how long I have.

Perhaps they don't know. But of course Peter has been wonderful and assures me there will be no pain."

"Lucky you, to have a surgeon for a son!" I have never liked Peter but it is good to know he is very much on the job.

"A perfect dear." She has turned away. "But, Harriet, you understand this. My real comfort is the crits, those two old cats who purr at the foot of my bed through the rather tedious nights. How awful it would be to die away from home." And then with a sudden mischievous smile she adds, "We need fur."

There is a pause now. I feel she has come and gone, energy flowing back after a moment of ebbing and I am happy to sit beside her in perfect peace, resisting the impulse to hold her hand.

"Dying is interesting," she says now, "for me so far a long farewell celebration of some sort. So many dear friends who come to tell me they love me. So I feel," and she smiles again, "it really must not go on too long!"

"Everyone feels privileged to have known you."

"Nonsense. Why, for heaven's sake?"

"I see yours as an exemplary life." For some reason the whole atmosphere permits this sort of statement, which I have not made before, but see clearly, as pale gold leaves fall one by one. "You manage to hold so much life in a single cup: helping Winston, bringing up the boys, gardening, giving wonderful dinner parties, and—what so few people know—working full time as a psychiatric social worker. How did you manage it all? Vicky always said you were incomparable, far too good to be a role model, as they say these days, because who else could have done what you did with such warmth and grace?"

Caroline shuts her eyes, much to my dismay. Perhaps she has fallen asleep. A truck comes roaring past and after the noise has stopped she says, "All that seems far away. Thanks for telling me, though! I'll try to remember who it was I managed to be all those years. But now," she says quietly, "I am somewhere else and enjoying making no effort at all."

"I must go," I say. "I mustn't tire you out."

"Oh, not before you have told me about the shop! I'm dying to know. You must indulge me, Harriet, so I can think about it after you leave."

"What can I say about the shop? It's an absolutely new, rich, and terrifying world."

"Terrifying?"

"Yes, because I am not ready for all the lives that pour in. It's what I wanted, Caroline, it's what I dreamed of, people talking, women coming in and meeting each other."

"Then why terrifying?"

It takes me a second to find the answer. "I'm finding out that my life with Vicky—such a good life it was—was walled in somehow. I had no idea what a lot has been going on, what problems these women face."

Caroline smiles. "Vicky herself was a kind of castle, wasn't she? Way up on a hill of her own invention, the publishing house."

"Yes, exactly. So we really only saw people rather like us. Vicky never considered herself part of any group, perhaps even a little superior to any group, such as feminists, for instance, and, God knows," I hesitate before the word, then utter it, "lesbians."

"And I can imagine lesbians and feminists flock to your store. All to the good, I should think. You are brave to do this, Harriet. I admire your undiminished zest for life, your courage."

"No, not really. I'm afraid of all the labels and the way women talk about everything. A young woman introduced her friend as 'my lover.' I was dumbfounded. I didn't like it, you see. I'm terrified because all my defenses are being beaten down, or simply disregarded," and I laugh. "I am an old fool. Oh dear," and I laugh again, "all I can think of is Philip Cabot saying of his brother Richard, 'There are fools, there are damn fools, and there's my brother Richard'! I'm brother Richard."

"Hardly. If I remember, brother Richard had outraged Philip by insisting that doctors must tell terminally ill patients the truth. He did so and made at least one painful mistake. He told a woman she was dying so she left her job, put her mother in a nursing home, and it all turned out to be a mistake."

"But really he was right; I mean Richard was. Peter told you, after all."

"I wanted to know, so I asked him. But he has not told me how long I have. How can he know?" She seems at the moment so much her old self that it is hard to imagine that she is dying, and again I feel the wall go up inside me, the wall against knowing something I do not want to know, that seems too painful to take in.

But Caroline changes the subject mercifully. "One thing about dying is that one can say anything, ask anything. One is immune from all the usual discretions and social necessities." She is now perceptibly a little out of breath and I know I must leave soon. "We've never talked about loving women. Did you feel guilt?"

"No. You see Vicky swept me off my feet. It all seemed part of her world, into which I was being taken by love, passionate love."

"I have more than once been in love with a woman," Caroline says. "I didn't feel guilty. As you say, it seemed so natural. Why I am telling you this is because I think all of us have it in us to be moved by the same sex and for a woman it is very different from loving a man passionately. It is not a choice, one or the other. Not for me, at any rate. Life is always more complex than we want to make it."

I am listening with all my being. While she has been talking, she has been looking away from me at the flowers. Now she turns and looks right into my eyes. "And so perhaps is dying, but Harriet," she says, "don't be terrified. The open door may be terrifying but it does lead somewhere. Right now it is leading you into unknown territory, just as dying is leading me. Let us rejoice."

"You marvelous woman. I must go now and let you rest." I lay the books on the table beside her. "A few books just in case you get bored and want a little distraction."

"I'm never bored," she says at once, "only I do get tired. I hate to say goodbye but, yes, it is time we parted." And she adds as I bend to kiss her, "Come back soon."

But I know in my heart that this may be goodbye. And I know, too, as I sit in the car, unable to leave the place, the street, Caroline, just yet, that she has said what she did to support me, to say I should accept myself and the world around me, the multiple lives, all the doors opening, and not close them ever again.

It is strange after that moment of truth and illumination that when I get home there is an anonymous letter among all the spring book catalogs from the university presses. When I lay it down I am shivering. It reads:

> Dear manager or whoever you are,
> This was a clean blue collar neighborhood until you and your ilk arrived. Now it is full of filthy gay men and lesbians. This is a warning. We do not want your obscene bookstore and we will do everything we can to get you out.
> A neighbor

I run down the stairs and find Joan preparing to leave as it is nearly two. "Read this," and I hand her the letter.

"Not unexpected, is it?" she says in her cool clipped voice.

"I'm scared, Joan. What do I do now? Wait for someone to burn the place down?"

"Take it to the police. I'll go with you."

"You're a trump," I say, thinking fast. The moment of terror is over and I am very angry. "We'll lock up and pin a sign on the door to say we'll be back soon."

"Good."

All police stations no doubt have the same dank smell, the same brown walls and battered desks we found in Somerville and, at least around Boston, the same Irish policemen, blustery, kind, and congenitally prejudiced against anyone deviating from the norm: black, Hispanic, or gay.

"Sit down," says the middle-aged sergeant in charge, looking us over with shrewd, not unkindly eyes. "What is the problem?"

"This is the problem," I say, handing over the letter.

He takes his time reading it and seems a little uncertain. Then he coughs and says, "Your activity has been brought to our notice," he says. "The people in your neighborhood are pretty square."

"But so are we," Joan says tartly. "A liberal feminist bookstore is a public service."

It sounds a little pretentious, but, after all, why we are in Somerville is not the point. "I came here to ask for protection from what looks like the lunatic fringe and I expect that fringe is in every community these days," I say as calmly as I can.

"Yes, well . . . Miss Hatfield, what can we do? I can't afford to have an officer patrolling the block day and night. If you call us, if there is some sort of attack, we'll come at once." But he does not look at me or smile at me and I sense that he is troubled by something. "What did the person who called our activity to your attention say?" I ask. "What is behind a savage blundering attack on two innocent booksellers?"

"Well . . . ," he pauses and frowns, "I was given a book bought at your store." He opens a drawer and brings out the evidence, Mary Daly's *Pure Lust*.

"Oh." I exchange a look with Joan. It is a rather anxious moment.

"It may interest you to know," Joan says, "that the subtitle of Daly's *Pure Lust* is *Elemental Feminist Philosophy* and that she teaches at Boston College in the department of philosophy."

"She does?" Absorbing this is as difficult as if Joan had called her a murderess. The sergeant, whose name I notice is Kevin O'Reilly, is clearly in a state of bewilderment.

"I think you would find it on the shelves of any reputable bookstore," I offer. "It has not been censored."

"May I suggest that you convey the information Miss Hatfield has given you to the person who brought the complaint?" Joan says.

"I'll do that." He is no doubt relieved to be able to do something. Then he smiles at me. "I had somehow expected some young dyke in trousers with a bow tie. Not," he adds with a patronizing smile, "an elderly lady like you."

Somehow it gives me a clue. "My guess is that that anonymous letter was written by an elderly lady."

"Elderly dames don't wear blue collars," he shoots back. So it was a man, after all. As I had feared. "My advice is to take some of those queer books off the shelves, at least for a while."

"That's not advice I can take," I answer. "I try at least to be open-minded."

"Well, have a good lock on your doors, and good luck to you. Call us if you need us."

So we go back to the store to find Martha waiting to hang her paintings, and two newcomers, an elderly woman and the stunning young black woman who had come the first day.

"Your dog has been defending the store," Martha says.

"That's a pretty forceful bark," the black woman says, and laughs as I unlock the door. "Do we dare come in?"

"Oh, Patapouf gets scared when she is left alone, not to worry," and indeed Patapouf is now wagging her tail as they troop in after me. It all feels so jolly and safe. It's as though the letter has been a bad dream. I remember suddenly that Sergeant O'Reilly did not give it back. Just as well. But when I mention it to Joan she offers to go back and get it.

"We might need it as evidence."

Back in the store, back in my own world, I am elated. It is good to be with three women who seem happy to be there, the elderly woman absorbed already in the poetry shelves. The black woman, whose name is Nan Blakeley, offers to help hang the paintings and that absorbs all our attention for a half-hour. Now that they are on the empty wall and I stand and look at them, I find I like them a lot more than I expected to.

"Beautiful," says Nan beside me, and turning to Martha, "Aren't you proud?"

"Sort of," Martha admits. "It's the first time I have shown my work, so . . ."

"I've always wanted to be a painter," says Nan, who strikes me as someone able to connect quickly, as she obviously has with Martha.

"Now you have worked for your keep," I say. "What can I do for you, Nan? I know you were here before. What are you especially interested in?" I feel it is a clumsy question and a little condescending. When will I ever learn? Learn the right tone, be at ease as Nan is?

"Oh, first of all black literature, especially autobiography by women. I saw that you had quite a lot when I came in the first time but I had to leave. So if I may, I'm just going to burrow in."

"I thought about putting all the black writers together and

then thought that all good writers should be placed together, not separated by race or even sex. Was that right?"

"Absolutely," Nan says. "Of course." She has taken Alice Walker's *In Search of Our Mother's Gardens* off the shelf and is sitting beside Martha, who seems lost in a trance, looking at the paintings. "What a wonderful title that is," she says.

"It's essays, actually, and very good they are."

"I guess I'll have to take it, along with Toni Morrison's new one—you must have that."

"On the table in front."

When she comes to the register with the two books she lays them down for me and then kneels down to pat Patapouf, who is asleep now under the desk. "Such a dear old thing," she says.

Somehow that gesture makes it possible for me to ask what I have been dying to ask. "I've been trying to guess what your profession is. Is that indiscreet of me?"

She laughs then. "You'll never guess!"

"A psychiatrist?"

This makes her laugh again. "No, I'm a housewife, mother of two little girls, so an amateur psychiatrist maybe. My husband is a physicist at M.I.T."

Martha hears this and comes over. "But what did you do before?" she asks.

"I was a journalist. Wrote a column for the small-town newspaper where I grew up in New Jersey."

"How could you bear to give it up?"

"It didn't seem important," she says. "I guess I just wasn't that involved." She is looking at Martha with real interest, trying to figure out perhaps why all these questions. "It's not like being a painter. Are you married?"

"Yes."

"Any children?"

"I don't want children. I know it sounds crazy and wrong . . . that's what my husband says. He says I'm not natural."

"You're in a tight spot," Nan says gently. "I don't envy you."

"It's tough enough being a woman artist. Children might make it impossible," says Martha with a slightly aggressive tone. She adds, "Where are your children now?"

"The smaller is in preschool. The other is in elementary school." She looks at her watch. "I guess I had better be off to fetch them. It's later than I thought." But she does not hurry out without turning back at the door. "Good luck!" she says. "Good luck to the painting!"

I am thinking what a charming woman Nan is as I go over some orders. My desk is a bit chaotic. Somehow I do not notice when Martha leaves. It is very quiet now in the store, but I am not alone and, remembering that warning letter, am rather glad not to be. But in a few moments the elderly woman has paid for Amy Clampitt's new poems, and now I am alone.

I look around the shop: books in their brilliant jackets, Martha's paintings, light and air. How can some brute want to destroy this? Already the atmosphere has changed for me. It has become a fort instead of an open, human place. But even as this thought crosses my mind I push it away. "They" are not going to change the atmosphere, I say to myself. We are going to hang on here.

For the next hour, with no customers to interrupt me, I manage to clear away most of the bills, and that helps. "Compose the mind," as Vicky used to say. Making order out of chaos does it for me. But remembering Vicky is not the best thing for me to do at the moment. She would be upset, horrified at what is happening. No doubt she would blame me for exposing myself as I seem to be doing without even realizing what a women's bookstore would involve, how much I would be asked to face in myself. Though she would have called that nonsense. Vicky did not want to think about what labels like lesbian, queer, deviant meant. We were as we were and to hell with everyone else would have been her attitude. But she would have approved of Joan—aloof, embittered, coping with a divorce and an unfair settlement. Vicky would have been quick to sympathize with her.

I wonder whether I am a coward not to have said to Sergeant O'Reilly that I am a lesbian, although—and here I cannot help smiling—a lady. For that might have changed his image of us a little. Yet, I know that I could not do that. To some women who have come into the store as a pair, I have talked about Vicky. But that is different, that is simply sharing.

Shall I tell Fred what is happening? The very idea makes me physically uncomfortable and I get up and get a dog bone for Patapouf as some kind of gesture to keep the devils at bay. My family had seemed to take for granted that Vicky and I were partners and had never asked an embarrassing question. And Vicky would have lied if they had probed. But if only the obvious, the exhibitionist, the aggressively role-conscious women "come out," how is a bridge ever to be made? And is it not precisely that bridge that I had envisioned, though not consciously, when I dreamed of a women's bookstore? As though somewhere deep down I want to be counted in, to be an active part of what is going on, want to make known where I stand in a discreet, unobjectionable way?

I wish there were someone I could talk to. Caroline! But Caroline is dying. I cannot drag her back into life. No, there is no one, and so I am thinking when Angelica walks in. "Oh Angelica!" I cry out fervently, going to greet her.

"Yes, Angelica . . . you sound marooned," she says, sitting down. "Nobody here, I see."

"They come and go. Today has been rather quiet. I even managed to clear my desk."

"Bravo!" She gladly accepts a cup of tea and I go out to put the kettle on while she talks to Patapouf, who has emerged from under the desk to be petted.

"Well, you seem to be well launched," Angelica says when we are settled with cups of tea. "It's a delightful atmosphere. What are those strange paintings, by the way?"

"A young woman brought them in. She's having a hard time being an artist and not wanting children, as her husband does."

"So you offered to hang her work? Of course you did."

"Yes. I am not crazy about it, but she needs support. If someone buys one, that will be great. And, besides, I am on her side."

"It's all happening, just as you dreamed it would," Angelica says warmly.

"Yes, but . . . ," and of course the story of the anonymous letter and Sergeant O'Reilly, all of it has to be told.

"Mmmm," Angelica says, not looking at me, a little shy, I think. "A dirty business, Harriet."

"The last thing I expected," I confess. "It really shook me up."

"An alarm system?" she says then.

"No, they always go off by mistake. I shall have stronger locks put on, and then we'll wait and see."

"Rather like sitting on a keg of dynamite. Why don't you and Patapouf spend the nights at my house for a while?"

That is so like Angelica, but it is not a solution, not really. "I can't run away," I explain.

"Hatred," Angelica murmurs. "Of course you are frightened." I sense that she is holding back.

"And confused," I say, "confused . . . It is also illuminating in a way. I have never felt like a leper before, an outcast. But huge numbers of people in our society do, of course. Maybe, for all we know, the blue-collars do."

76

"Come on now!" Angelica says, quite crossly for her. "You don't have to become a saint, do you, to stand firm?"

So at last I can laugh at myself and the whole stupid world. "I don't know," I say, pouring us another cup of tea. "I probably asked for this without even knowing what I was doing. A women's bookstore is going to attract all sorts of women. That is what I wanted, after all."

"But has there been an inundation of women couples?"

"No. A few. All charming so far. All people I want to know. It's the young who have no doubts, you see. They introduce a friend as their lover. I must say it does amaze me. It even shocks me."

"I don't like it, Harriet. It just seems so naked." And in Angelica's tone I recognize myself, the self of two weeks ago who has already begun to change.

"I like honesty," I say. "I like it that they include me. And that's what I want of this place: an open door and no judgmental values."

"You've come a long way, baby," says Angelica, mimicking the cigarette ad and teasing a little as she does so. And there it ends for the time being, Angelica insisting that she will call me every evening and that I carry a cane when I give Patapouf a last walk.

After she leaves and it is nearly six, I close up. Patapouf will have to wait until I can pull myself together. So far I have been too busy to be more than superficially afraid. Now I have the odd sensation that I mustn't move, and with Patapouf at my feet, I sit in the armchair by the cold fire for quite a while. I can hear footsteps on the pavement below, and once a motorcycle revving up and roaring away, people laughing, the grinding roar of the bus as it comes to a halt. These are familiar enough sounds, but I am ultrasensitized to another sound which, if it exists, is being drowned out. But, after all, who would try anything sinister at this time of night? I decide to walk Patapouf while there are still homecomers in the streets.

Whatever "they" will do or not do, they have invaded my life already and changed its atmosphere and that makes me furious. But out on the street with the old dog, and leaning on my cane while she smells every tree trunk, I am suddenly not afraid at all. Several people are neighbors, saying something friendly like, "How are you doing?" If there are enemies among the workingmen on their way, they do not show it. And suddenly the whole affair seems ridiculous. Two young women carrying book bags stop to ask me if I own the bookstore and beg me to stay open one night a week till eight or nine. They cannot know what a godsend they are.

"I'll think about it," I assure them, "when I can find an assistant to spell me and Joan. It is so good to feel the bookstore means something to you."

"We want to come and see," the tall one says, "but it's hard in the daytime. You see, I clean houses in the afternoons. I have to have a job. It's awfully expensive being a student these days."

"We clean as a team," the other girl says. "It's fun in a way."

"Look," I say on impulse, and because I like their faces, "I'll open up now for a half-hour for you." I have it in mind that they might be the answer to Saturdays, but it is a little soon to act on that impulse. At any rate they jump at the chance to come in and look around and bury themselves at once in silent roving from bookcase to bookcase, taking out a book now and then to look into, then carefully putting it back. Finally the tall one asks, "Do you have a book about those Welsh ladies, the eighteenth-century ones, who lived together in some remote place, but everyone knew them?"

"The ladies of Llangollen." I recognize them of course and go to the bookcase of biographies to pull out an English paperback. "This is what you are after."

"Oh my," the other one says, "how much is it?"

"I'll mark it down to five dollars. It's a little worn at the binding I see. Paperbacks do split rather often."

They exchange a look. "We'll buy it," says the tall one, burrowing into her jeans pocket. "Hot dogs for dinner, Fanny," she says to her companion, "but it's worth it," she adds with a smile.

As I make out the slip I am still uncertain about whether to ask them for Saturday help or not. Meanwhile I talk. "My friend Vicky and I went to Llangollen to see the farmhouse. We had a picnic in a field nearby, such lovely rugged country. But the house itself feels empty and strange. I felt that their ghosts had left, even from their big double bed with its dark carved bedposts."

"Oh, tell us more," says Fanny.

"Sit down for a minute. There is something I want to ask you. But first my name is Harriet Hatfield."

"Mine is Fanny Arthur, and my friend is Ruth Phillipson." I am relieved that Fanny does not say "and my lover is . . ."

"I'm happy to meet you. You appear to be one of those serendipitous happenings." Fanny is clasping the book in her hands. "How would you like to mind the store on Saturdays?"

They beam at each other. "We'd love it, Miss Hatfield, but . . ." She looks over at Ruth with obvious distress.

"You could even study. It's not been that busy so far."

"Fanny does not know how to say it, but you see, cleaning we make ten dollars an hour, eighty dollars on Saturdays. That would be too much, wouldn't it?" Fanny is blushing.

It is my turn to be distressed and to frown as I make quick calculations in my head. If we sold two hundred dollars' worth on Saturdays, and that is not really that much, would that cover their eighty dollars? Joan will be appalled, I fear.

"Oh dear," Fanny sighs.

"Well," I say slowly, still weighing the deal, still asking myself to go slow and be careful, "after all, I've found the right people for the shop, I think. I'll make a deal with you. Let's try it for a month, shall we? If you sell enough books it will work out for the shop. How about it?"

"It's wonderful, it's marvelous." Fanny leaps to her feet and does a little dance. "It's unbelievable."

"The only thing is we have to honor a promise about cleaning for someone this Saturday, so we can't start until next Saturday," says Ruth. I am entertained by the way she reacts as against Fanny's ebullience. Ruth perhaps is one of those people who reacts to good news with solemnity.

"But just imagine"—Fanny is not to be beaten down—"what it will be like to run a bookstore instead of cleaning out bathrooms!"

Patapouf, who always reacts to movement and gaiety, emerges from under my desk in a flurry of barks. "It's a deal," I say. But then I must tell them about the jeopardy we may be in. "You must give me your address, by the way, while I think of it."

"I live with my family," says Ruth. "I'll give you their address." So they are not a couple after all. Will they understand, I wonder.

"There is something you must know," I say, after writing their addresses down. "Sit down and let me explain."

They listen in silence while I tell them about the letter, about O'Reilly, and end by saying that the last thing I had imagined when I opened the store would be such hatred. I admit that I am frightened by it.

"Well, it's just disgusting," Fanny bursts out.

"It's the way things are," Ruth says quietly. "You see," she says slowly, feeling her way, "we are not lovers, just good friends. But so many people take it for granted that we must be lesbians, it upsets Fanny, and me too. So we get it the other way."

"The obsession with coming out, with being honest, telling the world. People just don't believe in a real friendship any more!" Fanny says. "It's out of fashion."

"So maybe you don't feel you want to hold the fort on Saturdays?" I am disappointed.

"Of course we want to come," Ruth says. "Fanny loves a fight!"

"You see," I explain, "I lived for thirty years with a woman, the publisher Victoria Chilton. When she died last year she left me money and that is how I can afford to run a bookstore at a perpetual deficit—at least so far."

"You mustn't think we are against such relationships," Ruth answers.

"For heaven's sake, of course not," Fanny says. "I feel any relationship that lasts thirty years must be real and fulfilling. I sort of envy you that, even though you must have felt cut in two when she died."

"I tell you what," I say, "think my offer over, talk it over, understand what you may be risking if you decide to take the job, and whether you can really live in the atmosphere here. Maybe you could come a week from tomorrow and let my manager Joan fill you in, and then see how it strikes you. Have a trial run. How about that as a solution?"

"But there's no problem," Ruth says in her quiet way.

And at this the whole situation strikes me as hilarious and I laugh aloud. "What a kettle of fish!" I say, still laughing.

"We had better let you go," Fanny says, "but we'll come on Saturday a week from tomorrow. You can count on us." We shake hands, and they leave.

When they have gone I turn out the lights and stand for a moment in the dark, looking out on the street—wondering who might be lurking there. Patapouf, sensing fear in the air, gives a loud, deep bark. "It's time we went upstairs, old dog."

I am suddenly so tired it is an effort to climb to the second floor. It has been an extraordinary day. One hard problem, one splendid solution. But when I call Joan to tell her about Fanny and Ruth she is upset.

"You can't mean you hired these women off the street, without knowing anything about them?" she asks, dismay in her voice. I had expected relief.

"I like them, Joan. I have to trust my instincts."

"Very well." But I can tell she is not convinced. "You are such an innocent," she says. "It scares the pants off me."

"I suppose I am an innocent. I prefer that to being a cynic." It is the closest we have come to a disagreement.

"I'll see you tomorrow," she says coldly, "hope nothing happens tonight." I sit down then and pour myself a double scotch. For once I do not turn on the news. The television can drown out slight sounds, and I must be alert. It is no way to live, but, strangely enough, when I get into bed after eating a poached egg on toast, I fall asleep at once.

The last thing I expect at nine the next morning, before Joan arrives at ten, is a ring at my door. And the very last thing I expect is to find Fred standing there with a parcel in his hands.

"Hey, what are you doing roving around here so early in the morning?" I ask, not very warmly.

"Well, let me in and I'll explain."

"Come up and have a cup of coffee."

"Thanks, but what I need right now is a pail of water, a hard sponge, and some detergent." My heart sinks. "I don't suppose you've been out yet, have you?"

"I was just going to walk Patapouf when you rang."

"Someone has chalked an obscenity on your windows. If it's chalk, not paint, I can rub it off in a minute."

"Oh."

"Angelica called me," he explains while I obey his orders, find a pail under the sink and fill it. "I happen to have a very strong lock on hand, came over to install it as a matter of fact." He smiles his secretive smile, then, "You have to admit I am a useful brother to have."

But I am cross, feel betrayed, and Fred is the last person I want around at this point. "Damn Angelica. She had no right to call you!"

"She was pretty upset," he says, "and she's a good friend. You need good friends."

"If there's any trouble the police will come." I am shaking with anger and close to tears.

"Come on, Harriet. This sort of thing is pretty hard to take. Don't get on your high horse with me."

"Oh, to hell with it, if you can rub off whatever those clods wrote on the window, I'll be grateful. But don't put me down as crazy or something. I'm doing what I dreamed of doing." I beg him not to tell Andrew. "Don't spoil it for me, Fred."

"Who's spoiling it, I or those clods, as you call them? For God's sake!" He stomps down the stairs and I put Patapouf on the leash and prepare to follow him.

When I get to the street I find Fred talking with two men in jogging suits. Whatever had been written on the shop windows has been erased. "Here's my sister. Harriet," Fred says, "meet Joe Hunter and Eddie North." Joe is tall, over six feet, with a short black beard, and he must be over forty. Eddie, much younger, is not as handsome, has blond, crew-cut hair and small, bright blue eyes. It seems in order to shake hands.

"We want you to know that we're nearby if you need help," Joe says, looking at me hard, though kindly. "I gave your brother my card with the phone number."

"Joe's a psychiatrist," Eddie says. "I work in the garage down the street. You are a brave woman to open a women's bookstore here. It's a tough neighborhood."

"So I am learning."

"These days," Joe says, "every neighborhood is tough for gays. People think they have a weapon against us now, and it's AIDS, of course."

Everything is happening so fast—Fred turning up, two gay men entering my orbit—that I do not know what to say, or how. "It's awfully kind of you to come," I say. "The best thing about trouble is that you learn who your friends are! Thanks a lot."

"We jog usually around half-past seven," Joe says, "so if there are any more remarks on your windows we'll clean up for you."

"Every day?"

At this Fred laughs. "You are a pessimist, Harriet. It may never happen again."

"Presumably it will," says Joe. "Well, see you!" And they are off.

Fred and I go back to my apartment now to have a cup of coffee. "Nice fellows," he says when we have settled at the table, "even though they are obviously faggots."

"The father of two has to feel superior, does he?" Keyed up as I am, I cannot let that tone of his pass.

"You may think you have to take on the whole world but you do not have to take your brother on, Harriet. For God's sake, woman!"

"Sorry, but you see I have had to absorb a lot in these first weeks. I guess I'm supersensitive."

"Now you have a handy psychiatrist. He might help."

"I don't need a psychiatrist, Fred. Who was it who said 'very few people can stand reality,' or words to that effect? I feel I'm beginning to learn about reality. And high time."

"And what is reality?"

It takes me a moment to answer and I drink my coffee in silence while Fred looks at me with an inquisitive, slightly patronizing air. "Whatever it is it is not the sheltered life I led with

Vicky. I'm suddenly in a big open space with nowhere to hide. And I'm meeting people who live in that open space and take the risks."

"At least you can have a proper lock on your door, so I had better get to work."

"I wish you understood," I say. "It would make it easier to thank you."

"How do you know I don't understand?" he asks, taking the lock, screws, a screwdriver, and a hammer out of the bag.

"I always feel that you think I'm daft, that, as they say, I need help. It diminishes me."

"That's your interpretation," Fred says coldly. "I'll be gone in a half-hour," and he runs down the stairs where I follow him, after washing the cups, and sit at my desk wondering why I have to be on the defensive, why he always manages to rub me the wrong way like a cat.

But there is no way to mend things now and I am glad when Joan arrives and I can go upstairs and call Angelica. I feel beleaguered. Joan is cross because of the Saturday deal; Fred is suggesting I see a psychiatrist; Angelica is betraying me . . . Oh dear, what is wrong with me? I ask myself.

"Why are you cross?" Angelica asks when she hears my tone of voice.

"You should not have called Fred."

"I felt so anxious, Harriet, and why not call your brother?"

"He's here now putting a new lock on the door in the shop. I am capable of doing that myself. My family are the last people I need to get involved in what is, after all, a problem I can only solve alone." I can hear my voice suddenly shrill.

"My dear, it is exactly because it is not a problem you can solve alone that I intervened."

"It was an invasion of privacy, Angelica. I don't care what you think or feel."

"I'm sorry."

"Whatever help I need must and will come from here, from the neighbors. Already a couple of men turned up to offer to help. They will erase any obscenities those goons write on my windows. You see . . ." But I have let the cat out of the bag by revealing there have been obscenities and have to explain that now. That done, I cut Angelica short by saying I have to go down and say goodbye to Fred.

I do not do that. I sit down in a state of great confusion and distress. The only thing that can help me, I know, is to be in the world I am trying to create—to be down in the store. There can be no salvation in arguing with a good old friend. Or with my stuffed-shirt brother for that matter. Joan, however, must be tamed somehow, and I invite her to come up for a sandwich lunch at noon and close the store for an hour.

Meanwhile I decide to take off until noon, get away for a couple of hours, take Patapouf with me, perhaps for a walk in the Mount Auburn Cemetery, where the trees must be already turning. There, perhaps, I can compose my mind.

7

For all the chaos inside me, outside it proves to be a perfect
morning, and, when I have parked the car and released Pata-
pouf, I stand there for a minute drinking in the light, one maple
brilliant yellow and beyond it a scarlet one. The dogwood
around a small formal garden near the entrance is the purple
and dark red Vicky had always remarked on, for we had come
here fairly often for a walk, especially in spring and fall. Her
parents and various aunts and uncles are buried here, but what
she enjoyed most was examining the amazing variety of
tombs—huge classic temples, Victorian angels on top of granite
peristyles, and even under what looked like a red marble table,
a large dog! The marvelous trees . . . Mount Auburn is really an
arboretum. The small ponds where ducks swim and dive for
morsels below the surface. Dug into the hillside surrounding
one of the ponds is a series of huge temples, which are tombs
with wrought-iron gates and family names carved into the mar-
ble. They look like a village of stone houses for the dead.

As I walk along with Patapouf decorously on the leash beside
me, I miss Vicky more than I have since her death. She would
have recognized a brownish bird who flies past and might be a

thrush. When I wander down a hillside to one of the ponds where we had often sat and picnicked on a stone bench, I sit down, trying to contain a wave of nostalgia for those safe days we shared, and to keep back the tears that are pricking my eyes.

But what keeps grief from engulfing me is my knowledge, my having to admit that Vicky would not have liked at all what has been happening at the shop. The idea of her disapproval sharpens my wits, for I begin to think of all the people who have already found refuge in the bookstore, the woman I had called a bag-lady at first, Martha with her conflict about painting, the two generous nuns who seem at this moment like sparklers lighting up the dark, the two lesbians and their dog, the older woman who is founding a home caretakers' organization as a way of handling her husband's death, the young women who are best friends and clean houses, and this very morning two men who appeared out of nowhere to give me support. "O brave new world that has such people in it!"

I exult in what has already been accomplished, and I exult to feel as alive as I do, as full of hope in spite of being under attack. My friends from Chestnut Hill may think I am crazy to have chosen to open a women's bookstore in this particular neighborhood, but I know they are wrong and decide to sing one of my Patapouf songs. Years ago when she was a puppy I used to make up songs for her, always hoping she would sing back. Her ears are attuned to my voice, and she just cocks her head and listens, half closing her eyes.

It is a little embarrassing in the middle of an aria to see a young couple approaching with birding glasses. No doubt they have not heard me, but I feel exposed enough to get up and leave by another path. It is time anyway that Patapouf and I go home to put a sandwich together for Joan.

She has news for me. A reporter from the *Globe* has called and wants an interview. I am pouring us a glass of California burgundy and when she says it my hand shakes. "Oh dear," I say, sitting down, "must I see this person? What did he or she have to say?"

"It was a woman called Hetty something or other. She wants you to call her." Joan looks rather somber. "Apparently word has gotten out that you have been threatened."

"Bad news travels fast."

"And the wrong publicity could wreck this place," Joan says.

"So you think I should not allow an interview? Go in hiding, as it were?" The minute I utter the words I know that I will see this Hetty person. But I sense also that Joan, for the second time, is violently opposed to my instinctive acts of this sort. "Oh dear, the cheese hasn't melted properly," I say, playing for time.

"It's a good sandwich," she says, frowning. "But yes, I'm against an interview now that undoubtedly is based on news that has little to do with the value of Hatfield House. It might bring in crowds of people you really don't want to attract."

"It's also a chance to state my position once and for all." I know we are at an impasse and decide to change the subject. "The two young women whom I am going to try out for Saturdays told me they are best friends but not lovers, you will be glad to hear."

"That's neither here nor there. How do you know they are reliable people? Their sex life seems to me to have nothing to do with it."

"I hate it when you are cross, Joan. It makes you sound so cold."

"Sorry, but I am, after all, involved," she says in, for her, quite a passionate tone of voice.

"If you don't like them after you have spent next Saturday teaching them the ropes, I'll find an excuse and not hire them after all. How is that?"

"All right," she says grudgingly.

I don't like feeling at cross purposes for she is the person I have come to depend on most, the efficient ally through all the problems. "You know, Joan," I say, trying to catch her eye, but she is not looking my way at the moment, "the reason we make such a good team is because we are so different. I may rebel sometimes at being held in check," and I laugh at the image of myself as a wild horse, "but I really could not manage without you at this point. I hope you do know that?"

"I don't have your verve, that's for sure," which is a large concession for Joan, who could have said, "I dislike your temperament," which perhaps would have been closer to the truth.

"Well, I had better go down, in case there are people waiting. Can you find your way out?"

"Of course."

I couldn't be gladder to see anyone than I am when I see Chris and Mary waving at me through the locked door. "How are you faring?" Chris asks. "We couldn't resist just popping in for a minute."

I rest my eyes on their already dear faces. How can I feel such intimacy so soon? "You can't possibly imagine how glad I am to see you," I say. "Oh dear, so much has happened since you were here."

"Like what?" Mary asks, sitting on the arm of one of the chairs.

"I'll bet a lot of people have come. Word gets around fast when there's a good thing going," Chris says.

"On the contrary, I am causing an outburst of hatred, a threat, and obscene messages written on the windows at night."

"No!" Mary's eyes are wide. "And whyever threats?"

"Outraged someone, and perhaps more than one someone. It is not what I have done, it is what I am," I say, suddenly overcome with the reality of what I am facing as though I were indeed a criminal. "They say the store itself is an obscenity and filled with lesbians and they don't want people like that in a nice, quiet, blue-collar neighborhood. There you have it!"

Chris looks thoughtful. "It's a bad time," she says. "You are reaping the seeds of fear."

"And then," Mary says, "people love to hate. It gets the adrenaline rushing, but it is frightening. What can we do, Chris? How can we help?"

Chris smiles. "It's a pity in some ways that we no longer wear the habit," she says. "Nuns are fairly respectable customers after all," and for some reason we all burst into laughter. It is such a grotesque idea that going back into the Middle Ages now would help bring people into the twentieth century. Their presence is a comfort, and I am happy that they stay on, looking at books for over an hour. They only leave when Sue Bagley appears, much to my dismay.

I pretend to be busy and, on an impulse, call the *Globe* and make a date to see the reporter on Monday morning, in my apartment. Is it a wise decision? As usual, I acted on impulse, but the young woman sounded warm and interested and said they would send a photographer, although I explained that I would rather not talk in the shop. It is agreed that he come later and take some photos of the shop with me in it, after the interview. Joan, I feel sure, will not approve. Why hadn't I asked the nuns' advice?

I am extremely irritated when Sue Bagley comes over to the desk and says with apparent pleasure, "So I hear you're in trouble."

"Bad news does get around fast, doesn't it?"

"A friend of mine saw some dirty words on your windows at dawn," she announces. "I knew something like that was bound to happen. People around here are nothing but hoodlums."

"On what do you base that view?" I ask coldly.

"The way they carry on in the streets, laughing and screaming ugly words. They never take in their trash cans, just let them bang around on the street. Drug takers, no doubt, too."

"Why do you live in this neighborhood if you don't like it?"

"My dear, it's cheap. That's why." She seems very pleased with herself this afternoon. "And why did you choose to open a radical bookstore in this neighborhood?"

Why did I? I really ask myself. "I don't know. I wanted lots of different kinds of people to use the store, and that is what has happened, as a matter of fact."

"Too many queers," she says.

"And what if I told you that I am, as you call it, queer myself?" I am cross enough to take the bull by the horns.

"Oh well," she says, a little taken aback, "you are old and respectable and no one would ever guess."

There it is in a nutshell. The image of gay and lesbian in the general public's mind is, of course, the young and exhibitionistic, the *outré* and the promiscuous, visible and shocking. And if none of the old and respectable like me ever admit what they are that image will reinforce discriminatory laws and the kind of ignorant attack I am suffering at the moment.

"That, Miss Bagley, is no comfort. It makes me see that I have been a coward."

"It is none of anybody's business what your private life is or was, and you'll do the shop no good if you come out with disturbing facts at this point. You're surely not thinking of doing so?" She seems for a change off her high horse and quite concerned.

"I don't know what I'll do. But one thing I know. I am not going to be driven out by those goons," and with that I turn deliberately to the papers on my desk. I need time to think, for it is becoming increasingly clear to me that the interview is a chance for action, and I must summon the courage to take it. I resist the temptation to argue with Sue Bagley. Somehow I sense that she has been hurt, that her aggressive behavior about lesbians is not entirely theoretical. I am in no mood for an outbreak of personal tragedy at this point.

The mail provides an excuse and, while I immerse myself in it, Sue Bagley leaves, in a mild huff. She expects to be able to talk at length when she drops in, but I am adamant this time. "I hope you will be sensible," she says at the door, "and not rush in where angels fear to tread."

In the mail I find a note from Joe Hunter, asking me whether I would care to come and have dinner with them next Saturday at six:

> . . . We have much to talk about, and we hope to lure you with Eddie's coq au vin. Don't bother to answer this unless you can't come.

Then a P.S.:

> Perhaps Patapouf could stay home and defend the shop. We have two Siamese cats.

It is my first invitation from anyone in the neighborhood and I feel very pleased, also because they have been so kind, those two. Patapouf, under my desk, is dreaming and gives two or three muffled barks.

The afternoon proves to be an unusually busy one so it may be a good thing that there is no time to think about the interview. Martha arrives at tea time with her husband in tow, a tall, thin, shy young man wearing dark glasses.

"I wanted David to see the paintings," she explains after we shake hands. And then, "See?" as they stand together looking at the wall.

"She is very talented, isn't she?" I say, standing beside them.

"I suppose she may be," David says. "At any rate she is consumed by it, and I have to admire that."

"But you don't really like them, do you?" Martha needles. She appears to be close to tears and they stand apart, not touching, the gulf between them clear to me in their unconnected stance.

He doesn't answer this probing question so I fill in for him. "They are strange and perhaps troubling, but the people who come into the store always look at them with great interest. They mesmerize . . ."

"I wish I understood them better," David says, turning to me.

"You don't have to understand," Martha says, and no doubt they have been through this before. "You just have to let yourself feel something when you look at them."

"I feel literally in the dark," he says bitterly, "shut out."

"Oh come on, David!"

At this he sighs and I am relieved to see him put an arm round her shoulders. "I'm impossible, I know."

"Yes," says Martha, extricating herself, "you make me miserable. It's not fair. I don't understand what *you* are doing but I don't rub that in, do I?"

"Art is not supposed to be closed to the common human mind is it? Physics of the kind I am involved in is, at best, open to a very few people with a certain expertise. Can't you see? There is a difference," and he looks at her now with a faintly patronizing smile. "We are not rivals, Martha. Can't you get that?"

"I don't know what we are," Martha says bitterly.

I wish I could make some brilliant remark that would close the gap but I can't. I am out of my depth.

"I've got a class in ten minutes," he says, "have to rush," and he is gone in a flurry, eager to be off the hook, of course.

"Sit down, Martha. Let's have a cup of tea."

"Oh I'm so furious," she says, "there are times when I hate David. He is so smug."

"Maybe just at sea," I venture.

"We do nothing but fight these days. It ends in bed and that's no good either." She raises her voice as I have gone into the little room to put on water for tea. "If we had a baby I would hate it, forced on me by his power of creating something, deprived of my power." She is unaware that someone has come in and cannot help hearing her outburst. Fortunately it turns out to be Marian Tuckerworth, and when I come back with the tea tray I beg her to join us, and introduce them.

"Thanks. I'm at a dead end. A cup of tea won't find a caretaker, but it will revive me."

I explain quickly what Mrs. Tuckerworth is doing, founding an organization to offer help to women who have become sole caretaker of a dying husband or other relative.

"It's proving next to impossible to find the right person, experienced enough, with some nursing experience, and," she adds with a smile, "above all, cheerful, if possible with a sense of humor."

Martha, still absorbed in her own problems, says, "If David jokes about having a baby I'll kill him."

Her intensity forces Marian to turn to her with obvious concern and interest. "I gather your husband is trying to persuade you to have a child. Hard to unpersuade him?"

"Impossible," Martha says. "He thinks I'm unnatural. Women were created to have children, you see, but," she turns to Marian and sets her cup down, "I'm a painter. I haven't even begun my career. I can't stop now for years and be a nurse, can I?"

I am glad to see that Martha is addressing Marian more gently, no longer apparently screaming from a hilltop as she had been a moment ago.

"Those landscapes," I make a gesture to the wall where they hang, "are Martha's work. You can see how talented she is."

"I don't know yet," Martha says, suddenly humble, "I haven't had time to find out."

"How old are you?"

"Thirty."

"Good heavens, then you do have time. Why not ask your husband to let you have five years and then have a child?"

"I'm not maternal," Martha says shortly. "It's not my thing."

"I'll tell you something," Marian says quietly. "I did not want children and fortunately for me, neither did my husband."

"What did he do?" Martha is visibly more cheerful. She has found an ally.

"He was a psychiatrist who specialized in treating cancer patients. He was convinced and proved it many times that cancer was often psychosomatic. He was a pioneer in that field."

"Why didn't you want children?" Martha asks.

"I don't know . . . maybe our marriage seemed complete, so much so that we were afraid of an intruder. Now I'm shocking you!" And she laughs her endearing musical laugh. "We were very happy," she adds, "until he was crippled by arteriosclerosis. He died of it after four years of hell, and I very nearly died I was so exhausted by the end."

"Why are you looking for caretakers?" Martha asks.

"So other women won't have to go through what I did."

"Oh."

For a moment we each drink our tea, the silence buzzing with all our thoughts.

"Organizing to make home care available is proving to be a great deal harder than I could have imagined. Medicare pays nothing toward it, of course, and there appear to be very few qualified people. We need people who will come into homes where a son has AIDS. Right now that is the priority, as you can imagine."

"I thought Hospice would come in," I venture.

"Sometimes, but not if it is to be a long illness. Emphysema, for instance, may go on for years."

"Oh dear," Martha sighs, "I wish I felt art was useful. I wish I could feel more justified."

It has begun to rain and several people have come in, partly for shelter no doubt. Suddenly the store is quite full and the time and place for intimate talk are no longer with us.

Marian gets up and brings a book on Jung to pay for, stops by Martha, who is sitting at the table where she can see her paintings, and says, "Stick to your guns! A child would not be the solution to whatever is wrong with your marriage right now. I feel sure of that."

"Thanks," says Martha, blushing, "you have made me feel less of a monster."

Marian has left but Martha stays on. I devoutly hope no one will make a negative comment about her paintings, and luckily no one does. And I settle back into the business end of the store, glad to be too busy now, too happily involved, to dread the Monday interview.

8

It is awkward not to see Hetty Rinehart, the interviewer, in the shop. Here, after all, I am in command and in my element. But I do not at all want Joan in on whatever I may blurt out, so the only thing is to greet Miss Rinehart in the shop, introduce Joan, and then take her upstairs. Either there have been no further insults written on the windows or the two kind strangers have washed them off by the time we open up.

Hetty is on time and while she talks briefly with Joan and looks around I size her up, a shock at first glance. Tall, she wears a blue-jean miniskirt, black silk stockings, heavy white Reeboks, and a long white sweater over a plaid shirt. Her wave of blond hair is cut in some absurd new fashion. Overall, a plain face diminished rather than enhanced by the way she dresses.

When we have settled in by the fireplace and she has taken out a pad and pencil there is a slight pause. Since she seems daunted I ask her about herself. "Have you been on the *Globe* long?"

"Two years. I graduated from B.U. in journalism and there was an opening. I've been lucky."

"Well, let's get going," I venture. "Why did you want this interview?"

"You're not at all what I expected," she says bluntly.

"Neither are you," I counter and we both laugh. "What did you expect?"

"I guess someone younger."

"The bookstore is young, but I am not. It's all new to me, all an adventure." This is bait and I hope she will take it. She does.

"I know," Hetty says. "I had heard about you from a friend of mine at M.I.T. and meant to pop in someday and see the shop. Then," she takes a deep breath and comes to the point, a subtle approach clearly not her forte, "I heard that you were being attacked as a lesbian outfit, that you had been threatened. That looked like news."

"It was news to me, I must say. I suppose I am an innocent abroad, but the last thing I expected was obscenities painted on the windows."

"Why not?" Hetty asks. "There's some sort of battle going on in society, isn't there? I mean . . . people are gross when it comes to homosexuals."

I have begun to like Hetty because she is so forthright, and therefore I too can come to the point without beating about the bush. "Why not? Well, because in the first place it is not what you called 'a lesbian outfit.' Some customers are lesbians and I welcome them, but they are not really the dominant group, you know. So far the shop has drawn a wide variety of women of all ages, married, divorced, old, young . . ."

"What was the attack actually?"

"An anonymous letter threatening to force us to close since we are tainting, if that is the word, a nice, clean neighborhood of working people who want none of us or the books we sell."

"I don't get it," says Hetty flatly, "except," and she looks me in the eye, "you are a lesbian yourself, aren't you?"

100

It was bound to be asked, that question, and there are a hundred ways I could fail to answer it. Joan's shadow crosses my mind—none of their damned business, she would say. "It's odd that no one has asked me that question before. When I was young it was not asked. Now it is and I must say yes. I lived with a woman friend, the head of a small publishing house, for thirty years. We did not think of ourselves as peculiar or out of the ordinary. We just lived our lives."

Hetty does not take her eyes off my face. She is listening intently and only looks down for a moment to scribble something on her pad. "Like Gertrude Stein and Alice Toklas?"

"I suppose so, though neither of us was or is a genius."

"What happened to your friend?" Hetty asks. "I gather you are alone now."

"Vicky died, very suddenly. I inherited money and so am able to do what I dreamed of doing, make a place that welcomes women of all sorts . . . and I'm pleased to say, as I did in answer to another question, that it is doing just that."

"I don't get what it is that makes your neighbors mad."

"Well, I was accused, when I went to the police station about that letter, of selling Mary Daly's *Pure Lust*," I smile. "You see, a red rag to a bull."

"Wow!"

"Mary Daly, as I'm sure you know, is a distinguished philosopher and a professor at Boston College. The title is, I suppose, a tease; the book is not about sexual lust."

"You took a risk selling that book," says Hetty. "Do you realize that?"

"No. I never thought about it. It is not obscene, but it does shake a reader up. I am all for people being shaken up."

"Will you be driven out?"

"Already some of the neighbors have come to offer their help. Two men go jogging early in the morning and offered to wipe

101

the windows off for me, for instance. I'll stick it out. I'm a tough old bird, and besides, I like it here. I wanted to get away from Chestnut Hill where Vicky and I had a big house and garden. The only thing I miss is the garden," I add.

"And you're not afraid?" Hetty pursues. "I would be!"

I look down at Patapouf, lying at my feet, her paws twitching in a dream. "I might be, without Patapouf, but she has a very loud menacing bark. That is a comfort."

"I can't figure you out," Hetty admits. "Why you chose a blue-collar neighborhood. You admit to being a lesbian but you are such a lady."

"You are teasing me, Hetty?"

"You might have evaded my question."

"Yes, I considered that. I knew it was bound to come up if I agreed to an interview." I am at ease enough now that it is Hetty really who seems the innocent abroad and I take time to think. After a considerable pause while she scribbles away on her pad, I say, "Many women have to conceal their private lives, for fear of being fired, so it is time for someone like me, who can't be fired, you see, to come out with who and what I am. Homophobia seems to be largely based on some way-out image of a lesbian as a girl in trousers and a man's shirt who picks up women in gay bars! It is odd that in Henry James' time what used to be called a Boston Marriage, two women living to-gether, was taken pretty much for granted. But when I talked to the police sergeant he commented just as you have that he did not expect a lady to show up under these shady circumstances. Don't you see, Hetty, I want it known that an elderly woman, as you see I am, can be a lesbian and certainly in the case of Vicky Chilton, my lifelong friend, a distinguished member of society. Isn't it time a whole submerged part of respectable society came out into the open?"

"But what does your family think about that?" Hetty asks. "I mean, don't they mind?"

I feel a second of terror and then laugh. "We have never talked about any of this. I have brothers and somehow the matter has never come up in so many words." And, having underlined "words" with my tone of voice, I see something I have not seen before. "Words, all the descriptive ones, from lesbian to dyke, from gay to faggot, are dangerous."

"Why, if they tell the truth?"

"Oh, but they don't. What they do is mark off about ten percent of the population as indecent, dangerous, and to be avoided if possible, fired if possible, pushed under the rug if possible. But it is not words that tell the true story, Hetty, can't you see? It's lives."

Hetty smiles. "How these dangerous people live, you mean?"

"Exactly. Those who have come into the shop seem to be leading exemplary lives. Wonderful women have come, a widow, for instance, who had to nurse her husband through a long illness and nearly died of that herself. Now she is founding a caretaking service to relieve women or men, give them a weekend off, or even a real holiday."

"Is she a lesbian?"

"Not that I know of. I see I am digressing. But not really. I want you to understand, Hetty, that the bookstore attracts all ages and kinds of women."

"That's not what brought me here," Hetty says, "but I think I am beginning to understand a little more than I did. I do admire your courage, that's for sure, and not only about sleeping up here every night, wondering whether some enemy is going to break in, or burn the place down."

It does sound scary, and I laugh. "You forget Patapouf, who has a sixth sense about any danger I might be in." Patapouf wags

103

her tail, hearing her name, and goes over to Hetty to be petted. "An old woman and an old dog against a lot of goons . . . ," and I burst into laughter. "You should have a story anyway."

I am pleased about the interview and tell Joan so after I have shown Hetty around the shop, pointing out what a variety of books and subjects we cover.

"Thanks very much," she says, shaking my hand.

"When will the interview come out?"

"I don't know. Perhaps in the Living section at the end of the week."

"Good luck, and goodbye then."

9

When Saturday comes I am too busy getting Fanny and Ruth settled in with Joan for their first experimental day to remember that the interview may be out. I can see that Joan is not showing any antagonism she may feel and the girls are delightfully enthusiastic, offering at once to tidy up the tiny kitchen, which I left in rather a mess the night before after a pileup in the store at the end of the day, a long line of people waiting to pay for books. I got rattled and forgot all about the tea things.

I feel supported and happy as I drive off to see if I can find a good bottle of wine for the two joggers, for this evening when I have been invited over to their place. It is a bright cool autumn day and I feel festive, on holiday because the girls have offered to keep Patapouf and to walk her at noon for me.

The *Globe* was delivered at the door and I had taken it in and looked at the headlines while I had my breakfast but that was all. I shall enjoy reading it later on when I settle in upstairs for a Saturday afternoon of leisurely reading.

In fact, I know nothing until the phone rings early in the afternoon and I hear Angelica saying, "Oh my dear, I am so

sorry." She seems very upset and it crosses my mind that some-
one close to me must have died.

"What is it? What has happened?"

"You haven't seen the *Globe*?" She seems incredulous.

"Just the headlines. Why?"

"There is a damaging interview in the Living section."

"Damaging? That girl seemed so sympathetic!"

"The headline is 'Lesbian Bookseller in Somerville Threat-
ened' and there is an awful photo of you at your desk."

I feel paralyzed and just manage to say, "Let me read it and
call you back, Angelica." No, no one close to me has died, but I
am exposed before millions of people. I find it difficult to unfold
the Living section, my hands are shaking so. I have been a fool.
The photo of me at my desk looking one hundred years old
makes me feel better. That old party does not look dangerous, I
tell myself.

And when I read the interview I realize that Hetty has been
fairly accurate in what she reports, including my statement that
it is time respectable older women came out. She tells about the
anonymous letter, my visit to the police, and, unfortunately no
doubt, the name of the book that caused the trouble. I am think-
ing very fast out of fear. What I realize is that, in talking to a
sympathetic young woman, in my mind I was talking only to
her. I had never imagined what it would be like to be quoted
and to have my thoughts available to tens of thousands of peo-
ple I don't know, more than half of whom, no doubt, are wildly
misinformed and prejudiced. I am shaken up all right, but I do
not feel that I have done anything to be really ashamed of,
whatever people may say. What to do now? First I have to call
Angelica back. She will be waiting.

"Well," I say, "Hetty quoted me pretty accurately, but I can
see how it may have caused a shock when you read it." I sound
cooler than I feel.

"You are simply either some kind of fool or some kind of saint," says Angelica, and that is very like her.

"So you see that I was trying to be honest."

"Oh yes, dear Harriet, no one could call you less than honest." The irony was heavy in her voice.

"Don't be cross with me," I say, "I just have to be myself."

"I'm not cross. I'm alarmed."

"I guess I'll have to say goodbye now. I must go down to the store." I am glad to put down the receiver.

I run downstairs with the *Globe*. "Hey," I say, taken aback by what seems like a crowd milling around, and go over to the register where Fanny is making out bills with a pile of books in front of her. "Perhaps," I whisper, "you had better see this."

"Oh, we've seen it," Fanny says. "Why do you think all these people are here?" She seems highly amused.

"A man brought it in ages ago, and Joan went off with it. She was very upset," says Ruth.

A solemn young woman in blue jeans and a leather jacket comes over and shakes my hand. "I think you are great."

She is joined at once by two or three other women, one about my age, who says, "Hurrah for you."

"You're a gutsy lady," says another.

I suppose this is the most unlikely moment in my life so far. What seemed a few minutes ago like a disaster is turning into a triumph.

The crowd is standing in the way of the table and chairs and my heart sinks when I see that Jonathan is sitting in one of them and Fred in another. "Oh hello," I say, "sorry I didn't see you at once."

Jonathan coughs. Fred is smiling his irritating superior smile. I sit down in the third chair. "I suppose you think this chair should be in a corner with dunce written on it," I say to Fred.

107

"Not really," he says. "You appear to have found a splendid way to bring in customers."

"Why are you here?" I ask Jonathan. I feel suddenly furious, hemmed in. I understand why Gide said *"Je hais les familles."* What business is all this of theirs?

Jonathan seems flustered and has risen to his feet. "I just wanted to be sure you were all right," he says. "I did not know about the threats."

"You didn't tell him?" I needle Fred.

"No, but we have been talking and Mr. Fremont thinks you should install a much more efficient security system than the primitive lock I put in last week."

"Nonsense. I would surely set it off by mistake, dunce that I am."

"Perhaps we could talk about it some other time," Jonathan says. "I'll call you," and mercifully he makes his way out, watched by all eyes, as though it had been he who uttered threats.

I go back to my desk without a word to Fred. "Well, let's do a little business for a change," I say to the three or four people patiently waiting to pay for books.

"We'll take care of that," says Ruth. "That's what we're here for after all."

"You've certainly had quite an introduction to the store! Saturdays are not usually like this."

"We're having fun," Fanny says.

On an impulse I suggest to Fred that we take a short walk with Patapouf. It is no place to talk if that is what he wants. And also I feel overcome by shyness. All this attention is really more of a shock than reading the interview was. I don't know quite how to behave, especially with Fred observing me, smiling his secret smile. Patapouf is delighted and precedes us, waving her tail in pleasure. She adores Fred.

"What an ugly neighborhood it is," Fred remarks, looking up and down the street littered with paper and beer cans, the Saturday clutter, and dismal shops selling liquor, or army and navy surplus clothes.

I have never really looked at it before, I realize. And in a way I like it. It seems a lot more real than posh enclaves of smart stores in Chestnut Hill. "It's not beautiful, but it's alive," I answer. "So what's on your mind, Fred?"

He slips an arm through mine and is silent for a moment while we wait for Patapouf, who has decided to sit down in the middle of the sidewalk, an awkward obstruction to the Saturday people milling around. "I'm trying to puzzle you out, Harriet. Why in heaven's name you chose to expose yourself when I should think you are already in trouble enough."

"I don't really know the answer to that," I say, and then add, "Our parents are dead, after all."

"What has that got to do with it, for God's sake?"

"Everything."

"They would have been shocked, but, after all, you have lots of family, nieces and nephews, to reckon with, Harriet."

"Are you shocked?" I am beginning to feel cornered and miserable. Had I said what I did on a crazy impulse? Must I be forced to regret it forever?

"I suppose I am," Fred admits. At least he is not sneering for once.

"But you must have known, Fred? After all . . ."

"Maybe. But I never thought about you as a sexual being, you see. Besides, it just doesn't seem to me anyone's business. That word makes what might have seemed normal, I mean two women living together in friendship, suddenly abnormal and peculiar and frightening, I suppose."

I see that Fred is unnerved for once, shaken out of all his superior attitudes, and I am glad. "Are you aware that this is the first time we have ever talked seriously about ourselves?" I ask.

"Really?" He frowns. "The thing is, Harriet, that as long as Vicky was alive you seemed secure, taken care of, and, let's face it, acceptable."

"Because she was so rich?"

"Maybe partly. And she was a powerful personality so we all took her for granted and did not ask ourselves embarrassing questions."

"Well, the family is allowed to cut me out, Fred. Besides, they don't read the *Globe,* do they?" I am laughing at him now and he winces. "You really can't face your little sister growing up, can you?" I speak on the tide of being my real self.

"It's not especially grown-up to blurt out unpleasant truths, is it?"

"When one is sixty years old and in a position to do some good by an unpleasant truth, maybe it is."

"What good is it to expose yourself to threats and insults?"

"If someone with money, who cannot be fired from a job, who has no children, whose lover is dead, comes out it may be one way to change the public mind about that word you can't bring yourself to utter. I said what I did in the hope of building a bridge across all this homophobia."

"All we need in this family is a martyr," he teases. This is the old Fred, at ease with me, so my laughter is spontaneous and we both laugh.

"Patapouf wants to go home," I say. She hates any exhibition of anger or hurt in those she loves and had been pulling at the leash Fred holds. "I'm having dinner with those two kind men, Joe and Eddie," I say, "you will be glad to hear."

"You seem to be making friends," he grants. "I was surprised at all that brouhaha just now in the store."

"So was I—thunderstruck, as a matter of fact."

We have reached my door, avoiding the few people standing outside the store. Fred gives me a funny little look, half amused, half something else I can't figure out. "I'll be off. I'm not exactly proud of my sister, but I have to admit you are quite a person, Harriet."

"Thanks."

It is odd to feel so close to tears. But after all it has been rather a strange day, half pain, half triumph, half good news, half fear. I feel all mixed up.

A little later Joe calls to say he will pick me up at six. I guess Joe is coming to fetch me so I will be protected. I go out rarely after dark, except to walk Patapouf. I decide to wear a red paisley dress and get out of my tweed suit and loafers for a change. And then, before I have a bath, I lie down on my bed and fall fast asleep.

Sleep doesn't always "knit up the ragged sleeve of care," but this little nap did me a world of good. Sometimes sixty feels young and sometimes it feels old, and when I wake up at five, I feel young and ready for anything. The curious effect of the last hours of crisis is a sense of relief. Something has happened that had to happen sooner or later, and now I am free in a new way and—I have to laugh at this—finally grown up.

So at a little before six I go down with Patapouf, who will guard the store while I am gone, feeling excited and happy to be going out to dinner with two new friends.

Fanny and Ruth are getting ready to close and there are only two customers in the store whom I am glad to see leave without fanfare. "What a day!" I say to Fanny, who is totting up figures. "You must be exhausted."

"Nothing like when we have cleaned two houses in a day," Ruth says.

"There!" Fanny closes the account book. "You know what you took in? Over a thousand dollars."

111

"I can't believe it," I say. "That is almost as good as the day of the opening party."

"People were so supportive," Fanny says. "It was awfully touching."

"We felt proud," Ruth says, "and Fanny was great when one older woman came in and asked for you and said we could tell you that she had not imagined a degenerate beast would move into the neighborhood."

"Oh my, I'm glad I was not here," I say.

"You know what Fanny said?"

"I can't imagine."

"She said, 'That's odd, that's what Hitler said of the Jews.' And several people milling around applauded. So that woman left, and good riddance we all felt."

"It's the start of what may be rather a long battle," I say, sitting down.

"Two nuns, Sisters of Loretto, they said they were, came by and told us to tell you they were thinking of you. They brought brownies—over there in a tin box."

"Degenerate beasts love brownies," I say, amused at the form Chris and Mary's support has taken.

And now here is Joe knocking on the door. I introduce them and leave Fanny and Ruth to lock up from the inside with Fred's new lock, and explain about leaving by my door. "See you next Saturday!"

"It's been a wonderful day," Ruth says, "maybe not for you, but we're grateful to be working with you."

As we walk along, Joe says that he came over twice to see how things were but there was such a crowd all seemed to be well. "No flack from that piece in the *Globe?*"

"Of course, but I have no regrets."

Joe slips his arm through mine but says nothing for a minute.

"You make me feel ashamed," he says then. "I couldn't help wondering if you had meant to be quoted or whether the reporter took it as open season on gays—or what?"

"Well, she did not misquote me, but I did not envision a headline, I must admit." I stop to shift the bottle from my left arm to my right and Joe notices and takes it from me at once. "It's wine," I explain. "I hope you like Vouvray."

"Love it. Eddie and I spent a week in the Loire valley two or three years ago. We were shown the caves back of Vouvray where they store the wine."

And then as he tells me more about that trip, which had taken them also to the Dordogne and south to Albi, we reach the Victorian house where they have an apartment on the top floor. The rather dingy staircase does not prepare me for the charm and style of their quarters, including two ravishing Siamese cats. It is appallingly neat, I think, guilty about my own lack of housekeeping skill, and it is peaceful and beautiful as well. The living room is dominated by a magnificent Navajo rug hanging on the wall. The furniture is modern, two armchairs echoing the blue bands in the rug, the walls white.

"I've never seen a Navajo rug with blues like that," I say. "It has to be an old one. Is it?"

"I bought it at an auction years ago," Joe explains, "for a hundred dollars, believe it or not."

Through an arched door I can see another room lined with books from floor to ceiling. "I brought you some wine," I say to Eddie.

"Oh wonderful. I'm making coq au vin for you. This will be perfect."

"What would you like to drink?" Joe asks when he has taken my coat and I am sitting on the nubby white sofa.

"Scotch with a little water."

"Ah," Eddie registers from the kitchen, "I was right. Joe thought it would be a martini!"

"Vicky and I used to drink martinis, so you were both right."

"That *Globe* reporter said Vicky was a publisher and I recognized the name," Joe says. "How hard that she is not with you now."

"Well," I fumble for the words and suddenly, a little shy, say, "Vicky would not have approved. We led middle-class lives in Chestnut Hill. It's her money, so sometimes I feel anxious. I mean, what would she say or think?"

"But surely you must do what you feel, not what she might have felt," Joe says. I remember now that he had said he is a psychiatrist, and the fact that he is does not alarm me as it might have. I feel very much at ease and am asking myself why, as I sip my drink and Joe brings in Brie and some water biscuits.

"What a wonderful atmosphere you create," I say as he offers me a biscuit and spreads it with cheese. "Thanks."

"Do we?" Joe asks.

"I feel I can say anything and you will understand, whereas my brother Fred dropped by to accuse me of letting the family down."

"In what way?" Eddie asks as he comes back to sit down with a martini.

"That awful word in the *Globe* headline. I find it hard to say it myself," and I realize that I am blushing.

"But did you say it to that reporter?" Joe asks. "If so, you are a brave woman."

"And the saints come marching in," Eddie sings, smiling.

"Watching all sorts of women come and go in the store, hearing their stories . . . I have learned a lot," I say. "I have changed, I guess. Some people would say not for the better. By the way, have you had to erase any obscenities lately?" They exchange a look. "I have to know," I say. "Come on, tell me."

"Only two or three," Joe says. "It's always the same crap."

I had felt so happy a moment before but now the reality hits me. Other people are being involved, other people at risk.

"Joe is a black belt," Eddie says, smiling happily. "One day we caught some young men at it and one of them called us a dirty name, and the next thing he knew he was flat on the sidewalk. What a moment! I had always hoped to see Joe do his stuff. I wouldn't have missed it . . . his face. Total amazement."

"Wow!" I say. "The stuffed-shirt lawyer who runs my business affairs came by and he wants me to have some fancy security system installed. Ha! I've just had an idea. Maybe it could be rigged to pour water on the head of anyone painting the windows. That and a siren going off at the same time." It is all so ludicrous suddenly that I am laughing almost hysterically. "Oh my," I sigh, "laughter is the only way I can handle all this," and now, because I really have had enough of it, "Let's change the subject."

I want to know more about Joe and Eddie, how they met and how long they have lived together. "It was so amazing the way you turned up to help me out, out of the blue like that. I can't get over it."

"Pure self-interest," says Joe. "We need a bookstore like yours, people like you. The neighborhood is changing. I suppose gentrification is a dirty word because it is putting workers out of some housing. But, on the other hand, the dreariness is beginning to be diluted, thank God."

It is Eddie who tells how they met seven years ago when he was a student at Rindge Technical School. Joe was for a time the school psychiatrist and had helped Eddie leave home where his father, an alcoholic, used to beat him mercilessly and had nearly killed him when he found out that he was gay.

115

I listen, once more confronted by how sheltered a life mine has been. These two men are very different. What holds them together? "Seven years . . . ," I murmur.

"People think gays pick men up all the time. Some do, of course," Joe explains, "but for some unknown reason, Eddie and I have felt happy being together, solidly happy."

"Your apartment makes one aware of that somehow," although even as I say it, I wonder whether it is not almost too neat, self-consciously so. "But are you both such good housekeepers? You put me to shame."

"It's a kind of outer skin," Joe says, "the apartment I mean. A kind of safety maybe, a way of living at the center of all we want from our lives, which are, of course, way out in the wilderness from society's point of view."

When I am safely in bed at home I realize that I have never before been with people in a social situation where I could talk as freely, rarely, if ever, felt cherished and applauded in the way those men had, so in a single evening they have become, amazingly enough, family. It is extraordinary to feel that way, to be knit together so fast, so soon.

I have much to think about and sleep very little all night. Twice Patapouf bursts into loud barks and that is unsettling, but nothing sinister happens. When Vicky and I were living together as lovers I never felt the slightest guilt or apprehension. It is true what Fred said, that she was such a powerful woman in her own right nobody questioned her life-style, as it is now called, or mine for living with her. The odd thing is that I felt no guilt or apprehension then, but since the word lesbian has been fastened on me like the "A" on Hester Prynne's dress, I do feel apprehension and if not exactly guilt, some self-questioning, although I am certainly not leading a lesbian life at present.

What this whole affair has done for me so far is to open me up for the first time to what society is doing to those who do live

such lives, often in perfect dignity; contributors to the civiliza-
tion as we are, how easy it is, still, to be unnerved, to be riddled
by self-doubt, and in some cases, self-hatred. Joe, later on in our
talk over dinner, had said something about how many of his
clients were wracked by guilt and fear, about how enormously
important it is for them to find a role model, to be witnesses of
an ongoing partnership. "And the problem is," he had added,
"that so many such partnerships stay hidden."

And I had said, "That's why I decided I had to come out, since
I have, comparatively speaking, so little to lose."

"Only your store, only your life," Eddie had said. "Don't you
see why the people turned out today to honor you?"

10

I am rather surprised when Andrew shows up this morning, which is Sunday of course. Ten years younger than I, a personnel manager for one of the high-tech establishments along Route 128, apparently always cheerful with a quirky sense of humor, it is strange that he has not married, but as he seems perfectly happy in his bachelor apartment, no one worries, and he is adored by his nieces and nephews. He and I have never been close, partly because he was intimidated by Vicky and perhaps did not like her or understand why I did. So it was a surprise when he came to the opening of the store and got quite absorbed in reading off in a corner. I have not seen him since, until today.

"What brings you here?" I ask when he has flung off his coat and sits drinking a cup of coffee at the kitchen table. He looks at me rather too intently for my comfort behind his thick glasses.

"Hot stuff in the *Globe* yesterday. So, my revered elder sister is a lesbian!" This comes from his exterior, always merry self and I know very well it is just a ploy.

"Quite frankly, Andrew, I dislike that word."

"And you are not alone. If you used it on purpose, if you came out, as they say, you are the bravest woman I have ever known. If it was not your doing, then you are the greatest fool."

I have to laugh, it all seems so senseless suddenly. "Probably a little of both. A brave fool. No, not exactly. You see, I am being attacked by these louts who live around here and are about as tolerant as crocodiles. I got mad enough to tell the truth. Some of the women who come here are lovers and even tell me so, but not all by any means. It's not in my mind to be labeled as a lesbian bookstore, but a store for all kinds of women and, Andrew, all kinds of women come here. So now there is a dilemma and I am hoist on my own petard."

I observe Andrew, who seems not to be really listening, bowed over his cup of coffee, playing with the spoon, which makes me aware not for the first time what beautiful hands Andrew has, the hands of a sculptor or a pianist. "What's on your mind so early in the morning?" I say, for I sense that he has not come with condolences but with something more important to himself.

"It sounds corny," he says, "but when I read that piece I had quite a strange reaction. I felt that I had a sister."

"You have always had a sister, though you never paid much attention to me."

"Vicky bothered me," he says. "You seemed so safe and protected from all that was going on in the world around you, the emergence of a feminist movement, the attacks on the patriarchy, with which, by the way, I heartily agree."

"I've learned a lot since Vicky died," I say.

"So now I have a sister," Andrew looks me suddenly in the eye with that troubling intensity with which he stared at me when he first sat down. "I can tell her that I am gay. I can at last tell someone in the family who can understand. Heigh-ho!"

Over the years it had occurred to me, of course, but then I had brushed the thought aside. "Well, thank you, Andrew.

120

That's one piece of good news that has come out of the *Globe* article."

"You call it good news to have a gay brother?"

"It's quite wonderful! I know it sounds crazy but I have been lonely, too, while all this bore in on me and I had to face all that I had not been willing to face as long as Vicky was alive. Emancipation is all very well, and healthy no doubt, but it is lonely, Andrew, isn't it?"

"Damned lonely," he says. "I'm sick and tired of being the odd man at dinner parties, of being teased by Fred about why I don't marry."

"Fred would find it hard to understand," I say quickly. I am thinking aloud for a moment and it pops out. "As far as the words go, 'gay' seems to me even worse than 'lesbian.' "

"Maybe," Andrew says, stretching out his long legs as though he were suddenly at ease with me and scratching Patapouf's ears while she groans with pleasure. "For some reason 'lesbian' seems primarily sexual."

"Oh dear, yes, I suppose so. I suppose that is why I have found it so hard, next to impossible, to say it aloud."

"We were brought up to total silence on such matters, weren't we?"

Do I dare ask now what Andrew's life is really like? Is he happy? Has he made his peace with his own self? Has he ever had a more or less permanent love affair? Asking myself these questions while he and Patapouf carry on their dialogue, I decide to tell him about Eddie and Joe.

"Last night I had one of the best times of my life, Andrew. You may not know that when obscenities were first defacing the store windows two men turned up one morning, saw them, and washed them off. Fred was actually here and met them before I did. And since then they have kept a lookout on their morning jog around the neighborhood and just clean up for me without ever mentioning it. Last night they invited me to dinner at their place. My first outing since the *Globe* revelation. They were absolutely dear, cooked a wonderful dinner. Eddie, the younger man, is the cook and made me feel loved and honored because I had come out, willingly or not."

"What do they do?" Andrew asks.

"Joe is a psychiatrist and met Eddie when Eddie was a student in mechanics at Rindge, helped him get away from a sadistic father, I gather, and they have lived together for years. Eddie is an auto mechanic. But the point is the marvelous sense of community I felt with them, the relief of being able to be open. It was heartwarming, Andrew. And such a beautiful apartment, austere and elegant. I was impressed." It spills out and Andrew listens intently but now he is silent, withdrawn, as he has always been with me. "Don't go away, Andrew."

"God damn it, Harriet, I'm fifty and I've never had a good relationship that lasted. I'm jealous, that's all."

"I'm going to ask these new friends up for dinner one of these days. Will you come and meet them?"

"What good would that do?"

"I don't know. It's just that we might as well all stick together."

"I'm a loner, Harriet. You know that. I've always been a loner."

And I remember how when we went off on a picnic *en famille* Andrew always disappeared into the woods or along the shore and seemed to choose not to be part of the fun. And his job, I suspect, is a lonely job, interviewing and selecting people for his firm, and not part of management except in a peripheral way. "I was so pleased that you came to the opening and then really looked at the books, as very few others troubled to do."

At this Andrew laughs his merry concealing laugh. "I was

forced into literacy by my shyness," he says. "Your friends were certainly supportive that day."

"Yes, I wonder what they are thinking now and who will be upset by all this. Angelica Lamb unfortunately is. She has been an enormous help, financially and in every other way."

"Let it rest—it's Sunday after all." And we share a rather long silence while he pours himself another cup of coffee.

"Why, then, no permanent relationship? Why the loneliness?"

"All I can think of is Yeats to answer that," and he recites in his clear deep voice:

> "Such body lovers have,
> Such exacting breath,
> That they touch or sigh.
> Every touch they give,
> Love is nearer death.
> *Prove that I lie.*"

I ponder the poem for a minute, trying to fathom what Andrew means by reciting it, how to respond. But I have to plunge in, of course. There is no cutting off this conversation. It has to take us wherever it is going. "But isn't it passionate love, sexual love, that dies with every touch or sigh? It seems to me a rather romantic vision, Andrew. It seems to me that love, which so often begins with sex, doesn't end there. Maybe you aren't willing to grow into that second phase which, I suppose, is friendship."

He sets his cup down and sits with his arms folded on the table and his chin resting on them, an attitude that strikes me as that of a young boy in despair. But as he says nothing, I press on. "What of friendship?"

"Oh well," he shrugs, "I had two or three good friends at

Exeter. They married, of course. Then I just didn't seem to belong anymore."

I wait. I light a cigarette and this gets an instantaneous reaction.

Andrew sits up and says sharply, "You still smoke, Harriet? For God's sake!"

"I realize I am a public nuisance," I reply, and can't help laughing. "It's the generation gap, Andrew. Women of my generation smoked and still do in private. You will just have to accept that your sister is an addict."

"I can't go along with someone who willfully commits suicide."

"We are not going to separate on that issue," I say, quite cross suddenly. "For God's sake yourself!"

"How did you stand Vicky's domineering all those years?" he asks, dropping the subject of smoking while I puff away.

"I guess it bothered me sometimes, but I truly loved her, Andrew, long past the early romantic years. We got built into each other's lives. We were rarely apart and the publishing business was extremely absorbing, you know. I felt we were partners."

Andrew lifts an eyebrow. "But she was the boss."

"And why not? Someone has to be the boss."

"Well, you are generous, I must say. I would have minded."

"Were you never in love with someone you wanted to be with day and night, to share a life with, Andrew?"

"Oh yes, but they were always married and quite content to have it that way. Anyway," he closes his right hand into a fist, "I'm on the way out. Fifty is simply too old."

"What an awful world then."

"You know, Harriet, I did not come here this morning to weep but to rejoice and praise." I sense him willing himself up from the darkness for my sake and I respect him for it. And yet we seem to be in hell together. And as though she senses that Patapouf gives a low growl and then goes to the door and barks. "Good old Patapouf, she'll defend you, in your awful world, won't she?"

"But it's not an awful world, Andrew. I'm happier than I have ever been. I know it sounds strange, but the bookstore is the most interesting thing I have ever imagined. Even the attacks challenge me to be more and to understand more."

"And you're not afraid someone will burn the place down?"

"Sometimes I'm a little anxious, but, after all, I could be mugged on the street. I could be hit by a truck. If one begins to imagine danger, the whole city is a battlefield these days."

Now the phone rings. I have feared it would for the last half-hour. It is Joan. I suggest she come over for brunch and then we can talk. Andrew has gotten up while I am talking.

"I'm off," he says, "but let's go on talking now we have begun."

"Let's."

"Have dinner with me on Tuesday. Can you?"

"What time?"

"I'll come and get you around seven. Okay?" Then just before he opens the door to leave he turns and hugs me hard.

"Thanks, Andrew." Here we are, I am thinking, fifty and just over sixty, and we have never hugged each other, not in fifty years. But there is no time to think more about Andrew because a second ring proves to be Angelica.

"I'm upset, dear Harriet."

"What about?"

"That *Globe* interview is damaging, to say the least."

"So you told me on the phone. But, Angelica, what did happen will amaze you. All day yesterday the store was full of people dropping in to salute me as a hero. Imagine that! It did me a world of good."

125

"But you are allying yourself with a tiny segment of the people who buy books. Maybe that tiny segment applauds you but maybe a lot of ordinary people will keep away."

"That remains to be seen."

"I just feel you are way off somewhere like a tiny sailboat disappearing over the horizon. It made me cry," Angelica says. "When I read it, I burst into tears."

"Come on, Angelica, I have not been sentenced to a term in jail."

"It could turn out to be a life sentence. That is why I cried." I wait as I really cannot think of anything to say that would improve matters, and she goes on, "I have no quarrel with how you choose to live your life, but I can't see and can't understand your talking about it in public. It's nobody's business but your own, surely. Vicky would never have condoned this kind of self-exposure, as you very well know."

"I am my own person, Angelica. I am not a shadow of someone else. And, let me try to explain, a lot of lesbians and gays cannot afford to come out publicly for fear of losing their jobs or being turned out of their houses or apartments. I can afford to be honest and therefore I feel I have a responsibility."

"You could be driven out of the bookstore."

"Yes, but if I were, I would not starve. Besides, Angelica, I want the store to be a haven where every sort of person can come and go and feel welcome. Can't you see?"

"I suppose it is admirable, but I just can't see it, Harriet. However, I am glad you got some support from your 'friends' yesterday."

The word "friends" was clearly in quotes and I react, "I had never seen a lot of these people before, as a matter of fact. Can't we just let this rest awhile, Angelica? I have so much else on my mind. Joan is coming for lunch, for one thing."

"Oh? And how does she feel about all this?"

126

"I haven't the foggiest idea. Two charming young women take over the store on Saturdays and they were here. I'll know soon enough."

I am now sick and tired of this subject, which seems to be taking over my life. With an hour to go after I put a salad together and get a frozen Welsh rabbit out for Joan, I sit down and make myself get to work. We have decided to change the window every three weeks and it is high time I put something together. At once everything falls into place and after discarding a few other ideas I decide that a window celebrating biographies of women might be fun and even attract some people who have not yet ventured in. I am making a list and full of all this when Joan arrives.

She seems quite herself, calm and detached, so why even mention the *Globe?* When we sit down with a glass of sherry while the Welsh rabbit melts in the oven I tell her about what we might do with the new window and she seems to think it a fine idea.

"It's interesting," she comments, "how many biographies of women poets have appeared in the last few years. Yet do people read the poetry? H.D., for example? Bogan?"

"I wonder about the poetry. Still, we have sold some Bogan and H.D.—the poems, I mean?"

"I think people are crazy about penetrating private lives these days. It's as though Pandora's box has been opened and things appear in print that would not have been considered possible even a few years ago." Now Joan is silent for a moment and I guess, of course, what is on her mind.

"You saw the *Globe* interview, I presume?" I ask, just to get it over with.

"Yes. That interviewer was a mischief maker. Too bad."

What a relief that Joan does not seem overly concerned or upset. "Well, what happened was a rush to the bookstore yester-

127

day to congratulate me. It was a bigger crowd than came to the opening. Really, Joan, I was awfully touched. They made me feel proud."

"That must have been gratifying, but . . ." She hesitates.

"But what?"

"There is a hazard, it seems to me, that what you founded as a bookstore for women in general may turn into a place of rendezvous for lesbians."

"Yes, I suppose that is a risk, but let's wait and see. You'll be here tomorrow and can check who comes. There are a few regulars now. They'll still come, and bring their friends, we hope. The new window should attract . . . after all, Beryl Markham, Isak Dinesen, George Eliot, Sylvia Plath, Emily Dickinson, Flannery O'Connor. We'll get hold of photographs wherever possible. Maybe that could be your job. The public library in Boston has files of photos, I believe."

"The publishers, more likely. I'll be happy to work on that."

"What would I do without you, Joan? Frankly, I was terrified that you might want to back out after yesterday's exposure in the *Globe*. You didn't call and I wondered . . ."

"Well, I didn't like it, that's for sure. It came at a bad time while you are already under attack. I *was* upset, but mostly for you. I love this job and neither goons nor malicious interviewers are going to deprive me of it, and that's that."

"I really don't believe Miss whatever-her-name-is was malicious. Partly it is a matter of generation. Her generation talk about everything in ways we never did or could."

"And don't reckon the consequences."

"I'm an optimist, you know. And Joan, I might as well say it. For me it is a relief to have come out and to be honest about my life-style, as it is called these days."

"You are an innocent, aren't you? Sometimes it staggers me."

"Why? Is it bad to be an innocent? I suppose you are right. I am one."

"Innocents get beaten. Look at me."

"But they survive. I do look at you."

To my amazement Joan has tears in her eyes. She is so much more vulnerable than I am, I suddenly realize. She has been so badly hurt.

So we eat lunch and indulge in concentrated shop talk for an hour. "I really can't wait for tomorrow" are my words as she leaves.

11

Because I want to get the books ready for the new window, Joan and I have agreed that we will exchange our stints and I'll take over the store for the morning, then, after one, Joan will come and help me set the books out—quite a job.

It is raining, a somber day, but I feel elated and eager to see who may turn up. Sure enough, the sisters do, and then Patience and Alice, and I introduce them to each other. While I work they begin to talk about Paris. It is a peaceful start to the day, and I am having fun piling up the books for the window, and making decisions. There are so many fine biographies of women, far more than I can use.

Patience, who has been sitting on the arm of Alice's chair, notices that the fire has not been laid and offers to do it for me. I go out to the shed to show her where I keep the wood, taking the key to the padlock with me. "It's wonderful to have friends drop by," I say. "Already it feels like a kind of meeting place. Aren't those nuns grand?"

"What do they do?" But before I can answer, we see that the shed has been broken into, the door simply smashed and the wood stolen.

"Darn it, that's a mean thing to do!"

For some reason Patience laughs at me. "You're so reserved," she says. "Darn it, indeed!"

"It's the goons who write obscenities on the windows and I'm going to call the police." I am not so much angry as sick. Will we ever get out from under this kind of harassment? Should I get a lawyer? Tell Jonathan? My head is in a whirl as we run back into the store. I tell Patience to explain what has happened while I call the police. "He's sending an officer over," I tell the four women, who are now standing.

"What a nasty thing to have happen!" Alice says.

"It's just part of a cabal against me and the store. They are trying to force me to leave the neighborhood. Whoever they may be, they think this is an obscene business."

"Not really?" Alice says. "You can't be serious."

"Homophobes," Sister Mary says. "Harriet's really under siege. What can we do?"

"Stick around. Nuns are good moral support," and I smile. "I'll be happy to introduce you to the officer if he ever comes."

Meanwhile, of all people I do not want to see, Sue Bagley has walked in. "What's going on?" she asks, sensing at once that something has happened and eager for excitement.

"The fireplace wood has been stolen," I say coldly.

Alice, no doubt sensing that I am not eager to go into the matter now, says that she and Patience will be glad to replace the wood. "We have friends in the country who cut their own. It won't be that expensive and maybe Carl will not only bring it but stack it for you. How much will you need?"

The relief of the practical! "Half a cord. That's marvelous."

"Everyone has wood stoves these days. It's hard to come by in the city," Alice explains to Sue.

"Who would steal from you?" Sue Bagley asks, giving me a

sharp glance. She obviously is dying to be let in on whatever is up.

"God knows," I say, "but there are plenty of hooligans in this neighborhood, as you yourself have told me."

"Where can you keep it now where it will be safe?" Patience asks.

"The cellar. It will mean carrying it upstairs, but I can manage. And Joe and Eddie will help me."

"I didn't like this book," Sue Bagley says, taking Mary Daly's last one out of her bag. "Too deep for me. I could hardly understand a word of it. So can I exchange it for something else? I'm sick and tired of all these women philosophers popping out of the woodwork. Give me a good solid biography."

"You've read the Dinesen, of course?"

"No, as a matter of fact, I haven't. I was put off by the movie."

That transaction completed, Sue Bagley leaves with the biography just as a uniformed black officer walks in.

"Good morning." He takes out a pad and pencil and reads my name. "Which of you is Miss Hatfield?"

"I am. Come with me, Officer. I'll show you the scene of the crime." I am happy that he is black. I do not expect to be browbeaten or treated with contempt, and I am not. He is courteous, listens, and looks at the damage, making copious notes, but when he has all the information I can give, he is not helpful.

"We can have no idea who is responsible for this theft."

"Also breaking in," I say. "Don't forget that door was smashed."

"Didn't you hear anything?" he asks. "If you could have called us when it happened."

"Now I remember something did wake me around four, but it had been clearly not inside the house so I went back to sleep."

"And you have no clue?"

"Well, I assume they're the same people who have threatened me with an anonymous letter. You must have that in the record, Officer."

"Someone brought in an obscene book but they did not give us their name," he says.

"I do not sell obscene books," I say.

"Excuse me, but that's what it says in the record."

"Then the record is inaccurate, as I pointed out to Sergeant O'Reilly some time ago."

"That is not in the record."

"Well, is there anything you can do?" Sister Mary asks.

"You can't let this woman be threatened and do nothing at all, can you?" Alice interjects.

"We'll come right away if there is trouble," says the officer, closing his notebook and slipping it into his pocket.

"You mean if she catches someone stealing, hangs on to an ear, and at the same time makes a phone call to the police, you will come?" Patience asks and we have to laugh. It is all so maddeningly absurd.

When he has left, Patience suggests that she and Alice go off right away and see about the wood. The sisters are reluctant to leave me alone, but I tell them no one will try to break in in broad daylight, and no doubt there will be customers in and out all morning. It is nearly eleven and, after hugging me with real warmth, Sister Chris admits that they will be late for a doctor's appointment. So they leave, and now, quite suddenly, I am alone.

I decide to bring Patapouf down. She has been asleep upstairs. I find I am feeling quite shaky, and she will be a comfort.

So I am sitting at my desk drinking a cup of coffee a half-hour later and still wondering whether to call Jonathan when Martha Blackstone walks in looking so awful that I get up at once and go to her. "Sit down, Martha. Let me get you a cup of coffee." She must have fallen downstairs, I think to myself. She usually has quite an air about her and dresses with flair. I have never seen her in pants till now, and her shirt looks torn at the neck. "Sit down and rest your bones."

At this she gives me a wan smile. "They sure are sore."

"I'll only be a minute." It seems a good idea to leave her alone to pull herself together, and when I come back with a cup of coffee for each of us she is putting on lipstick and, looking in the small mirror for that purpose, sees her face.

"My God, I have a black eye!"

"Compose the mind," I say, "and when you can, tell me what on earth has happened."

"Harriet, I don't quite know what has happened," she says. "I didn't know what to do, where to go, so I came here. At least my paintings are here. I have some identity here."

I can't believe that David has beaten her up, but there seems no other possible explanation, unless a stranger attacked her in her apartment. I am in no way prepared to meet this. In fact I am terrified of saying anything for fear it may be way off the beam, so I drink my coffee. One part of me is saying, Why do I let myself get involved with people I don't really like? Because, I answer myself, pity is the trap. I remember the first day she came and started almost at once to complain that she did not want children, that her work must come first. I could see her distress, but somehow it bothered me that she was willing to talk to perfect strangers about it. Nan Blakeley, the handsome black woman with two little girls, had been there another day when Martha was complaining, I remember, and laughed about being quite content to be a housewife.

Finally, as the silence grows, I lift my head and see the misery. "Was it David?" I ask.

"Yes," she says, slowly, as though she cannot believe what she is saying. "My husband pushed me up against the refrigerator and hit me so hard, so many times, I fell. I can't believe that David could do this. He said awful things and then he walked out, leaving me on the floor."

"What made him get into such a state?" I ask.

"Oh, it's been brewing. David can't talk about things, you know. He shuts up and broods."

"Every marriage carries a lot of tension, doesn't it? I mean, there's always an outburst sooner or later, and sometimes it clears the air."

"Violence doesn't clear the air," Martha says, still in that cold bitter voice with which she has told the story. "I have to leave. I can't go back there."

"Not now, anyway."

"Never, because I'm not going to change and he's so furious because I won't. I won't go along with having a baby and imprisoning myself for years. I can't, Harriet," and now at last, the tears fall. "He says I am abnormal, not a real woman. He treated me with contempt."

"You know that is frustration and anger. He's probably feeling pretty sick himself."

"Maybe he is, but there's no turning back now. Can't you see?"

"What I think I see is that you should talk to a psychiatrist, and if possible with David. I have a friend whom you would feel comfortable with, I think: Joe Hunter. He's quite near here. Why don't I give him a ring and see if you could make an appointment?"

"First I get battered and then I'm expected to strip myself naked and talk to a stranger. I'm not that crazy."

I don't mind the anger. It is a lot healthier than cold bitterness. She is not acting now. She is outraged. "Let's be practical, Martha. Do you have any money?"

"About five hundred dollars in my savings account."

"So you could go to a hotel, or motel, which might be cheaper, at least for tonight. Have you a woman friend you could call? What you need right now is support, and not to be alone. Oh, I wish you would see Joe!"

"I don't need anyone but you."

"But I'm an old woman and a busy one. What you don't know yet is that I'm sort of in a fog myself. Thieves broke into the shed and stole all my firewood last night. The same people, I suppose, who have been threatening to drive me out."

"Dirty work," Martha says, but her mind is not on that, of course. "I wish I could just stay around here today, sort of pull myself together."

I knew this was coming, and I shrink from it. The kind of warmth Martha needs I do not have in me to give. I want to get at arranging the new window. I want time to absorb all that has been going on, the shocks of this morning. I have anticipated today as a respite, a quiet time of gathering myself together— and the store.

Martha is watching me intently and when I do not respond she says, "I guess I'm asking too much. You've been awfully good, showing my work and all. I suppose I've locked in on you like a limpet on a rock," and for the first time she smiles, and I can smile at last myself.

"The trouble is I'm no rock, Martha. Besides, if you won't talk to Joe, I do think you should see a doctor, have someone look you over and do something about your eye. What about the Harvard Infirmary? I tell you what," for I am beginning to see light, "Joan will be here any minute now and she'll take over. I could drive you there, see what is what, and then take you home and help you pack a suitcase and get you settled. How does that sound?"

"Wonderful." Tears are flowing again.

I decide to send Martha upstairs to my apartment while I

confer with Joan, who has just walked in. I need badly to get away from Martha's problems for a few minutes, and I hope she would like to have a chance to wash and lie down on my bed, or so I suggest.

Joan and her cynical outlook on women's lives are a tonic, and her fury about the stolen wood does me good. I call Joe at his office and he is on the job at once, saying he will try to get in touch with David and tell him where Martha can be reached. "My guess is David is in a pretty bad way himself by now, and," he adds, "I can see Martha at four if you can persuade her to come. She's in a tough situation, isn't she?"

"Joe, I'm at sea," I say. "You know all about these things, and I feel ignorant and cross with both of them at the moment."

I tell him about the wood and he says, "Hey, you appear to be on the front line in several wars at the same time!"

"Thanks, Joe, but I've got to go now and try to be a nurse."

At this he chuckles. "Not quite in your line?"

"Not at all in my line, I'm afraid." But I did open the bookstore as a haven for women, I remind myself, so I am getting exactly what I asked for. Perhaps it does have its humorous side.

As often happens, what I had dreaded turns out to be illuminating. In the first place, Martha is silent as we drive to the infirmary, and the fact that she is, that we are in a shared silence, does something new for my state of mind about her. I like her better than I thought I ever would. Of course, she is very nervous about being examined and we have to wait almost half an hour, sitting beside a boy who looks young even to be a freshman and is on crutches, a broken ankle playing ice hockey, he explains.

When Martha comes out after a fairly short time, she looks relieved although the black eye is still visible behind her glasses. She doesn't speak till we are in the car. "The doctor said I was lucky. No broken bones, only bruises, a strained muscle in my left arm, and this damned eye—I'm supposed to put raw steak on it."

"Would hamburger do?" For some reason my question sends Martha into almost hysterical laughter. "What's so funny?"

"It's so like you," she says. "You're so practical. Of course you are thinking that hamburger is cheaper. Admit it!"

"Yes." She is right, of course. "Old New Englander that I am!"

Now I sit in the car while Martha goes in and packs, after making sure that David's car is not in the yard. It is wonderful to be able to sit still with nothing to do but wait and think things over. In a way it is wonderful, but I find almost at once that the episode of the wood has damaged my sense of myself, of being myself after the *Globe* article, of somehow living my life as I want to live it. What if there are people around, and there appear to be, who do not want me to live the life I imagine, who will do almost anything to break it up, to harm me and the store? What then? I have kept fear at bay lately, but now, on this disturbed morning, maybe just plain fatigue has let it come in again. I light a cigarette and smoke it slowly, but it does not calm the strange palpitations in my chest. I can feel the sweat on my upper lip. What can I conjure up against this tide of fear?

Joe and Eddie, of course. They are there. They arrive like guardian angels when I need them. Andrew, yes, he has become an ally and a friend after all the years when that seemed impossible. Even Fred's teasing cheers me up. After all, I am not alone and it is interesting that these defenders turn out to be men. But I have left Joan out, and she is surely the most vital person for brushing off the moths.

Nevertheless I wish I could catch one of the hooligans and get the police involved. Being a sitting duck is not easy for me. I need action. And what will they attack next? And how many of them are there who consider the neighborhood their possession and look on me as evil and damaging to it?

Homophobia—the word had not been in Vicky's or my vocabulary. Now it is beginning to loom rather large in my consciousness. The word causes conflict for me because I did not intend the store to be a meeting place or rallying point for lesbians. I did not want to be pushed into a corner. At this point Martha startles me.

"Hey, here I am! Sorry to have kept you waiting so long."

I have been literally lost in thought and have no idea how long she has taken. "Where are we going?" I ask.

"I think that motel, Quality Inn, on Mass. Avenue. Old New Englanders appreciate that it is cheap."

"You direct me."

Martha has brought only a small suitcase and a tote full of painting things, and I judge both to be good signs. One, that she does not mean to leave for good and, two, that she may even try to paint in the motel. Things are looking up. I park and go with her to be sure they have a room and, while she signs the register, I take a pad out of my purse and write down Joe Hunter's name and office address, which I fortunately remember is not far from Harvard Square, and note that she has an appointment at four, if she wants it.

"Are you going to be all right?" I ask, as we stand waiting for the elevator. I hand her the note, which she reads without comment and puts in her pocket.

"I think I'll go to bed and sleep," she says.

"Good."

"Thanks for everything."

I flee. Maybe it is not the kindest thing, but I feel I have to. I want to get back to the store. I want to get away.

In the car I remember that the Blackstones have a cat called

Tuggle. What about the cat? Well, David will presumably come home sooner or later. Why ever do I remember the cat? And why does an animal in distress affect me more than a person in distress?

When I get back to the store I am delighted to see that Marian Tuckerworth is sitting talking with Joan. A grown-up person is a relief at this point. I have liked her from the first day she came in and asked me the question "Why a women's bookstore?"

Joan gives me a message from Joe to say he has reached Mr. Blackstone and not to worry. Then she asks if I have had any lunch.

"Good heavens, no. No wonder I felt sort of shaky in the car just now, waiting for Martha! Hunger explains what I imagined might be fear."

"Let me go out and get you a sandwich," Marian Tuckerworth says at once. And I am almost as eager to get my teeth into a ham and cheese on rye and a chocolate milk as I am to get my hands on all the books and start arranging the new window, so I accept her kindness gladly.

"Well," says Joan, "it's been quite a day, so far!"

"Now we can get back to what really matters. Let's see what the new window will look like. Oh," I see Joan has managed to clear out the old window for me, "that's great. We can begin right now."

It is an immense satisfaction to stand in the window while Joan hands me George Eliot, Virginia Woolf, Emily Dickinson, Mrs. Pankhurst, Gwendolyn Brooks, Sylvia Plath, Louise Bogan, Sylvia Townsend Warner, Maya Angelou, Willa Cather—a litany of names. But pretty soon I am taking up too much room and have to sit sideways while I shift the books around.

"It's a window on women's world, I see," says Marian Tuckerworth, after she has stood outside looking in for a moment. "I highly approve," and she hands me a brown paper bag.

141

"Let's sit down. I'm ravenous." And in the next breath, "What do I owe you?"

"Nothing, Miss Hatfield. I'm only too glad to have been of use."

While I eat my sandwich and drink a glass of milk from the fridge in the kitchen, Joan and Marian talk. Marian is still having trouble finding volunteers for caretaking and she turns to me to thank me for having suggested she read a new book called *Women, Take Care* from OWL in California. "Older Women's League," I explain. "Their motto, 'Don't Agonize, Organize,' makes a lot of sense, doesn't it?"

"It's clear," Marian says, "that organize is just what I have to do, and that means a board and some professional who can size up volunteers and perhaps even train them. An office, I suppose. Oh dear me, there is a huge abyss between a good idea and a working organization, isn't there?"

"How will you finance all this?" Joan asks.

"I don't know. But I do have some contacts in the banks, and maybe I can extract at least interest and advice. I think I can put a hundred thousand into the till myself. That way I can go ahead without waiting."

"Hey, that's a lot of money," Joan says. "Should you invest so much? What about your own old age?"

"But if I can show how great the need is and prove that such a center for helping caretakers really works it will be easier to raise money from outside."

"Hospice began in a small way and look how it has spread," I offer.

"What will you call the organization?" Joan asks.

I am so delighted to be talking with Marian about such a serious matter I forget how tired I am. "Why not be blunt? Caretakers Help, Inc."

"Well, it needs thinking about. How about your coming on the board, Miss Hatfield?"

I swallow. It is suddenly clear to me in a bright gaudy light that I have become something of a pariah. "I don't think that would be a good idea, Mrs. Tuckerworth."

"Why not? And do call me Marian. I feel we are old friends."

"Well, Marian, you are going to have to appeal to solid citizens for money, and solid citizens are going to need help. My name might scare them away."

"Oh it's not as bad as that, Harriet," Joan quickly intervenes. "All this will blow over."

Marian looks mystified.

"Let's drop it," I say. "I can give you some names that would be of help. Angelica Lamb, for instance."

"Splendid. I recognize the name, of course," and Marian gets up to go. "Thanks awfully. You have cheered me. I had begun to feel rather overwhelmed, standing at the foot of Mount Everest alone."

As she goes out Nan Blakeley comes in. I had hoped so much she would come back, and here she is, looking quite beautiful in a red coat and red shoes, smiling her expectant smile.

"Miss Hatfield, I've been trying to get back to this heaven for days, but little Serena has flu. She's the one who is only four, so I couldn't. Then my mother flew in from New York and she's reading nursery rhymes to Serena. I want my kids to grow up with poems in their heads right from the start."

"Well, I was hoping to see you again," I say.

"Good. I looked at the window. It's stunning. There are so many women's lives I know nothing about. Do you have extras for sale? I wouldn't want to spoil that window!"

"Of course. What is your pleasure?"

"Maybe that big fat biography of Willa Cather."

"That I can provide."

"I read a lot of her in college—I went to Hunter—but somehow not a biography, though I suppose it's clear that the Nebraska novels, anyway, have elements of autobiography." She is standing by my desk as we talk. "I'm babbling away, I'm afraid, interrupting your work. You just can't imagine the relief it is to be in an adult world for a half-hour! Talk about books! Oh my!"

"I'm not working. It's been a humdinger of a day so far and talking about books is what this old body needs. Come over and sit down, why don't you?"

"You can't imagine how sustaining this store is. It does me good just to know it's there when I get to cooking macaroni and cheese or even making a milkshake—all poor Serena will eat. I'm a good mother, I think, but oh dear me, I'm not a good housekeeper! And the things I like to cook are not the things small children like."

"But your husband does, I trust."

"Oh yes. Phil, he comes home ravenous and we eat after the children are in bed—late—but then we open a bottle of wine and we feast."

"Sounds good to me," I say, basking in this happy, buoyant woman's presence.

Now I see her hesitate and look at me for a second as though she were making a decision about something. "Somebody told me you had been threatened. Or is that just gossip? And if not, why would anyone threaten you? I'm curious. Maybe I shouldn't ask."

"Some goons in this neighborhood think I'm a bad influence who sells obscene books."

"You must be kidding!"

"Well . . ." I wonder how much to explain. "You may have noticed that some of the women who come here are couples. And maybe you saw that interview in the *Globe*?"

"No, I must have missed that. We read the *Times*. I buy the *Globe* only once in a while."

I glance over at Joan and she shakes her head. Oh dear, what

144

can I say? "In a nutshell, Mrs. Blakeley, homophobia is the answer. I lived for thirty years with Vicky Chilton until she died. I'm a lesbian."

Nan takes this in and frowns. What is she thinking? "I see," she says, and meets my eyes, such a questioning warm look we exchange. "I suppose sometimes that must be something like being black. I'm black and I know what it is to arouse curiosity, pity, and sometimes hatred, or even worse, being patronized. You just have to grow a tough skin or the shell of a turtle," and she smiles that warm smile that touched me from the first moment I laid eyes on her. Now she says, "You must miss your friend a lot. I wish I had known her."

"She was a powerful woman dedicated to publishing books she believed in." I smile at her. "And like you I was glad to take care of things and not be a professional. The publishing house was, I suppose, our child. Never thought of that before, but I see it's quite true. I miss Vicky but I am rather enjoying not being anyone's housekeeper, gardener, and general factotum anymore. Does that shock you?" for I catch a questioning look in her eyes.

"Not at all," she says. "I admire you for being able to build a new life."

Because I catch some ambivalence in this answer I think it over. "Sometimes I think I haven't even begun to mourn Vicky. I plunged into the whole business of the bookstore a few months after her death and it has been so absorbing, so enriching, Mrs. Blakeley."

"Do call me Nan."

"Then I'm Harriet, and we are friends."

"You must come over some afternoon and see the children and maybe Phil could get home early for a drink. That would be fun." She looks at her watch. "Heavens, it's nearly five and my mother will be dealing with some kind of uproar. I must run."

145

I persuade her to wait a minute while I find a copy of the Cather biography. "It's expensive, I'm afraid."

"Never mind, I've earned it. I tell Phil my salary as a home-maker should be at least ten thousand dollars and he has to agree though he doesn't want to."

When she has left I say to Joan, "Joan, I'm a wreck. But isn't Nan a wonderful woman? I do enjoy her."

But Nan's visit is not, as I hoped it might be, the end of a demanding day. For just as I am about to go upstairs Patience dashes in for a minute to ask if it is all right if Carl delivers a load of wood tomorrow morning and charges seventy dollars. "That's good news," I say, "I paid a hundred and forty dollars for what was stolen. Great day! Joan will be here and can pay him when he comes."

"Good, Alice is out in the car, and I must run."

"There appear to be quite a few guardian angels around," Joan says. "It's not such a bad neighborhood after all."

"Well, yes and no. The enemies have not been routed."

"Shall I call you around ten to see if all is well?"

"I expect to be fast asleep by ten, so don't worry."

As usual, at around five, people begin to pile in to buy books, and for once I am glad to make my escape.

I lie down on my bed with Patapouf beside me and let the waves of anxiety and fatigue rise and fall inside my head. I al-most never think about myself as sixty years old, but lying here, it comes to me that I am driving the old body rather hard. I am stiff from lifting and arranging the books. And under that irritat-ing pain, which makes it impossible to get comfortable, is—and it really can't be kept at bay—anxiety. What are those goons plotting now to try to drive me out? Smashing the windows of the store? Setting it on fire? The possibilities are endless. I try to shut them out by calling the Quality Inn and asking to speak to Martha. She has checked out an hour ago. So presumably David has persuaded her to go home with him and perhaps Joe has helped with that decision. In the end there is nothing to do but get up, make myself a stiff drink, and take a look at the news on television. And this I do.

But these days the news is hardly soothing—a black man beaten up in the South End, the terrible starvation in Ethiopia, another rocket blown up on its way, though that perhaps can be considered good news. Finally I make myself a cheese sandwich and drink a glass of milk. Now at last I go to bed but I keep waking to listen for any strange sound and there is so much traffic it is hard to tell if some truck braking might not be someone with evil in mind. There is the sound of broken glass now and I hurry downstairs in the dark. But it turns out to be from a collision of two cars down the street.

This will never do, I tell myself severely. Either you learn to live with anxiety or it will drive you nuts. Finally I fall asleep, only to have a strange dream about Vicky. She is shaking me awake and is very angry and keeps saying, "You fool, you fool, don't you have an atom of common sense?" But what her anger is about is not clear. And I suppose my aching arms are at the root of the nightmare.

I wake up crying and can't stop. I do not cry often or easily so it upsets me to feel so weak and defenseless, with even the Vicky of my dream turning against me. And maybe for good reason. It is true what I said to Nan. I have not really mourned her. I have buried our life together deep in my unconscious. I do not want to think about her. And no doubt the unmourned get their revenge, which is guilt.

12

After the tears, I must have slept hard because I wake up at half-past seven, late indeed, as I often wake at five and like to have time, unhurried time, in which to pull myself together. But the morning after my nightmare about Vicky I do not want to get up. I want to lie in bed and think, and so I do, grateful that there is no reason not to, since Joan will be opening the shop and my stint won't start till two. Patapouf is still fast asleep under the bed, a late riser in her old age.

I make some coffee and take it to bed with a hard roll and marmalade. It is the first morning since the store opened that I permit myself the luxury of breakfast in bed. But it is not exactly pleasure after all, rather a need to think about Vicky and me, and our relationship, to look at it from the point of view of the new Harriet, one she did not know, I realize, for the more I consider it the more I see that I have changed in some fundamental ways since Vicky's death. Whatever guilt I feel must be from the idea that I have been leaving her all these months, that I have cut myself off almost entirely from what she and I shared for thirty years.

Instead of looking back with nostalgia to our ritual tea by the fire with Patapouf and the old cat who has since died, I am engaged in pouring tea for total strangers, women off the street, anyone who happens to be around when the water is boiling. Instead of ordering an expensive but glorious tree peony— Vicky always teased me because when we went over garden catalogs my mouth watered, as though we were ordering food— instead of that self-indulgent pleasure, I am ordering books, tons of books, many of which she would have referred to as by "another one of those loony lesbian feminists."

I am breaking out of the tight circle in which we lived very happily all those years. I am choosing to ally myself with, in some cases, social pariahs. Vicky, I tell myself, was not really a snob, but she expected the amenities to be observed, and she wanted to see people who shared her own interests. She liked men better than women, and preferred women who held positions of power to her colleagues' wives.

Whatever would she have made of Chris and Mary, going off to El Salvador to help rebuild the villages destroyed by the army? She might well have said, "Why don't they mind their own business? There are plenty of needy people right here in Dorchester." And as for Sue Bagley, she would have given her short shrift, as I sometimes want to do myself. She might, on the other hand, have understood Martha better than I do. "Oh Vicky," I murmur, and again those tears that shot out of me in the night begin to flow. What is happening to me?

Is it grief, as Nan and so many others would think, those who have commiserated with me in my widowhood? But is it grief I am feeling? No, I know it is not exactly that. Perhaps it is guilt for having been able to cut myself off with such objectivity from a good marriage, as it surely was. Joan, for instance, is mourning what has been taken from her. Maybe death is easier to handle than divorce. I wonder . . .

I rarely felt anger towards Vicky and when I did she closed

the door on it and waited, as she said, for my "mood" to change. It was useless to argue that I was not in a mood but outraged because, for instance, she had just fired the gardener without telling me. He had cut off all the aster buds thinking they were seeds. It was extremely irritating, but it was really not his fault. "We have to have people around who know what they are doing," she had said.

"The buds do look a little wizened at first," I had explained. Danny, the fired gardener, was quite an old man and had worked for us for ten years, after all.

"I'm too busy, Harriet. I can't take time to argue with you," and she had closed the door to her study.

But why am I remembering that sort of thing and not all the trips we made to Europe together, and the warm family atmosphere she was brought up in and the huge old mansard-roofed house in Brookline? Her father and mother, especially her father, were the only people I ever knew who could tease Vicky and bring her down from her high horse. And they took me right into the family, even to Vicky's mother saying at the start, "Don't let Vicky order you around, will you? She is an only child, you know," and she commended me for the strange reason that I had brothers.

"I'm afraid I'm used to being ordered around . . . a girl, with two brothers, you can imagine."

Vicky just smiled and paid no attention. "I am who I am," was her refuge before any serious attack, "and I'm not about to change."

What she did do was to treat me always with tender respect, and that was quite new to me and very dear, for I rarely got that at home, except from my father. In some ways, I recognize on this morning of reflection, Vicky was rather like my father, going her own way, but in such a charming and secure manner that it seemed quite all right. After all, who was hurt by that? No

151

one. My father, who had been greatly loved, exuded warmth and good will, and so had Vicky.

"What would I ever do without you, darling?" was often her last word at night, as we curled up together in our bed with Patapouf at the end, and sometimes the cat, Porteous, purring between us. That is what I have lost, and what I miss, the tender loving, the physical closeness long after the first passionate year was over. So very slowly now as I lie here, allowing thoughts to take me where they will, I do come to the place of mourning. There will never again be that kind of sharing—of that I feel certain. I cannot imagine anyone ever sleeping in my bed again. My life from now on will be dispersed among a great many people, friends, strangers, strangers who will become friends like Joe and Eddie, but there never again will be that strong loving arm around my shoulders, and for a half-hour I feel the loss. I let the loss in and don't lock it out as I have been doing. And I weep good tears.

I know I am weeping partly for me, for me who will never again know that sort of absolute love and security, that fortress against the world that two people who are truly married become. I feel vulnerable for the first time since Vicky's death.

So with that in mind, I make myself get up and begin to face this day, wondering as I dress what the new Harriet will do with it, and what she will have to meet. And there on my calendar I see that it is Tuesday already and I am to go to Andrew's for supper. What an occasion! One thing about my years with Vicky was that we did not see much of my brothers after my mother and father died. When they were alive there had been large family gatherings which Vicky only rarely wanted to attend. I was astonished when Fred showed an interest in the store, and now Andrew recognizing the special bond he and I share. I look forward to seeing where he lives, what atmosphere he has created for himself alone, but he is clearly not a happy man, sorry for himself, eating himself up with angers and constraints. We were none of us brought up to handle being outside the norm and Andrew has no doubt walled himself in in order to survive. Well, we shall see.

There is now the welcome sound of wood being stacked in the cellar and I hurry down to thank Alice and Patience's friend. He proves to be a grizzled man in a red shirt with a boy with him who looks only about thirteen. They introduce themselves as Carl and Mike.

"How about a cup of coffee and a piece of coffee cake?" I ask, but they are anxious to get home and refuse the offer.

"The other lady gave us a check," Carl explains.

There is something comforting about a cellar well-stacked with wood and I tell him how grateful I am, what a lift it has given us to be able to replace right away what has been stolen, and at such a good price.

"Glad to oblige." He explains that the top layer is seasoned and what is under that had better be given six months before it is used. "You could start a fire all right, but it takes some skill. In the top layer there's some apple. That'll make a sweet-smelling fire for you any day now." And Mike, eager to have me notice it, points out some white birch.

The woodpile has taken on during this talk a personality, a reality all its own, and I savor it. When we part we shake hands and Carl gives me his phone number and says to call when I need another load.

When I go upstairs to the store, there is Martha, who rushes at me and gives me a warm excited hug. "I've just sold a painting!" she says. "I can't believe it—a sort of bag lady, dragging in parcels. She wanted to buy it and I let her have it for ten dollars a month."

Of course I recognize the woman, she who does not like Gothic novels, but her buying a painting does surprise me.

153

"She's quite a character . . . comes in often to sit down and wait for her bus."

"She said it was the roots of the trees that fascinate her, the thought that trees are as wide around under the earth as above it." For me there has been a nightmarish quality to those roots. How wrong my perception of them is! "She said it was an archetypal image. Oh she talked on and on, and then I drove her to her apartment because she really couldn't carry it and all those parcels. She lives with her husband who is bedridden, a terribly depressing place, filled with books and magazines and the hospital bed taking up half the living room—her husband, a wrinkled old baby, whimpering in his sleep. I couldn't wait to get away, but I must say she has guts, that woman. Imagine living like that, and all they have is Social Security plus a very little in savings they have to draw on, she says."

The last thing I expected was to see Martha in a state of euphoria, interested in someone besides herself, and I am struck dumb.

"Oh Harriet, I am so excited I forgot to tell you the most important thing. David came to the Quality Inn before four and persuaded me to go with him to Dr. Hunter's. At that point I didn't know who I was or what I wanted, so I agreed. I was awfully glad to see David, to see him not angry for a change, and very subdued."

"The world appears to be turning right side up again. We have wood and Martha is all right," I say, turning to Joan, who gives me a surreptitious wink. "How did you like Dr. Hunter?"

"I liked him. He wants us both to go back next week. He doesn't say much. I guess I talked a lot and he listened, but his listening was very supportive. I mean I didn't feel he was judging me or David and when it came to David's hitting me so hard, David cried. Nothing is settled but we are going to try to be gentle and not argue for a week."

"That," I say, "is optimistic." I am slightly irritated by Martha's state of mind, so positive and on top of things, when I remember what she put me through yesterday.

"I know," she says, giving me a wary look. "I don't know what I would have done without you. You saved me from despair, Harriet. I'll never forget it."

"I'm glad if I was of help, but now, Martha, I really have to have a talk with Joan about business matters."

I feel ashamed when she has left and I turn to Joan. "How do psychiatrists manage not to be bored?"

"My guess is they sort of black out until a real clue is uttered and then they wake up."

"I made that up about a business talk."

"But," Joan says, "it's high time we did have a talk. So much has been happening lately I didn't want to add another anxiety or burden, but we have been losing money. That big sale on Saturday after the *Globe* mess just about saved us."

"Oh well," I say, "I told Jonathan we would probably lose money for a year at least, so he is prepared."

"But are you prepared?"

At this I have to laugh. "Of course not. I hoped I might be wrong. Now we must think about getting the store known. What about a small ad in the *Globe?*"

"Worth a try."

"What about a poster we could pin up here and there? At Sage's, for example?"

"That might work. Do you know anyone good at that sort of thing? What we need to think about is a logo or some kind of device."

"Oh." I ponder this. " 'Good Books for Good Women,' " but as soon as I utter the words I see how ridiculous they sound and so does Joan, so we can't stop laughing. "Andrew might know someone at that high-tech place where he works. I'll ask him

155

when I see him tonight. Meanwhile I had better have a look at the accounts."

Joan suggests that I take them upstairs so I will not be inter-rupted, and so I do. What becomes clear almost at once is that the big expense is ordering. I have been ordering anything and everything that looks interesting. Two of each except for obvi-ous best-sellers when I order five. Maybe I have been extrava-gant, but we found early on that publishers are maddeningly slow about refilling an order, so I choose to avoid that by order-ing a lot. My instinct is to go on as we have been doing for six months, meanwhile stimulating sales in every way we can.

It is not hopeless but I realize that I have not put my mind on the business and it is high time that I do.

13

When I walk into Andrew's apartment, high up on the wrong side of Beacon Street, I don't know what to expect, but whatever I was expecting was not this rather cozy Victorian atmosphere, comfortable chairs upholstered in red velvet, thick tapestry curtains that shut out the traffic, books everywhere. It is a studio, really, with just one bedroom off the big room, lighted chiefly from the large skylight.

"What a beautiful room, Andrew."

"You're surprised, I hope. You didn't think your brother had taste," he teases.

"I knew my brother had taste, but this seems so . . ." I hesitate before a word that might offend. I censor *conservative, nostalgic, enclosed, secret,* and finally Andrew supplies the word himself.

"Esoteric?"

"Maybe."

"I planned it around Father's English desk. When we divided up the family stuff I got that and the two Victorian chairs."

"It's a sort of private re-creation then. I did think of the word 'nostalgic' when I was looking for a word."

"Maybe nostalgic for something that never really existed. You know as well as I do, Harriet, that I never felt at home in that house, so I made this into what feels like home to me now. I love this place," he says. "Sit down and tell me what you would like to drink. I have a bottle of champagne on ice but if you would prefer scotch or a martini, that's available too."

"Champagne of course. This is a celebration, Andrew, isn't it?"

Suddenly he smiles his warm smile which lights up his narrow dark face as though in smiling a mask slides away and the young ardent boy under it looks out. "It is for me. I never in my wildest dreams thought you and I could have anything in common. You appeared to live somewhere far away on a peak with Vicky, so serene and safe. There was no room for misfits."

As the champagne cork pops I say, without thinking, "Pop goes the weasel!"

"Hey, it's Mumms, no weasel. Have a taste!" and he hands me one of the now old-fashioned wide champagne glasses I much prefer to the fashionable flutes around these days. For a second as we lift our glasses, I meet Andrew's eyes, those very dark eyes, and we look rather than speak a toast.

"Pure bliss," I say, setting my glass down.

"You know, you are looking extremely well, Harriet. Has anyone told you that?"

"People don't make personal remarks to the manager of a bookstore," I say demurely, "but at sixty one comes into one's face at last. I was, you have to admit, a rather plain person in the old days. Whereas you, Andrew, were always tantalizingly handsome and I envied you."

"And now I'm a seedy old man," he says with sudden bitterness. *"Sic transit . . ."*

"Nonsense. I still envy you that tall slim figure. Women must be crazy about you as they always were." But of course that is the wrong thing to say, the habitual trite thing people in our society say without a thought.

"Men no longer are," he says, frowning and drinking half his glass down. "In the bars I'm treated like an old professor who is patted on the back and chivvied."

"Then why go to bars?"

"Because that is where gay men meet sexual partners. Honestly, Harriet, you are an innocent old body, aren't you?"

How many people have called me innocent lately? It is getting to be a bore, and the tone this time is not charitable, "old body" indeed. "Can't you meet men at your job? I mean, does it have to be bars? I'll tell you one thing, Andrew, I am proud of having been part of a gay marriage, a marriage that lasted thirty years."

"But at what cost?" he needles.

"Don't put me on the defensive. That's over. I'm leading a wholly different life."

"Exactly. After being in prison for thirty years you're out in the real world."

"True." I have to grant it.

"We may be brother and sister, Harriet, but you have to realize that men are different from women. Thank God we can talk about it, but the gulf is there—when I can I pick up a young man for the night, or with luck, for a month or so, but it doesn't last."

"Hasn't AIDS changed that—that easy casual sex?"

"Yes." Andrew fills my glass and his and sits down opposite me, stretches his long legs out, and looks over at me having apparently dropped his aggressive stance.

"It seems so wasteful," I say. "I mean, to get involved for such a short time."

"Oh, but one is not involved," he says quickly. "It's the lure of the stranger, it's the perpetual adventure."

159

"You miss then what a long-term marriage is all about and I can assure you that it is not primarily sexual."

"It sounds boring," Andrew says. "You know all about each other. What is there to discover? What do you go on learning?"

I do not have a quick answer to that question so I am rather relieved when Andrew says he had better get the Dover sole into the broiler. "I won't be long, so just relax and look around."

I want to look at the books, a whole wall of books to the back ceiling, with an elegant English ladder with which to reach the top shelves. The books make a statement about the homosexual writer and artist. Gide is there in the beautiful Pléiade edition, Julian Green's journal, E. M. Forster, of course, all of Virginia Woolf, Vita Sackville-West, W. H. Auden, Isherwood, Ackerley. When Andrew comes back I am up on the ladder in order to examine all of Proust, beautifully bound, and his biography, and have taken out, to glance at, a collection of Proust's essays on art, in French.

"So there you are," he says, bringing in a plate and laying it on the table in the corner next to the kitchen. "What an agile sister I have!"

"The ladder is wonderful and the way one can shift it along."

"Yes, I designed it myself. I like to rove around the library, as you can see." He smiles up at me. "But now you must come down. Dover sole is on the table."

"My brother appears to live very well," I say as I sit down to a blue linen cloth, matching napkins, elegant glasses on long thin stems. "You make me see what a lower-class existence I lead these days."

"Really? Do you feel *déclassée,* as it were? I am fascinated." He is teasing, as I had been, but as he pours the Vouvray, which happens to be my favorite white wine, I am thinking about this.

"What I have been discovering since I opened the store is that that whole world of Chestnut Hill, which resembles this elegant table, is something I have left for good."

"Why leave it?"

"Because it feels limited finally. Or perhaps not quite real."

"This table is very real," he says, teasing again. "Does reality have to be poor and ugly? What's unreal about Dover sole and Vouvray?"

"It's delicious, Andrew. I'm a spoiled old creature, spoiled and awfully glad we can talk."

"Even though you bring out the worst in me?"

"Do I? How so?"

"The snob, I suppose. The slightly superior person, at least in his own eyes, who has a penchant for garage mechanics and sailors."

"I wonder why? My new friends Joe and Eddie come to my mind because Joe is a psychiatrist and upper class, I suppose, and Eddie is a garage mechanic. As I told you they have lived together for years and create a marvelous atmosphere. They are the ones who jog every morning and wipe off any obscenities people have written on the store windows."

"Very nice and clean. But you see I have no wish to harbor forever the men I pick up in bars."

I feel that Andrew is daring me, is asking for scorn or contempt, and why that is I cannot understand. His face looks pinched suddenly, and old. What I see in it is something close to despair. And here we are across the blue linen, the light shining on our glasses, but despair has joined us in the last few seconds, and for the first time I feel at a loss. Andrew has become a stranger with whom I cannot make contact. "Only connect," but that is what he seems unable to do in his life and I, at the moment, seem unable to do in regard to him.

161

"Forster's great love, I think I read somewhere, was a police-man."

"Yes indeed, that is common knowledge."

Andrew, his eyes half closed, has become a turtle I think, but now he decides to break the spell. "I wonder what it would be like for me if my private life was exposed to public view as yours has just been—what it would do. Of course the first thing would be that I would lose my job, not exactly a hilarious matter. How did you feel when the thing exploded in your face, Harriet? You seem almost unbelievably unscathed, secure, glad even, to be who you are." I don't know how to answer this right away and he breaks my silence himself. "Please try to talk about it."

"The best thing about it, or next to best, is that it brought you over, that you wanted to tell me about yourself. Isn't it rather wonderful to be sitting here like old friends?"

"Yes," he says, filling our glasses. "I'm amazed that you are here, that I am suddenly not alone, that there is family." I see tears in his eyes. "But tell me now what the best thing about it is—granted that this is the next-best thing," and he lifts his glass in a toast.

"The best thing, I suppose, is the sense of freedom. And the way people have reacted. I was bowled over by the support, the way people came to the store, many who have become old cus-tomers by now, and treated me as a hero. Every homosexual these days feels in some way at risk. Maybe when an old lady comes out it makes them feel less isolated. I don't know. What I do know is that I myself am in the clear. And I'm well aware that I am partly because I am not now associated with anyone. I don't have to protect Vicky from malicious gossip, for example. For me it is good to be as old as I am, and alone."

"And your own employer, as well," Andrew nods. "I can't help envying you, I must say."

"I live in a much wider circle than I have ever known. Oh

Andrew, I'm almost ashamed of how good it feels—my life, I mean."

"Yet you are in some ways at risk yourself. That is what seems admirable and brave."

"Yes. I get anxious at night. But there is Patapouf, you know. She would bark."

"Do you really think those goons, as you call them, are going to leave you alone eventually?"

"Joe, who is a black belt by the way, knocked one down the first time he and Eddie caught them writing on the windows."

"How satisfactory that must have been!"

"Yes, for him. But I expect it created rage and someone will pay. I just have to put it out of my mind, and luckily that is easy, except at night, because I am awfully busy."

"And at night?"

"I am dead tired. And I go to sleep more often than not almost at once." I don't really want to talk about fear, so it is my turn to change the subject. "I wish you were not so lonely, Andrew."

There is no answer to this. Andrew busies himself clearing the table and bringing on dessert, chocolate meringues with some sort of special raspberry ice cream. It is awfully good and I tell him so, and say no to coffee when he asks if I would like some. "If permitted I'll smoke a cigarette when we move back to the library."

Andrew is pleased. "Still crazy, after all these years," he sings. "It makes you more bearable. Otherwise you are a little too good to be true."

"Oh come on, Andrew." I get up and we move back to the comfortable chairs. "Before I forget, we've got to make the store known in some way. I'm looking for a logo and someone who could design some really smart posters. I wonder if you might know someone. Maybe at your firm?"

"Let me think about it. But how in hell can you advertise a bookstore for women and make it attractive?"

"It is Hatfield House: A Bookstore for Women. What's wrong with that?"

"Nothing, I suppose," but "everything" is clearly in his tone. "HHBW—maybe a design could be made around the initials. Why not let me have a try?"

So we part with something to be created and that seems to me a good augury. Andrew insists on following me home in his car to be sure everything is all right. I am grateful because I rarely go out at night, partly because opening my door and going in alone is a little scary. But when Andrew waves goodbye and shoots off in his BMW, and I have taken Patapouf for a very short run, I sit down in the living room, a little amused to contrast its utilitarian look with Andrew's elegance, but I do not feel happy about him.

Patapouf comes and begs for her evening treat of a dog bone while I smoke a last cigarette. How easy it is to keep a dear dog happy, to know exactly what she wants, and how hard and complex the needs of a human being! On the surface Andrew is leading a pleasant enough life, if a rather self-indulgent one, but what emptiness and self-disgust there are just under the surface I can only imagine. When he smiled at me and teased me he was his old self and looked ten years younger than his fifty years, but the minute he was serious his face looked taut and unhappy. He is not, I decided, at home in himself. And I wonder why I am. Is it, I wonder, harder to come to terms with male homosexuality than female? And if so, why?

But now I remember Joe and Eddie and what seems a very good life they lead together. Maybe it is easier to be an old gay woman than an old gay man. And why is that? Maybe because it doesn't matter as much to a woman to become physically less attractive? Do women feel rejected by the young of their own sex in the same way? How am I really to know? It all comes down to Andrew's having failed to make any lasting connection with a lover. He is floating along on the surface. I had Vicky all those years as my loving companion and dearest friend. And I realize that the last thing I want or need now at sixty is another such intimate relationship. What I have felt since I opened the store is a lot of admiration, more certainly than I deserve, and real affection on the part of the nuns, the young lesbians, the two friends who come on Saturdays, Eddie and Joe. How lucky I am!

What makes me sad, I realize, once I'm in bed, is simply Andrew himself, gay or not. Living alone is not the easiest thing in the world, but doing it with grace is a matter of character, no doubt, not sexual preference. Angelica, for instance, comes to mind like a burst of sunlight. She manages to balance out solitude and even loneliness against a passionate interest in what is going on in the world. One may laugh a little at all the volunteer work, the committees, the endless meetings she attends, but her gray eyes widen when she talks about the homeless, or the need for planned parenthood, and she is vibrantly alive. She works much harder than many professionals do.

It makes me wonder whether Andrew has not settled for a job that means security but after some years is no longer a challenge. He has all those marvelous books. Has he dreamed of being a writer himself? I see that I have a lot to learn about Andrew. At sixty I seem to be learning a lot, chiefly learning, in fact. Growing up! It may appear humorous to some people, people who tease me about my innocence, but it makes my life extremely interesting. What more can one ask at sixty?

So I go to sleep finally, on a wave of, not exactly happiness—what then?—fulfillment of a rather special kind.

14

It seems fortuitous when Caroline's nurse calls me this morning to say that if I can, this is the day to come and see Caroline briefly at around half-past ten. I have been so busy for the last ten days that I have hardly thought of Caroline and I am appalled, as though the dying are kept alive partly by the thoughts of others. Or death is eased by those thoughts. I am very relieved that I can see her once more, beloved woman that she is. I want to bring her flowers, something light and airy, that tiny yellow orchid on a long spray, if I can find them. The local florist is not very sophisticated, but I'll go to Harvard Square. Strange how just thinking of Caroline makes time that has been clobbering me lately quiet down and I feel I am on the slow peaceful ebbing of Caroline's tide. It's a chilly dark day so we won't be able to sit in the garden. Those days may be over for her, I am aware.

The atmosphere, when the nurse comes to the door, is subdued. "You must stay less than a half-hour, Miss Hatfield. Doctor's orders. I'll take the flowers and put them in a vase for you," she says.

"Thanks, something small, Nurse. You can cut the stems."

Suddenly I feel panic stricken. I am opening death's door as, according to my directions, I open a door on the second floor and there is Caroline in a big bed, sitting high up on pillows piled behind her. "Darling, I am glad to see you. I wanted so much to come out but didn't quite dare."

"Thank you for the books." Caroline looks wan, her eyes the only thing in her face that has not changed, yet they are circled in shadow. I am amazed that her voice is the same as ever, as though a voice could be like a heartbeat, what remains when the body itself is diminished, is fading away. "I liked Freya Stark," she says, "maybe because I could read it a paragraph at a time—and because she deals with all the things I have been thinking about," she stops a moment to catch her breath and then says, "except one."

I have been standing. Now I pull a chair up close to the bed. "And what is that one?"

Caroline reaches out and just touches my hand gently where it lies on the counterpane as I lean forward. "Why women love women. Will you talk to me about this?"

I am flustered. "The trouble is, Caroline, dear Caroline, that I have thought much too little about it!"

At this she smiles. "Admirable. You have lived your life rather than thinking about it, but when someone sticks a label on you that sets you apart from most of the rest of us, isn't it difficult to handle?"

"Oh, you read that *Globe* interview." The light is dawning.

"Susan Whipple, who comes and reads to me, brought it along one day."

"What did she say?"

Caroline smiles a mischievous smile. "You can imagine and I'm not going to repeat."

"I am learning to get used to the label, Caroline, but of course most people I know can't deal with it at all, and perhaps that is

168

partly why I decided to open a bookstore as far from Chestnut Hill and all it represents as possible."

"Yet I am told that you are getting threatened in that new neighborhood. Your Chestnut Hill circle might not approve but they would not threaten."

"Somehow, maybe for Vicky's sake, I don't want polite evasions. I'd rather have a rock thrown at the window."

"I can't help being anxious about you, Harriet." She settles back on her pillows, a little out of breath. "I would like to manage to live till things down there are settled, till I know you are safe."

I feel a lump in my throat as I say, "They will never be settled, Caroline. That is the fact."

"You are brave, dear woman, very brave," and she sighs.

"You must think of me as happy and—if I say so myself—useful. All sorts of amazing things happen every day. After that *Globe* piece Andrew came for breakfast the next day to tell me that he is gay himself."

"Surely you knew that?"

"We were never close. I suppose I didn't think about it much one way or another." I see Caroline look over at the clock on her bedside table. "I mustn't tire you out."

"I do use up my little bubble of energy rather quickly," she admits, "but I so want to go back to my question, the one you did not answer—why women love women."

I answer it first with a silence, then I ask, "Maybe you can answer it better. You have been in love with a woman."

"My guess, Harriet, is that a multitude of women have felt the attraction, the need, whatever it is, and cannot face it, so bury it and pretend it never happened."

"And they are the furies," I say.

"Yes, they do become the furies—at least at times. What cannot be faced must be destroyed."

I do not know what to say or how to say it, but I feel that it is mandatory that I try at least to answer Caroline's question. "For a woman, another woman is not primarily a sexual object, whereas for a man she often is. A woman wants to be recognized as a person first, to be understood and cherished for what she *is,* and especially perhaps in middle age she may find this kind of understanding and recognition from another woman, a woman she admires as I admired Vicky."

"Yet Vicky did swallow you up, didn't she?"

"Yes, that is one of the things I am learning now. I was rather happy to be swallowed up when we first met. She made everything easy, she was so incredibly sure of herself, no guilt, not a shadow of a doubt about her way of life."

"Money helps," Caroline says meditatively. "I find it difficult to unravel all this," her voice growing faint. The nurse knocks softly and comes in with the little orchids in a narrow Chinese vase. "How lovely! Did you bring them, Harriet?"

"Yes, I did."

"Like tiny saffron butterflies on their long stems."

"I'm afraid it is time for a rest," the nurse says and I get up at once.

"I have failed to answer the question," I say, bending down to kiss Caroline's cool cheek.

"Never mind. It will keep."

At the door I stop to wave, but Caroline has slipped down into the pillows and her eyes are closed.

"Don't come, Nurse, I'll find my way down."

Outside I sit in my car for quite a while, thinking about Caroline, wondering whether I have just seen her for the last time, heard her musical voice for the last time, and I weep tears of comfort that I have known her, and for some reason that she admits the love of women in her own life, so rich and full, for she surely has loved Winston and her two brilliant sons. Yet . . .

It is much too simplistic, what I said to her. I am ashamed now, for certainly Winston recognized and cherished Caroline and she always has seemed a whole person in her own right. Yet...

A certain tenderness, a certain reciprocity, not having to make allowances for the male compulsions and fundamental sense of superiority. What man does not have it? Gay men included.

Still, I remain at sea, old innocent that I am.

15

It is time for a lull and I am happy to have the afternoon ahead of me here at the store, for once hoping that not too many people will drop in needing to talk. Looking at the calendar I can't believe it is October already. Vicky and I always drove to Williamstown for a weekend of leaf-seeing at about this time, but there is no one I want to ask to do that with me now.

I am not surprised when the phone rings and it is Jonathan to persuade me to take out more insurance just in case. He assures me that the stolen wood is covered. "Until those oddities who are threatening you can be taken care of, it would be wise, Harriet."

I am so amused at the word "oddities," so typical of Jonathan's way of talking, that I laugh aloud.

"Why are you laughing? I am serious."

" 'Oddities' is such a peculiar word to describe them."

"What is your word then?"

"Goons, gross goons."

"Oh."

"I see that even my vocabulary is changing lately. Yes, gross goons. It is a comfort to be well insured. Thanks, Jonathan."

After his call I fiddle around with ideas about how we might advertise the store and it comes to me that so far not one of my Smith classmates has dropped in, and there are certainly many in this area. Once Andrew has invented a logo I am going to have something printed that I can send out to my class and those of the year ahead of me and the year after. Of course they are all grandmothers by now but a few at least should be interested in a women's bookstore. I am jotting down some notes about what to say when a young woman I have not seen before pushes open the door. She is a round young person, which I like, and is dressed in a dark blue coat and white turtleneck sweater. She smiles at me shyly. I think she may be a nurse.

"I wonder," she asks, "if I might sit down for a few minutes. I've been up all night and thought the walk back from Central Square would do me good, but I feel rather weak in the knees suddenly."

"Sit right down, you are welcome," I say at once. I am dying to ask what she has been doing all night but don't quite dare. I say, "It's a little early for tea, but I'll be glad to share a cup with you. You do look worn out."

"Thanks, but I'll be on my way in a minute." She looks at me for a second, asking herself, perhaps, whether to say more. Then she looks down at her gloved hands and says, "You see, the person I was with all night died an hour ago. I'm coming from the hospital."

"How awful for you."

"No, it is a blessing."

"Are you a nurse then?"

"No, I work for Hospice. I've been on this case for months, going every day to look after Mrs. Dolan, whom I grew to love. She was afraid of dying alone, you see."

"Didn't she have any family?"

"Only a brother in Los Angeles and he couldn't come. She's

been in the hospital for three days. We tried hard to keep her at home till the end. That's what Hospice aims to do when possible, as you probably know."

"How hard it must be for you, helping people to die. I do admire you. May I ask your name? Mine is Harriet Hatfield."

"Mine is Bettina Morgan. You are kind to listen when you surely have better things to do."

"I am honored to hear all you care to tell," I say rather lamely.

"I suppose a lot of women come who find it rather wonderful to be in a bookstore like this, where there are books about themselves."

"That's my idea—and it seems to be working out. It's quite an adventure, as you can imagine, for an old person like me."

This remark makes Bettina smile. "There are days when I feel very old and I am only thirty."

"Tell me a little about Mrs. Dolan. I would like to know about her and this last night."

"She was nearly eighty and very frail. She had lung cancer but I think her heart may have just given out. She had the hands of a woman who has worked hard all her life. She had worked in a laundry, then nursed her husband after a stroke. Her hands were crippled by arthritis so it was not easy to hold one and not hurt. But I did learn and held her in my arms when she was afraid." The story pours out and I listen. In these few minutes I have come to like Bettina a lot. "I'm tired because what I did all night was sing to her."

"You sang all night? How did you ever do it?"

"I don't know, but when I stopped she would reach out and touch my sleeve so I knew I must try to remember another song. I sang everything you can imagine from hymns to popular songs. I sang 'Let It Be'—you know that one Paul McCartney sang. I sang it several times. Mrs. Dolan's eyes were closed but she was listening and I knew she was by that tug at my sleeve."

"Where were the nurses all those hours?"

"Oh, they came and went. You know how it is. Her heart was being monitored. They looked at me sometimes as though I were crazy, but I paid no attention. Mrs. Dolan and I were alone on that journey together. That's all that mattered to me, you know."

"I don't know, but I can imagine. The only death I have been close to was the friend I lived with for many years and she died of a heart attack in a few minutes. It was a terrible shock. We had no time to say goodbye. It was like a cliff falling into the sea without any warning." I had not talked with anyone before about this and it surprises me a little to be doing so now.

"That is a good death for the one who goes, isn't it? We see so many hard deaths. You must take it as a blessing," and Bettina looks at me shyly but with understanding.

I feel tears pricking my eyes. "Yes, it is, but the survivors are not prepared. I sometimes think I haven't even begun to come to terms with it. I simply went on into a wholly new life without looking back. I have not yet mourned, not really."

"Mourning takes time, too," says Bettina, clasping and unclasping her still gloved hands. "I really loved Mrs. Dolan," she says. "I hope I helped her go easily at the end. Her heart stopped, you see, and since her eyes were closed I only knew she had gone when the nurse who was monitoring her came running in and took her pulse." Now quite suddenly the round face crumples and she brushes tears away. "It seems so wrong that her brother, who said he couldn't come while she was dying, is flying in for the funeral. I can't understand that. It hurts."

"I'm going to make us a cup of tea," I announce, feeling she perhaps needs to be alone for a few minutes. I like this person, I think, as I put the kettle on. She is not sentimental, but she is very aware. I know that by the way she listened to me just now about Vicky. And I am thinking about Caroline, too, and that I am witnessing an extraordinary death, since she has had time to savor her friends, her garden, her sons, her whole life as she slowly leaves them, but that is because Caroline is such a remarkable woman, containing as she does a fulfilled life, even to her love of a woman.

I bring the tea in and a few cookies for it looks as though Bettina has had no breakfast.

"Thanks. How kind you are," she says, blowing her nose. Her gloves are lying on the table and she is relaxed, I can see. Before pouring I ask whether I can put a little rum in it and she smiles and says, "Please do." That means going upstairs and on an impulse I bring Patapouf down with me. She goes right up to Bettina, wagging her tail. Patapouf always knows when I like someone and does not bark.

"Oh, what a darling dog," Bettina says, rubbing behind the dog's ears in a way that is rewarded with some licking. "Is she very old?"

"About fifteen, so we don't have all the time in the world."

"She must be a comfort."

"Oh she is. I don't know what I would do without her. When things get tough she calms me, balances me. Animals are so easy to make happy."

"Compared to people, yes, I know. I wish we could have a dog, but I have to be away from the house so much and my friend Helen works too, so we have a cat instead. He is very beautiful, a black cat, and we call him Patrick."

"I have been wanting to ask how you manage the transition. It must be strange when a patient dies and you are left dangling, and then I suppose very soon are called to someone else. So I am glad to hear you have a friend."

And I am thinking, here, as in the case of Joe and Eddie, is an exemplary life. If only more people knew this! If all the labels

177

and fears and stereotypes could be exchanged for a few exemplary lesbian or gay lives, the actual lives lived, what a difference it might make.

"I read that interview with you in the *Globe*. I suppose that is why I felt drawn here, to stop here today," Bettina says, and having said so, is too shy to say more. "The thing is that the people we serve are so different one from another. I suppose that helps in a way. I think my next case will be a spastic boy about twelve and the problem we have there is the parents. They have been quite good at taking care of him, but now he is dying of cancer of the marrow of the bones, they are finding facing that very, very hard. His mother looks at him and starts crying, you know."

"And you are going to walk right into that frightfully difficult situation. You are brave!"

"Not till next week," Bettina says, brushing aside praise. "It is my life, after all. It is what I have chosen—and perhaps it has chosen me. Who knows?"

"I am awfully glad you came in today," I say, "and that for once we have not been interrupted by an eruption of customers. That does happen, you know."

"I expect so." I see her hesitate before she asks, "Are you really being threatened by ignorant people, and how do you handle that? That seems to me much harder than what I handle—very much harder."

"Why do you say that? I go along doing my job as best I can."

"Exactly, and that takes guts," Bettina says.

"It's the other side of the coin that brought you here this morning. I have no regrets."

"But you live alone."

"I have Patapouf."

"An army with banners," and Bettina laughs, stroking Patapouf's head. She is lying under the table. "Well, I must get myself together," she says, putting on her gloves. "What shall I take home with me to read?"

"*The Stones of Ibarra.*" It pops out as the perfect book for Bettina. "Here you are." I take it from the shelf. I see her hesitate when she looks at the price. "It's a present," I say. "I want to give it to you."

"Oh my, you'll never make money if you give books away."

"Take it," I say, slipping it into a paper bag.

"How can I thank you for this morning and the book?"

"By coming back and telling me about that boy later on."

"Oh, I shall."

"But now get some sleep, Bettina. Curl up with Patrick."

"I'll do that, but first I want to play a record, the Fauré Requiem, for Mrs. Dolan."

And now she is gone. I am amazed that she has chosen one of my favorite records, amazed and pleased. Bettina is one of the best things that has happened lately, I say to myself. No wonder she feels an affinity with that tender beautiful music. It is like her.

16

After locking up at six one evening I take Patapouf for a brief walk. Now in October the days are getting shorter and it is nearly dark. Patapouf is in the mood to linger and smell one small area like a guard dog looking for cocaine. But it is restful not to hurry, to observe the people coming home with their lunch boxes, the students on bicycles weaving in and out of the traffic, old women carrying packages of food, and that makes me think of the old woman who used to come and sit waiting for her bus. I have never asked her name, and I wonder whether she is ill or her husband worse. I should have asked her to sign the book but I forgot. In fact I don't believe anyone has signed it since the opening. Stupid negligence on my part. Tomorrow I must take a look, and if Joan is forgetting too, we must put it in a prominent place and try to remember. It will eventually become a mailing list. I intend to send out a monthly bulletin recommending certain appropriate new books.

I am thinking about the store rather happily as Patapouf and I wander along. And I am wondering why it is that I am only afraid when I am locked inside the house. I sometimes take Patapouf out quite late in the dark and am not afraid at all. I

suppose inside I feel I am a target and more or less defenseless
in spite of all the locks. What is going to happen? Things appear
to have quieted down since the wood was stolen. No more anon-
ymous letters or window writing. It is too hopeful to think the
goons may have moved away themselves. No, that is not possi-
ble.

Several times I notice young men go past; just now two do,
nudge each other, and laugh when they see me with Patapouf.
Are they the criminals? One has red hair, a freckled face, a
black leather jacket, heavy high boots. The other has a crew cut
and wears a brown sweatshirt with a death's head painted on it,
jeans, and dirty white sneakers. Is it worse to imagine your
enemy than not to imagine him? I have not before ever consid-
ered a person on the street as a possible enemy.

The neighborhood has become familiar. It is beginning to feel
like my neighborhood. I am happy here. I love being among so
many different kinds of people. On this walk I have seen no one
in any way like me or our Chestnut Hill neighbors.

I wonder now whether Angelica is really so upset that she has
deliberately not called in days. Is that possible? How can I lose
such a truly kind and bountiful friend, simply by being myself,
the self I have been through all the years. She must have known
about me and Vicky, after all. Oh, but we were safe and Vicky,
at least, notable. Now I am dangerous, marked like a wild ani-
mal some people wish to exterminate because the species is
accused of killing sheep: a coyote. Who does the lesbian
threaten?

I have my head down thinking these disagreeable thoughts
and am startled when Chris stops me, and Mary is behind her.

"We hoped to find you," Chris says, "because we are going
back to El Salvador tomorrow. We wanted to say goodbye, but
we couldn't make it before six."

"Oh my goodness. You are leaving tomorrow? I can't believe

it!" I can't bear to have them go—and especially into danger. "Walk back with me. Come up to my apartment and have a drink. Can you?"

"We'd love to," Chris says at once.

"We still have to pack, Chris," Mary reminds her.

"Maybe you shouldn't, but please do." And after exchanging a look, they agree and we walk quickly back to the store.

"How fine to live over the store," says Mary as they look around while I pour out sherry and open a tin of nuts.

"I thought so until the threats began, and I think so now really because I can hear anyone trying to break in and call the police."

"And you still don't know who 'they' are?" Chris asks.

"I have no idea." It is not the time to talk about me and I raise my glass. "Let me drink to good luck on your perilous journey."

"We are anxious to get back," Mary says quickly.

"We are so afraid the villagers who have come back to the ruined village will be attacked again," Chris adds.

I can feel the tug inside these two, the pressure to go where the need is, a need they have seen and know well. "I imagine your presence itself helps. The Duarte soldiers may hesitate if they know you are nuns," and then I remember, "but that didn't stop whoever killed the Maryknoll sisters. How stupid can I be?"

"It's a dirty business," Chris murmurs. "So few people over here have any idea what is happening. We were sold Duarte just as we were sold Pinochet."

Mary says more quietly, "We hate not to be proud of our country. Corruption everywhere you look and the wild hunger for material things that eats people up, even more in a neighborhood like this perhaps, where people look at television and can't have what they see there."

"It's hard in El Salvador, but," Chris hesitates, "how can I say it? The people we work with anyway are so moving, they have so little, but they sing all the time, even in the jails they sing, and they hope. How can they hope? I sometimes don't know. After Cardinal Romero was murdered the hope flickered for a time. We saw it flickering, and very nearly flicker out."

Their faces are so serene and so alive that for a moment I envy them.

"But," Mary intervenes, looking at her watch, "we want to know about you. Have there been any more incidents?"

"No, as a matter of fact. And my lawyer tells me insurance will pay for the wood. But I am in suspense for I can't believe whoever they are will be satisfied with stealing wood."

"I know," Chris says, "that is why we hate to leave."

"I'm going to miss you. You have been a wonderful support from that first day of the opening when Chris had the wit to take the guest book around and get it signed." This makes them smile. "And," I add, "in a way I envy you. You know you are going to be useful. You go where extreme need exists."

"Yes, but we can do so very little when you come right down to it. It is often terribly frustrating," Mary says. "Whereas you are in the front line right here. You don't have to go to El Salvador to know you are needed."

"Can you believe this bookstore is needed, needed enough to justify my selfish desire to own it?" I ask. "For goodness' sake!"

"For goodness' sake, yes," Chris says, half laughing. "In the times we've dropped by we have seen a lot happening—that young painter, for instance, and that fine woman who is setting up a caretakers' organization. They all gravitate here and meet here, meet each other."

"And," Mary says, "you are a haven for the frightened gay people, the women full of guilt and dismay because they love a woman. We have seen that, too."

"You have seen a lot with your bright eyes. I still have my

184

doubts. One of my best friends has more or less withdrawn since that newspaper article." It would hurt to say Angelica's name, and I do not. Now I ask what I have wanted to ask for weeks. I turn to Chris, the elder, "Do you really believe it is all right for a woman to love a woman?" Is it a mistake to ask it? I hardly dare look at either of them.

"We do believe it is all right," Chris says and adds with a rueful smile, "although doctrine is adamant on this subject."

"How do you reconcile yourselves with that?"

At this Mary laughs. "We don't."

"The Church is a patriarchy, after all," Chris says, "and so has to be wrong about some things."

"Such as women priests."

"Of course." She is thoughtful, not smiling now, and takes a last sip of her sherry before setting the glass down and saying, "Oh dear, I wish we could talk on, but we have to get going. We leave very early in the morning. Only," she changes her mind and decides to speak out to me and I am grateful, "in a way, homophobia seems rather like the fear of communism. Both are rooted in pathological distortions of reality. It seems only natural that an evil dictatorship like that of Somoza should be followed by a shift to the extreme left and if we had supported that shift maybe they would not have appealed to Russia for help."

"I see that, but, Chris, the gay world is something else. They are not going to change radically, are they? But why is the fear pathological? I wish I understood."

"Because," Chris says quietly, "it is a fact that one-tenth of all creatures from the worm up are homosexual. God created the world as it is. Did He not know what He was doing?"

"Dear heart," Mary says, tugging at Chris's sleeve, "we have to go."

There is just time for a warm hug from each of them and they run down the stairs.

I live these days in a state of perpetual astonishment and the last few minutes have been astonishing. I suddenly remember something that Ramsey, the Archbishop of Canterbury, said years and years ago and that I copied out. It was: "It is a mistake to believe that God is chiefly concerned with religion." It makes me smile with pleasure now as it did then and while I get my supper together I feel happy and relieved.

It is the right end to this good day when the phone rings just before I go to bed and it is Angelica's voice I hear: "When are you coming over for supper, Harriet?"

"I began to think you were shutting me out."

"I've been frightfully busy, as a matter of fact. We have to get a new director for the Cambridge settlement house and there have been a lot of interviews." After a brief silence when I think we might be cut off, she says, "I was troubled, I admit. But we are friends for life, aren't we? I don't shut friends out."

"Neither do I, even when I am chastised for being myself." I can't help saying it but wish I had not.

"Maybe friendship has to accept the unacceptable sometimes. Do you agree? I'm an old-fashioned critter, Harriet, and you seem to be way off somewhere in a new age."

I have noticed before that sometimes it is possible to say things on the telephone one would not say face-to-face. "I wish that were true, but I can't see much progress as far as tolerance goes. The new age remains totally old-fashioned about some things—blacks, for instance, and gays. Being in a minority sets one up for persecution of one sort or another."

"That is rather extreme."

"No doubt it is. But let's talk, Angelica. How about if I bring Patapouf over tomorrow night?"

"Splendid."

"I'll bring a bottle of Vouvray."

17

I woke at five this morning, in a state of extreme anxiety, of tension I could not control, so it is no surprise when the phone rings at eight and it is Peter, Caroline's son, to tell me that she died in the night, peacefully in her sleep. He and his brother Alan had been with her earlier in the evening and she seemed extremely tired, so they had tiptoed out before nine, and were called at midnight by the night nurse. Peter is quite calm and voluble, and he agrees with me that she has had a wonderful death.

"And that is surely partly due to having a doctor for a son."

"Yes, I could monitor pain. She suffered very little except for shortness of breath. We couldn't do very much about that."

"When is the funeral?"

"At two tomorrow afternoon in Appleton Chapel. There will be only music by her wish," and he adds, "Of course we hope you will come back to the house afterwards—just family and the dearest friends."

"Thanks, Peter." I put the receiver down and stand here by the table for a long minute. One is never prepared, is one? I feel as though the whole geography of the island on which I live has been changed.

I arrange with Joan to change shifts with her tomorrow. Now there is nothing to do but go on living, but as I drink a cup of coffee, make my bed, tidy up, get dressed, and take Patapouf out for a short walk, I keep asking myself questions. Why was Caroline so precious? so rare? I have no other friend like her, none as admired, as cherished for what she was. And that, I tell myself, is partly because she was so open to life, never judgmental, and hugely amused by some things that might shock most women. She was an observing participant, and maybe that is rare: to be both involved as she surely was and also detached. And where has she gone? so peacefully in her sleep?

The last time I saw her before her illness was at Vicky's funeral and it all comes back to me, the strange inappropriate yet supportive bustle immediately after a death. Caroline brought three dozen *madeleines*. The house was filled with formal arrangements of flowers so it did not feel like our house at all and I wandered in it, suddenly a stranger, not knowing what to do, receiving endless sympathy and not myself able to shed a tear. I felt guilty because I enjoyed the *madeleines* so much. The only person remaining in Vicky's family was an ancient aunt whom I hardly knew, whom we called on about twice a year in her vast Beacon Street house filled with bad nineteenth-century paintings. She seemed as lost as I was that day and I corralled Andrew and Fred into taking her under their wing and seeing she was introduced to anyone they knew. But my family had not been close to Vicky—my parents were also dead by then—so the hundred or more people who showed up after the funeral came out of respect for Vicky as publisher: other publishers, agents, authors, but hardly an intimate among them, except for Angelica. I felt abandoned, Vicky's life finished, and I left dangling with no life of my own to take refuge in. It did not help that Patapouf, not used to such large numbers of people invading her territory, barked almost without ceasing, and even though she was tied up outside it was irritating.

At that point I was near to tears, not of grief, but of exhaustion and nervous tension in that busy scene which did not really concern me. That was when Caroline caught my desperation and whisked me off to a corner of the library where we sat down, and I managed to drink a cup of tea and devour a *madeleine*.

"It's been so sudden, Harriet, hasn't it? No time to get used to Vicky's dying. I do feel for you."

Vicky died of a massive heart attack in the ambulance on the way to the hospital. As I remember it today I have prickles up and down my legs and arms. "I can't even cry," I had said. "I'm just dangling somewhere up in the air. I can't seem to land."

"People keep saying to me what a wonderful way to go." Caroline had reached over and taken my hand. I still remember the warmth of that hand clasp and how it somehow brought me back to reality. "But," she went on, "in a way it is to be deprived of one's death, of experiencing it, if you will. I myself would like to have time to say goodbye."

"Vicky hated saying goodbye, you know. I think for her it was best. What am I going to do, Caroline?" and it was not grief but terror that possessed me at that moment, holding Caroline's hand like a drowning person. "This huge house, servants . . . I can't maintain it of course. My own income is minimal. Where shall I go? What shall I do?"

"You'll find out, darling Harriet. After a while you'll know what it is you really want to be and do. But for now you must try to be patient with your inner self, not make quick decisions, let life do it. Life is rather good at filling up the gaps, as I discovered when Winston died."

"But you had the boys."

189

"Yes, and very little money to bring them up on. So, because I had to earn, I got into a job I really love, social work, of all things! It never would have occurred to me that I could be good at that, and love it. It has changed my life in a radical way."

"How?"

"It balances off the social side of me. It makes me feel human and useful. Now when I give a dinner party for Mrs. Elliot and Robert Coles and the Marshalls I feel I have earned it."

We were interrupted by Andrew, who suggested I had better come into the drawing room and say goodbye to the aunt, who was being helped into her coat. But the moment with Caroline had saved me from drowning and I shall never forget it.

The aunt, on the other hand, kissed me coldly on the cheek and said, "I always thought Vicky would kill herself with that publishing business. She worked much too hard," and she had looked at me with a penetrating glare, as though I were somehow responsible.

I had wanted to say, "It's not my fault." Instead I had murmured something polite. "She loved her life. She had what she wanted, after all."

"And paid a high price for it."

"As people usually do for a great life like hers." And then Andrew had come to my rescue.

I have not felt close to my brothers but I have to admit that they were an enormous help that day—an interminable day which ended by Mary bringing me supper in bed.

Here I have been wandering off into the past and it is high time I pull myself together. Caroline was right that life would fill the gap. I could not have imagined how right at the time, nor what a sea change I have been experiencing, what a different person I have become to that one who wandered a big house in total panic and who later said goodbye to a garden with tears pouring down her cheeks as she picked a sprig of mint, of lavender and lemon verbena, and crushed them in her hands. Leaving the garden had felt like a little death. How could I know what a rich adventurous life I would find, or what I would become?

It is strange how close I feel to Caroline, as though she were at my side or somewhere very near. And I think she will always be there. Who was it who said to me long ago, "the dead help the living"?

Late this afternoon I am downstairs in the store, when Martha, whom I have not seen for quite a while, comes in. What's wrong now, I ask myself, and not altogether kindly, because I'm in the midst of writing an ad for the Cambridge *Chronicle*. "Well, hello!" I say, not getting up from my desk. "How are things? Haven't seen you for ages."

She sits down and throws her large black hat on the table. She looks pale but not hurt at least, and maybe I am imagining that something must be wrong. "Are you busy?" she asks, standing now at one of the book tables and picking up books at random. One turns out to be absorbing and she sits down to read. I go back to work, making it clear, I hope, that I am busy. "I have something to tell you when you can spare a moment. No hurry. I'll just read."

But in a moment someone else will push open the door and make it harder to talk, so I get up and join her at the table. "So what's on your mind?"

"I'm pregnant." She says it in a small cold voice.

For a second I really do not know what to say or how to react. But of course Joe is the answer. "Have you talked with Joe about this?"

"What can he do about it?"

"What can I?" I say a little sharply.

"You always seem to be the source of wisdom to me," she says.

"This time I'm the source of mere astonishment. I gather you are not happy to be having a baby."

"You know I don't want one," she says quite crossly. "I told you when I first came in here that David and I were at logger-heads, that he wants a child and I don't."

"That was theoretical, Martha. You could decide not to."

"Apparently I couldn't. We use contraceptives of course. So why did this have to happen?"

"Does David know?"

"No." I take this in and wait for what she might have to say. "I can have an abortion and he will never know."

Bravado? Was she really considering that? I remember all I have read lately in my explorations of feminist philosophy. Women are too often betrayed by their bodies. But Martha took precautions and still she is caught. What can I say? "Theoretically an abortion makes sense, but actually does it? Inside yourself does it?"

"How can I tell? All I know is that I have work to do and if I have a baby I'll be caught for years." She sounds definite and hard.

"If you have an abortion you think you won't be?"

"Hundreds of women have abortions, Harriet. You are behind the times."

"Yes, I guess I am. All this is new to me. I have never had to face such a decision."

"There are advantages to being a lesbian," says Martha.

"No doubt there are." I am not going to be drawn into an argument. "Also I am over sixty, so the whole idea is outside my ken."

"I came to ask you to lend me the money to do it."

Now I am staggered. I feel a little as though someone had

asked me for money to buy cocaine and my reaction is impulsive and quick, "I can't do that, Martha."

"Why not? I thought we were friends."

"You say I am a source of wisdom. I do not believe it is wise to help someone do something one can't understand or believe in. I don't want to be part of this, a conspirator behind David's back. I think you must see Joe. I'll gladly pay for that, Martha, if you don't want David to know." I hurry on, as I see she is red in the face, blushing or furious, I cannot read the message. "Joe at least has knowledge and experience to bring to bear. For all I know he may be on your side."

"He's a man, Harriet. Men do not understand anything about a woman's body and what it does when you cannot control it, when you are being forced against your will into a radical change of life, into bondage."

Am I wrong? Is she right? Am I imagining she will have regrets when she insists that she won't? What would Caroline say, I ask myself, she who was so tolerant, so all-accepting? I cannot answer that. I am in the dark.

"You are silent."

"I'm upset, Martha. If you counted on my help and feel let down, I can't blame you, but . . ."

"Very well, you can't do it. Maybe I just have to fall downstairs or drink something. One reads about such things."

"I am not responsible, Martha, for whatever you decide to do and you can't threaten me." I am angry now myself. I am being blackmailed.

"Please don't be angry," and she begins to cry, pulls her hat off the table, and uses it to hide her eyes in a violent gesture, rejecting me.

"Listen, we can find a woman psychiatrist for you. Tomorrow night I'm having dinner with an old friend who will surely know someone you can talk to in confidence. I meant it when I said I would gladly pay for that."

"I hate you for being so good," she murmurs. "You always win, don't you?"

"Oh for God's sake, Martha, it's not a matter of winning. And besides, I'm not that good," and I manage a laugh. "No fool like an old fool." I feel I have made a complete mess of this conversation out of sheer ignorance.

I am mighty glad when the old bag lady comes in, delighted of course to find Martha there, since she bought that painting. "Oh Mrs. Blackstone, how glad I am to see you again! I brought my ten dollars for you, too. I was going to ask Miss Hatfield to give it to you."

"I feel bad to take your money," Martha says, suddenly genuine and herself because, I suppose, her painting is concerned, not her mixed-up life with David. I am delighted when she calls the old woman by name as she takes the ten-dollar bill and says, "Mrs. Stoneworth, this is the first money I have ever earned. Maybe I should frame it."

"Put it in the bank," Stoneworth says, "put it in the bank." She has now settled with two large packages on the side of her chair and looks at her watch. "I have to keep an eye out for the bus."

"I'll do that," Martha volunteers. "I'll just stand and keep a lookout and help you gather things together when I see it."

Mrs. Stoneworth sighs, "Thanks, dear," then she murmurs, "Coffee's gone up again, hamburger is out of this world." This, I think, is addressed to me for then she turns around so she can see Martha and tells her that she wakes every morning and sees that painting and thinks about roots. "It starts the day right, makes me feel strong. I don't know why."

"I hear it," Martha cries out, "we'd better get going," and somehow everything is gathered up and off they go.

194

I have just time to say to Martha, "I'll have an address for you day after tomorrow, so be sure to call, won't you?" But there is always the risk nevertheless that she will rush off and have the abortion, and I wonder whether I should call Joe. But I must not believe for a moment that I am in any way necessary or the source of wisdom poor Martha imagines me to be. I'm not God and it is not for me to take decisions out of her hands.

So I sit down again at my desk and rough out another ad, this time for the Smith *Quarterly*. It would be fun to get some support from my classmates, who have presumably not all read the *Globe* interview.

That has proved to be more troubling than I cared to admit at the time. I notice that something in me cringes still at being identified with a suspect and beleaguered minority. I do not feel comfortable with it. I have to admit this.

18

Here I am at Angelica's, basking in the open fire with Patapouf lying at my feet, basking in the charm of this big living room I know so well: over the mantel the Sargent portrait of Angelica's mother as a glowing young woman, a small Vuillard of an intimate interior where a husband and wife appear to be breakfasting, the easy unselfconscious warmth of it all, emerald green velvet armchair and sofa, English chintz pillows here and there and repeated in the flowery curtains. I sit and dream while Angelica is making our drinks in the pantry. When she comes back I look up at her as she hands me my scotch. I smile with the joy of being here. "It's heaven. I don't suppose I have felt this laid-back since I opened the store!"

"It's heaven to have you come. Just like old times," she says, taking her Dubonnet over to a chair facing mine, "but, darling Harriet, must you use expressions like 'laid-back'?"

"I saw you wince. Oh dear, well, I am taking in the language of my present environment. That is inevitable."

"Was it wise," she asks, after a short pause while we sip our drinks and settle in to the pleasure of the occasion, "I mean wise to try to educate through a feminist bookstore in such a mixed neighborhood?"

"It wasn't wise, but it is not they who are being educated. It's I, Angelica, and being educated is what I need. I learn something new every day. I live in a perpetual state of astonishment."

Angelica cannot help laughing and I know I sound absurd— innocent abroad, as I am told I am almost every day by someone or other. And so it is natural to tell her about Martha's dilemma and ask her advice about a possible therapist. "Poor woman," Angelica says instantly and I realize this is something, an unwanted pregnancy, that she deals with often at the family planning agency. She is on the board. On this subject at least Angelica is far more with it than I am. And after a few seconds' thought she comes up with a name and writes Dr. Frances Willoughby down on a card with her phone number and I slip it into my purse.

"Thanks. I knew you would be able to help."

"You don't sound very sympathetic yourself," Angelica says.

"Oh dear, how perspicacious you are! Martha has attached herself to me, you see, but I do not really like her. She seems terribly selfish, for one thing."

"But you gave her wall space for her paintings. That was generous."

And I tell Angelica about Mrs. Stoneworth, how strange it seems that she fell in love with that painting, and how at first I thought she was a bag lady, and how she hates Gothic novels and reads history. "Maybe I just don't understand creative people, whereas you always have." And that is true. The young artists and writers Angelica has helped are innumerable. "For instance, I am really drawn to a stunning young black woman, Nan Blakeley, who gave up her career as a journalist to marry and now has two little girls. She is so warm and alive she lights up the store." I want to talk about Nan as I don't, really, about Martha. "I have never had a black friend till now, but Nan is going to invite me to meet her husband and little girls some evening when he gets home early enough. Can't you see how happy I am these days, Angelica? It is a *vita nuova*. It nourishes me."

"You look ten years younger," Angelica says, smiling. "It's quite visible that you are happy."

"I wish I were younger though. I get flattened out at times."

I am aware that we are picking up the threads of our long friendship one by one, but somewhere there is a knot that has to be untied. How to approach that?

It is Angelica who does it. "The bookshop seems to be a store for lesbian women to patronize? At least so I hear."

"And where do you hear that?" I am instantly on the defensive.

"Word gets around," she says tentatively, "and of course that interview in the *Globe* exposed you and what your chief interest is."

"What rot! I am not chiefly interested in lesbians or the very little lesbian literature there is, not at all. The store is a feminist bookstore, which means there are a lot of philosophical and sociological books about women, 'herstory' as against history, books most women do not even know exist. You'd be amazed, Angelica, at all I have learned by reading them. The subject is inexhaustible."

"I don't doubt that for a moment." There is a silence now. We are each wondering how to tackle the essential thing. "Of course," Angelica says slowly, feeling for words, and it reminds me of a game where you pile up small sticks until finally one makes the whole structure fall down, "I always presumed that you and Vicky were . . ." Here she hesitates.

" 'Lovers' is the word," I suggest with a smile.

"What I can't understand is your willingness to exhibit what most people consider a private matter."

I stand up now and back up to the fire, a move that startles Patapouf and makes her give a short bark. Angelica and I exchange amused glances, and the ice is broken.

"Patapouf senses danger," she says gently. "Well, go ahead. Enlighten this old-fashioned porcupine."

"As a lesbian—and believe me, Angelica, it is still hard for me to use the word—I am part of an absurd minority that threatens a lot of ordinary people just in the way the black minority does. The difference is that blacks can't hide, nor can Orientals, but homosexuals are not visible targets."

"So why make yourself one? You are already paying a high price for it—those threats."

"Because I am comparatively safe and because I am not the stereotype. No one can fire me; I am not young. I am—don't laugh—a 'lady.' So can't you see that I must stand up for the hundreds of women who can't, who don't dare because for them the risk is too great?"

"No one can fault your courage, Harriet. I admire you for it. But . . ."

"You don't like to have to admit that lesbians are and always will be a part of our society and it's high time this was accepted."

"I suppose so." At this moment Alice comes in to announce that dinner is ready and Angelica says, "Give us a few minutes, Alice, we haven't quite finished our drinks."

"Now I'll tell you something," Angelica says and it is clear that she has had it in mind and wants me to hear whatever it may be. "Sit down and listen to me." She leans forward in her chair, her hands clasped on her knee. "Ever since this whole business began with that article and all the talk I have had to

200

listen to ever since, I have found myself examining my own relationships with women since I was a child."

"Good, and what have you found?"

"A lot of things I had buried. For instance, that I adored the headmistress at Winsor School and used to write her what amounts to love poems when I was about thirteen. I used to wait for her to leave school and sometimes walk a little way with her, as she lived nearby. Holding her hand very occasionally was a tremendous excitement—I can't find the word—stirred me to the depths."

"And," I suggest, "you were not afraid because you were too young to have been brainwashed. And you did not feel guilty, did you?"

"No, as a matter of fact, I didn't. I felt elated and privileged."

"So you do understand that a woman can be drawn to another woman."

"In a way, I suppose I do. But I was a child, Harriet. It's rather different, isn't it?"

"In a way it is, but what seems to happen as one grows up is an increasing fear of one's own feelings. If you had felt as you did then when you were in college it might have been more troubling."

"My dear, it was," Angelica says. "In my sophomore year at Mount Holyoke a girl called Emily fell in love with me, I suppose, and I was in a state of such ambivalence toward her that I think I must have been cruel. I was terrified because I found I rather liked being kissed, but at the same time it was too disturbing, so I went to the college psychiatrist, who was a man, and he assured me that there was nothing wrong with me, but possibly Emily needed some help. She did not come back for the junior year and I have no idea what has become of her. I have never told anyone this, Harriet. But I've been rather upset since that article appeared in the *Globe.* I guess I am still too disturbed to be quite reasonable."

"But you are honest. So many women are not and perhaps they are the ones who take it out on lesbians like me because it makes them feel safer."

"Anyway, I feel better for having told you," Angelica says, and as Alice hovers in the doorway, she murmurs as she gets up, "The problem is sex, isn't it?" It is such an obvious conclusion that I can't help laughing. "Oh I know I'm an old fool. And come to think of it the first time a young man kissed me, I felt just as upset as when Emily did."

Later on, over a demitasse in the library, we talk about Caroline and decide to go together to the funeral, which is tomorrow.

"Nothing shocked Caroline, did it?" Angelica asks me when we have settled and Patapouf has been given my dessert plate to lick. "How did she learn not to be shocked? I feel like such a dodo because I am shockable, as you see."

"What a splendid woman you are!" I am happy that we can talk again, that we are friends after all. "As for Caroline, perhaps she was unshockable because she had allowed herself to experience everything without questioning, accepting what she felt. It was so beautiful when it came to dying, wasn't it? She became as open to death as she had been to love all her life." I would like to tell Angelica that Caroline had loved a woman, but I refrain. I have had enough of this conversation, I think, and it is time I go home and face entering the dark house alone. "You know what I think, Angelica? Simply that everyone is capable of many kinds of love. It's all there waiting in each of us for that magic touch that wakes up everything we have in us."

"Yes, and it is something I have not known—the magic touch. Sometimes I mind. I feel deprived."

"But you mustn't," I say quickly. "You have given to friend-

202

ship all your life what some people can only give to a lover, to a husband. I love you for it."

She is embarrassed and laughs her embarrassed laugh. "So I'll see you tomorrow. We'll meet in front of the Coop and walk over to the chapel together."

It is a comfort to have Patapouf sitting beside me, her big head staring out the window, as we drive homewards. If there is anyone lurking around she will bark, I tell myself. But when I draw up into the parking place to let her out, the person who is waiting for us is Joe. "Good heavens, Joe, were you waiting for me?"

"Maybe I was. I went out for a walk and ended up here but didn't see a light upstairs and your car wasn't here, so I thought I'd hang around, see you safely in. Want me to take Patapouf for a short walk?"

"Dear Joe, I'll come with you." It is clear that Joe has something on his mind. He does not talk and I am silent as we wait here and there for Patapouf to perform. Finally I have to ask, "Is anything on your mind, Joe?"

Now he faces me and hesitates before he says, "Harriet, I hate to lay this on you, but I know you are a real friend. Eddie has been diagnosed as having AIDS."

I am silent, too shocked to utter a word. I look down at the pavement, then reach out and take Joe's hand and squeeze it hard. "But how could it happen to Eddie? Is he on drugs?" I don't know what to ask or to say and no doubt am blundering.

"Not that I know of," Joe says.

We walk on in silence. "Of course maybe they'll find a cure in time."

"I doubt that. There is a drug that appears to prevent the pneumonia that in the first years was one of the most common causes of death."

"That is something anyway."

"It costs one hundred and eighty dollars a week. We are lucky to have that kind of money. Think of all those who don't."

I am quite aware that Joe is holding back on something he may not want to talk about. "Dear Eddie. It's not fair, Joe. That's all I can think," and then, as he is still walking along in silence, his head bent, and we have turned now toward home, "Can Eddie still go to his job? I mean, can he, at least for a while, lead a normal life?"

"We'll learn that. He is at present very difficult to live with and very angry."

"Oh."

"You might as well know, Harriet, that Eddie has always cruised around, picked up men in bars, and when I began to love him, not just want him, I had to accept that."

"How can one accept that?"

"One accepts what one has to accept. I am ten years older, Harriet. I thought he would outgrow the obsessive desire for conquest. I was betting on the long run . . . and now," his voice is hard, "love can't win after all. There's no time."

"He needs you, Joe, and it is going to be dreadfully hard."

"I know something about that—a third of my patients either have AIDS or their partner has it. I dream about it in my sleep."

"It's no fair," I say again. "It's no fair."

"I get the answer from all sides, anger at the heteros who use AIDS as a stick to beat gays with. I handle that every day."

"Is Eddie's anger about that?"

"No. His anger is against me because I don't cruise and am safe, or so he imagines." Joe gives a bitter laugh. "I'm the cross he bears, the well man whom he has to live with. Christ, what a mess!"

We have reached my door and I ask him to come up but he explains that he has to get home. "By now Eddie is sorry for all he has said to me, I expect, and needs a little TLC."

"You are good, Joe. He is lucky to have you, and I must say that I have held you and Eddie in my heart as an exemplary couple. You have been a comfort to me. Tell Eddie that."

"He likes you," Joe says. "Give me a hug and I'll be off."

I feel a great warmth in that solid, unsentimental hug, and I feel honored that Joe has felt he could confide in me. There are, after all, advantages in being an old person. If you can be a rock and not fall apart.

I remind myself that I must not forget to give Martha that psychiatrist's name, but I don't dare call now as David presumably is there. Tomorrow morning. I write a note to myself and leave it on the breakfast table where I can't fail to see it. And also remind myself that I am to be in the store tomorrow morning so Joan can take over for the afternoon of Caroline's funeral.

But once in bed I can't sleep. I listen to Patapouf's snores and for a while breathe in and out in their rhythm but that does not help. I am simply out of breath. What would Caroline say about Joe and Eddie? Is fidelity essential to a viable relationship? I should have thought so. Without fidelity how can one feel secure? Once in the thirty years I lived with Vicky she went away for a month to Paris, pretending it was a business trip, so our friends were told. I knew that she had fallen in love with a Frenchwoman who ran a bookstore. Oh why do I remember it now? Until now, I have buried all that. It was ten years ago or more. I couldn't eat and lost twenty pounds in that month. I learned that jealousy is the most destructive emotion there is, because it can't be sublimated. It is simply a poison. Vicky wrote me almost every day and often wrote "Have no doubts, I'll always love you." That was like acid on a wound. I could not even cry.

When she came back I felt like a prisoner, walled in. It took a year for me to unlock myself and begin to have faith that she meant it when she told me it was finished with Claire. A long awful struggle, but she won me back in the end, of course. I worked things out in the garden, which was splendid that autumn. I took refuge in the housekeeping routine. I slept alone. When we finally made our peace and could lie in each other's arms we both cried with relief, and though the crack in the glass could not be mended, the glass did not break and we drank from it. In any good marriage one or two excursions may take place, but at a very high price, as I learned, and I think Vicky learned. But what if I had had to accept a whole series of brief attachments, one-night stands? What if she had said, "That's the way I am"? I could not have accepted it. I know I could not.

How does Joe achieve enough detachment to accept? How many gay men have to and do? Their physiological makeup is so different from a woman's. It is not *vive la différence*, but *hélas la différence*. Vicky used to tease me because I had never wanted to be a boy whereas she had even coaxed her mother into letting her wear boys' sailor suits in the summer. That was long before jeans and must have caused a sensation on Mount Desert. But now with all I have been reading lately I see that she was old-fashioned. Lesbian women today talk about being whole women, not about being imitation men like Radclyffe Hall. It is a different universe we live in now, thank goodness.

I am taking refuge in the past, I tell myself, in order not to have to take in what is happening to Eddie. I cannot even imagine such a death as his is bound to be. And finally at 3 A.M. I sink away from it into troubled sleep.

19

I feel blurred this morning, unready for the day, but there is the note reminding me to call Martha and at about nine, when I have had breakfast and taken Patapouf out for a few minutes, I make the call. No answer. Well, she may have gone for a walk, who knows? I keep thinking about Eddie and that blocks everything else. I must learn more about AIDS. I must try to understand what Joe and he are facing so that I can find ways to help. I wish Bettina would come back. Maybe she has had an experience with AIDS, or knows of a support group, although Joe of course will be looking into that. Someone is being poisoned right around the corner and there is nothing we can do. All I can think of is Camus's *The Plague* and what fear can do to a city when the plague enters. I must have it somewhere. Vicky and I felt it was the greatest work of art to come out of occupied France. AIDS is our plague and it is moving in.

It is comforting to go down and open the store, but when I unlock the door and open it I find an envelope has been slipped under it. Inside on a large sheet of paper in large red printed words it says: "You feel safe, but we are going to get you." So, it is all beginning again! Things have quieted down lately, a remission, but this other plague has not abated. I feel the sweat on my upper lip. It's Joe I need to speak to but God knows he has enough on his mind without my problems. I call Joan who says she'll come right over. "There's nothing you can do," I say.

"I can take that sheet to the police station," she says. It is a relief to know she can and will do that. I am in no state to confront the police this morning. Besides, I am tending store.

The first arrival is Bagley and I cannot say that I am glad to see her, but for once she turns out to be enthusiastic about what she has been reading, one of the Amanda Cross mysteries, and wants to try another. I suggest *The Question of Max* and she gets out her purse, murmuring, "Books are too expensive, Miss Hatfield."

"I know. It's awful, but as it is I am not yet breaking even."

"You should have a rental library the way they used to have in England."

"Well, you know, I have thought of that but I don't know how Joan and I could manage it as well as everything else."

"Plenty of people come here. When I go past there is always someone talking with you, and I presume buying."

At this I smile. "Well, sometimes they are buying. Sometimes they just want to talk."

"I see that and sometimes I think you are simply a sucker for any odd person who needs an ear." Sue Bagley has to have an ear herself, I am thinking, but chiefly for purposes of complaint, or setting herself up against most of what she sees. A form of ego, I suppose, a small exercise of power.

It is not a good thing that at this moment Martha walks in, luckily not visibly upset for once. "Oh, you're the painter," Sue greets her. "Have you sold any?"

"Yes, I have sold one. Isn't that amazing?"

"Congratulations," Bagley says grudgingly.

I interrupt, fearing she may have something derogatory to add, by handing Martha the note with the woman psychiatrist's phone number on it. "The friend I told you about gave me this last night. I hope you will act on it, Martha." She slips it into her purse without saying a word.

"Miss Hatfield is up to something," Bagley says. "I wish I knew what is going on. Nobody ever tells me anything."

"Sometimes what is going on is none of your business," Martha says.

Sue Bagley laughs at Martha's angry tone and says, "The only business I have is other people's business."

I find I cannot be cross for long with Sue Bagley. Together we watch Martha, who has gone over to look at her paintings and is standing there, her hands on her hips, thinking heaven knows what.

"You're a damn good painter, Martha, so have no doubts about that," Bagley says in very good humor now.

It's not being connected that makes her often so difficult, I decided long ago. She has to crash in because no one invites her in, an elephant in a china shop. And now they both sit down at the table and Martha, in a very fragile state of balance, I realize, asks, "Do you really think so? You're not just saying that to be polite?"

"I'll tell you, Martha. When I first saw the paintings I didn't like them at all. They bothered me, but every time I dropped in here I looked at them again and they began to grow on me, so today I came with the idea I might buy one."

"You did?" Martha's eyes fill with tears. "I can't believe it."

"I'm surprised," Bagley says. "If I had a talent like yours I wouldn't have any doubts."

"That's what people think," Martha says, "but I guess most artists and maybe writers, too, live in a perpetual state of acute anxiety. Is this worth doing? Have I the right to do it? Shouldn't I be doing something positively useful, like working in a hospital?" I have not heard this side of Martha before. It is rather a relief; for once her insistence on herself as *the* important thing is opening out a little. Is this what the ordeal of her pregnancy is doing? She turns to Sue now with great intensity. "If you had a talent, Miss Bagley, would you go so far as to abort a pregnancy because you feel your work must come first?"

Sue is flustered. Who would not be? It is a direct challenge and one rather hard to meet or to parry. "How am I to answer that? I am a spinster and have no talent except as an accountant," but she stops now and looks straight at Martha. It is a compassionate look, one I have not seen in her eyes before. "That is your problem, is it?"

Without looking in my direction—I am now sitting at my desk pretending at least to work—Martha says defiantly, "I took care of it yesterday. I had an abortion."

"That took courage," Bagley says. "I admire you for it."

"I felt like a caged animal," Martha says.

It amazes me that these two have reached such a point of intimacy. I have been an antagonist lately for Martha but here in Sue Bagley she has apparently found an ally.

"But you're married, aren't you?" Bagley asks. "What does your husband say?"

"My husband will never know. I hope he won't." The tears she has held back till now flow and she blows her nose. "Sorry," she says. And then, "It's your kindness that makes me cry."

I wonder whether anyone has ever said this to Bagley before, and she leans over and clasps Martha's hand. "You're a strong person and you made the right decision." Now she draws her hand away and looks over at me, appealing for help but I am silenced.

"Miss Hatfield wanted me to see a psychiatrist but I didn't

want to be opened up and examined. I suppose I wanted to do something, not endlessly talk about it."

"I understand," I say quietly.

"Well," Sue Bagley says, "how much do you want for the painting on the left, those winter trees against a troubled sky?"

"I sold the other for one hundred, but the abortion has to be paid for . . ."

"I'll offer two hundred if that is acceptable."

"Thank you. It will help—mostly that you believe in my work. I'll never forget it," Martha says.

What an odd example of what is known as the sisterhood they are, I think, as they go out together for lunch, the dry cranky spinster and the tempestuous young woman determined to go her own way.

My thoughts about this interesting event are abruptly interrupted by Joan's arrival. I take the anonymous threat out, handling the paper it is written on as though it were dynamite. "Here it is."

"What creeps!" she says. "Something has to be done about this now. I'm off to the police station and this time they are going to take notice."

"Good luck. I'm glad you are an optimist." But when she has left, striding up the street alone, I feel that sweat on my lip again. Fear. For what can the police possibly do? There are no clues. Possibly the sheet of paper has a fingerprint on it; more likely the anonymous criminal wore gloves.

On an impulse I call Andrew at work and ask whether he could come by on his way home. "It's another threat and I need your advice." He says he'll be here by six if not earlier. He offers to spend the night, says he has a sleeping bag in the car. But the whole beastly thing cannot be solved by Andrew or anyone else standing guard permanently. Something has got to happen.

I force myself to go over the reorders and make a few phone

calls on business matters while I wait for Joan to get back, but my head is full of too many things: Eddie's plight, Joe, the funeral this afternoon. I am in a thicket of disorder and pain and end by just sitting at my desk and doodling the heads of strange animals. I discover that it is not a bad way to relieve tension and I am quite pleased by the odd animals I am creating.

Joan comes back with a paper bag containing cheese and ham sandwiches and two milkshakes. "You'll need lunch before you go to the funeral," she explains, setting them out on the table.

"Thanks. Great idea." And when we have settled down at the table, "What happened? Did you see Sergeant O'Reilly?"

"Yes. The first thing he did was just glance at that dirty sheet and lay it down as though it were nothing. Then he said, 'I am very busy today on a drug case, Miss—' He had forgotten my name and I said, 'Mrs. Hampstead' with heavy emphasis on the Mrs. I suggested that it was high time the police department put its mind on your problem. What are drugs compared to a life at risk and the life of an elderly person who has never done harm in her life."

"You did?" I am a little shy hearing this.

"Yes, I did, and I told him something about what you have achieved, how many women of all kinds come to the store, what a center it is for lonely women, for young married women, for women of all races and ages. I felt it was a stirring speech," Joan says with her ironic smile, "but I do not believe he was paying the slightest attention. He simply repeated what he had said to us when we first went, 'The police are here when you need us. If anything happens let us know.' I pressed him, demanding that he try to think of possible people who might be involved: 'You must have some idea where these threats come from?' 'Sorry, ma'am, but we are not omniscient.'"

"The old runaround." I am unaccountably in a state of acute distress. It comes out in a question. "You don't really think my life is at risk, Joan, do you?"

"Well, I said it powerfully to wake Sergeant O'Reilly up. Maybe you are not in danger, but these attackers are lunatics likely as not. Half the people around here carry guns."

"Yes, I suppose so."

"Oh dear, I have made matters worse, I see. What I really think is that whoever these goons may be, they are not murderers, but they want to drive you out. They want to make you leave here. They want to close the shop down." She looks me straight in the eye, with warm concern. "Please don't imagine they are killers. I simply cannot think that, and you must put the idea out of your mind."

"Easy to say," but I look at my watch and never finish the sentence. "Good heavens, it's ten past one. I am meeting Angelica at the Coop at half-past and must find parking space."

"I'll be here when you get back. Not to worry."

It is bliss to get away, to run away into the safe world of the Coop, where Angelica, looking very handsome in a black suit and a large black hat, is waiting for me. "Sorry I'm late. I was held up."

"We have plenty of time," she assures me and we walk sedately, arm in arm, waiting what seems hours for a chance to cross Mass. Avenue and get into the Yard.

"I might as well be killed by a truck," I murmur, half to myself.

"Whatever do you mean by that?" Angelica lets my arm go.

"Nothing," but I can't leave it at that and suddenly the humor of the whole situation strikes me and I laugh aloud. "It's just that those goons are threatening me again and it suddenly struck me as funny that, after all, there is danger everywhere, even cross-

213

ing the street these days. So why worry about possibly getting shot?"

"Ha, ha," Angelica responds, with heavy irony, "I'm glad you can think that humorous. I don't."

"Forget it! I'm keyed up. Being a sitting duck is not really my line."

We are climbing the steps to the chapel and the sound of the organ playing Bach's "Sheep May Safely Graze" pours out and silences us. I do not laugh this time but I do find it amusing and swallow a smile. I myself am no doubt a sheep but I can no longer safely graze, and it brings back a joke of my father's, "In Kansas only the cows browse." Oh dear, I must not give way to unseemly behavior.

We are ushered to a pew near the front where of course we nod and are nodded to by half a dozen people we know. Seated, with the great music filling the chapel, I am relieved. I can sit here in peace. I can think about Caroline. I have nothing to fear.

After the funeral I had been expected to go back to the house, but I tell Angelica that I feel I must get home, back to the store for some reason. The wonderful timeless peace I felt in the chapel, the deep rejoicing that a person like Caroline had come into my life, has given way now to an attack of anxiety. These anonymous letters take their toll. I remind myself that Andrew is coming. I shall not be alone after Joan leaves.

Still, I am always happy when I push the door open into the store, so peaceful and exciting, as Gertrude Stein once said of Paris. There are two people I have not seen before reading at the table, and as soon as Joan catches my eye she makes it clear that there is some problem. They do not look like our kind of people, I think to myself. One is a rather heavy woman in a dark blue suit, wearing a broad-brimmed red hat, and the other one an extremely thin woman in a starched collar that stands above her mink cape.

214

Joan comes forward from behind the counter and says to the women, "May I introduce you to the owner, Miss Hatfield?" They do not get up, but stare at me as though I am not quite human. "Harriet, this is Mrs. Thomas and this is Mrs. Ferguson."

"How did you happen to find us?" I ask blandly. "I am always interested, since we are so new and just being discovered."

"Someone warned us that a subversive bookstore had opened," says Mrs. Ferguson, "so we thought we had better make an inspection."

"And what did you find?" I ask, keeping contempt out of my voice, I hope. Since neither answers I pursue the subject myself. "This is a feminist bookstore, which means that many of the books here concern the problems and needs of women. I might suggest that you take a look at this one, for instance." And I hand over *Women, Take Care,* the book addressing the need for caretakers to spell the many many women who have to take care of dying husbands or mothers or aunts and have no help at all.

It is truly providential that at this moment who but Nan Blakeley comes in with her two little girls. "Oh Nan, how I have missed you! Where have you been?" and quite spontaneously I go over and hug her. "And you brought the children."

One of them, long-legged in a short red tunic, not at all shy, about seven I imagine, speaks right up. "We had to come. You see, Momma talks about this place."

"She says I can choose a book," the younger child, in a pale blue tunic and blue leotard, announces. "Can I go find it now?"

"Just a minute, kids. First you must meet Miss Hatfield. Harriet, this is Eve and this is Serena. Eve and Serena, this is Miss Hatfield."

They stare at me and mumble, "Glad to meet you," suddenly overcome with shyness, each clasping one of her mother's hands.

"Now you can look. See? The children's books are on the low shelves over there."

Eve sits in the small armchair I have provided and Serena sits on the floor. They become completely absorbed and, rather unusually, do not take one book out after another without really looking at it. Serena is now lying on her stomach deep into the story of Babar. I wonder what Eve will choose. It is all like a reprieve and even the two women are smiling.

"What about Martha?" Nan asks in a low voice, her back turned to the ladies. "I have been worried about her."

"She had an abortion the same day," I whisper back.

"I thought she would, and I have something to tell her that may help."

"Sue Bagley came in this morning and bought one of her paintings, if you can believe it. They went off to have lunch together—an odd couple if I ever saw one."

Nan laughs her open, delighted laugh. "That is very good news!"

I take her hand and draw her over to the table to introduce her to Mrs. Thomas and Mrs. Ferguson. They are wide-eyed, clearly, at a black woman so well dressed and at ease, hesitate whether to shake hands, and then rather self-consciously do so. My only wish is that they go away. I want to tell Nan about the new threat, so I decide to take the bull by the horns and ask, "Have you found what you were looking for, Mrs. Thomas?"

"We were informed that this was a meeting place for gay and lesbian people. There are people in this community who don't like that," Mrs. Ferguson answers. "We did not see any religious books." Mrs. Ferguson is gathering momentum now.

Nan is observing them with kindly disbelief and exchanges a mischievous amused glance with me. "May I ask who sent you here?" she asks.

"The Women's Auxiliary at Our Lady of the Sacred Heart.

Someone told them they had better look into this corrupting influence on our young people."

"And that somebody was?" I press the question. We may at last get a clue.

Mrs. Ferguson is flustered and gets up. "I really can't tell you that," she says, "it's a private matter."

"Well," says Nan, "let me tell you a little bit about what this bookstore has meant to a happily married black woman."

"I've found the book I want," Eve interrupts, coming to show us a book of poetry in a bright red cover. "It's poetry. You can read it to us, Momma. We can learn it by heart. There's a poem about a lamb."

Serena is less happy. "There are so many books about Babar, how can I choose one?"

"You may choose one today and next week you may choose another," says Nan firmly.

"I don't want to wait till next week." Serena is close to tears.

"Now, kids, I want you to go back and sit quietly because Momma has something she wants to say and it is important." Nan turns now to the two women. "On the whole this is a rather dreary neighborhood. There are plenty of bars for the men but where can women go to browse and talk to each other? Where can a woman find books that really speak to what interests her, what she needs to know, and meet other women who are longing for someone to talk with? For instance, a young painter who feels isolated, and then Miss Hatfield hangs her paintings. Imagine what a lift that is!"

I am so happy and feel so supported by Nan's clever defense that I can't help smiling, and of course it is splendid that she came with the children.

Ferguson and Thomas exchange a glance.

"For me it has been an enrichment, I must say."

I can't help putting my oar in now. "So many interesting

women have come, so many women who have a lot to give and a lot to give each other."

"The Women's Auxiliary fulfills that purpose for us very well," Ferguson says with bland self-satisfaction.

"But if you will forgive me for saying so, you would meet each other anyway, but all kinds of women come here," I say.

"I can see that," says Mrs. Thomas, glancing over at Nan.

"Well, I think we had better be going now," says Mrs. Ferguson.

"I do hope you will spread the word about the bookstore, that we welcome diversity and discussion. It is an open door." I guess by the way they put on their gloves and nod a goodbye that they have been somewhat nonplussed. "It makes me sad when my good will is misread and I myself treated as some sort of unwanted intruder."

"It's not you, Miss Hatfield," Mrs. Thomas says, "it's the people the store draws in."

"What don't you like about them?"

It is Nan who lifts her head from a book she has been immersed in. "That they are black?"

"Oh no, we have black members of the church. We feel it is very important to include minorities."

"Then who are these unwanted people? I'm a fairly steady customer and I've never seen anyone pushing crack!" says Nan.

"It's gays and their possible influence on our children. I'm afraid you can't deny that you have a good many gay customers," says Mrs. Ferguson, still at the door, which is half open so she is turning back to say this and it gives it a slightly unpleasant thrust, as though it could only be said on the way out.

"I don't deny it for a minute. They are welcome, but they do not dominate the atmosphere by any means. Did you notice the window as you came in? All those great women . . . it was fun setting it up. I felt so proud." But these tentative gestures of friendliness are no use, of course. I am facing a door barred and locked against me. "Well," I add, as the door is slowly being shut and they are almost out of hearing, "goodbye and I hope you'll come again." Now I turn to Nan and give her a spontaneous hug. "You were wonderful."

"They were incredible, weren't they?"

Now the thought occurs to me, "But they can't be the threatening ones, can they? I had another anonymous threat, you know."

"It has occurred to me that it might be a woman, by the way, but these two seemed rather vague and not the plotting kind. They will make a big fuss at a *kaffee klatsch* and that will be it," Nan says.

"Let's hope so," and I add, "It shouldn't but it does upset me and makes me feel a little sick. Let's have a cup of tea."

"What is so depressing is ignorance, isn't it?" Nan murmurs.

"I was tempted to say that I am a lesbian myself but thought better of it. That could be so distorted in the telling." I am weary of all this. It's been going on too long. Let the store flourish in peace, I want to say, leave us alone, but this is the effect of fatigue and fear, a poor mixture, as I am well aware.

I hate to see Nan and the children go, but she suddenly sees the time and hurries them off.

20

Now in October the dark creeps in and makes one feel the day is over, whereas, I realize looking at my watch, it is only five. Four to six are apt to be the busiest hours.

"I'm suddenly out flat," I say to Joan. "Be an angel and put the kettle on, will you?"

"You get an anonymous threat, you go to a funeral, you meet prying old women on your return . . . and you are amazed that you are done in!"

"It sometimes feels as though each day were a lifetime."

"Sit still and I'll bring the tea. I could do with some myself. That O'Reilly is a frustrating man. Oh how I wish we could once and for all catch whoever it is!"

"It has occurred to me," I say with my head in my hands, "that not doing anything except continue to threaten may be their strategy—drive us out by creating an impossible psychological climate."

"It could very well be," Joan says from the kitchen.

"Anyway, Andrew is coming around for supper so I won't be alone this evening. And that reminds me I must call Joe and see whether I could bring Andrew around. It may be that Eddie doesn't want anyone to come, but I have a feeling it might do Andrew good to be with them, and he perhaps even help them." We drink our tea in silence. One of the wonderful things about Joan is that we can be silent for considerable moments without self-consciousness. That is one of my tests of friendship . . . and how rare it is! "Of course, it may be too late. Joe says Eddie is angry and on edge. Why wouldn't he be hard to get along with?"

"What a nightmare," Joan says, "and so unfair. They seemed such a happy, civilized couple. It shouldn't have happened."

After Joan has gone home and I have locked up downstairs I do call Joe and he seems amazingly cheerful. It is because Eddie has marched at the State House in Boston, and is filled with angry pride.

"Angry against fate?" I ask.

"No, against the heterosexual world which has simply taken a righteous view of AIDS as punishment for sinners and refuses to admit that it is a universal problem."

I ponder this news. Andrew doesn't quite fit in from what I hear but I decide to risk it. "My brother Andrew is coming tonight to defend me. There has been another threat. It does make me feel rather naked before the wind, I must confess."

"The strategy is to terrify, is my guess," Joe says. "If you tough it out as you are doing, they may give up."

"That's what I say to myself. But, Joe, I have wanted for a long time to introduce Andrew to you and Eddie. I thought maybe if you became friends—and God knows he is lonely—he might be able to spell you when Eddie needs someone there, as I expect he will eventually. Is that a crazy idea?"

"Not at all," Joe says with real warmth. "Why don't you bring him over after supper? It may prevent another fight. Eddie takes his anxiety out on me these days, but he is fond of you, as you know, and will love to meet your brother."

"Splendid. We won't stay long because . . . well, I'm afraid something will happen if I'm not here. The whole place could burn down in a few minutes."

"It's gone on long enough, hasn't it? I mean the suspense and anxiety. I hope and pray one of these guys will get caught, and soon."

"But how will they ever get caught? The police couldn't care less." I sense that Joe has enough on his mind without my problems and end the conversation as soon as possible, but not before he has again made me promise to call at any time of night or day if I should need help.

"I'll get there faster than the police at any rate."

When I put the receiver down I feel both warmed and chilled, warmed by Joe's unfailing response and kindness, and at the same time chilled by my exposure and fear in spite of friends, in spite of Andrew. When I come right down to it, I am alone, alone against an unknown, possibly dangerous antagonist.

On the one hand, the store is being built into the community. A large part of my dream is coming true. On the other hand, I am myself despised, even hated, for being myself, for having loved a woman, for being honest about that. Tonight I am more aware than usual of what this does to any sense of wholeness in my endeavor toward the community. I am torn in two.

"It's not fair, Patapouf," I say, bending down to rub her soft furry head and ears, finding what comfort there is in the dear creature who would not allow me to be attacked, who would defend me, old and lame though she is. At the moment she is making her groans of pleasure, and the moment is soothing.

"Maybe I had better take you for a short walk before Andrew

223

comes." Her immediate response is to heave herself up, wagging her tail hopefully. I put on a coat and we trundle down the stairs. As usual at this homecoming hour the street is full of people and I am glad to be outdoors.

About a quarter of a mile from the store there is an empty lot, overgrown, full of debris, and this is one of Patapouf's favorite places, because of the marvelous and varied smells she finds there, from old rubber tires to bits of wood that are sometimes chewable, and delicious coarse grass. She has found an ambrosial tuft now and is determined to chew it bit by bit, but I'm anxious to get back and not keep Andrew waiting, so I give the leash a tug. At that second I hear a shot and pull hard on the leash. We must get out of here, I am thinking, and fast, but Patapouf is lying down. When I kneel, sensing something is very wrong, I get blood on my hands as I lift her head and I can see her suffering puzzled eyes. Now she goes limp suddenly and I scream, "Help! Help!" and people materialize around me.

"Are you all right?" It is an old man who kneels down beside me, very concerned. "You're covered with blood! Were you shot?"

"I'm all right. It's my dog. They got my dog. Someone call the S.P.C.A., and fast, for God's sake!"

Suddenly there is someone crouching down beside me and I realize as I feel his arm around me that it is Andrew. "I'll take care of this," he says. "You must get home, Harriet."

"I can't leave Patapouf. Someone is calling the S.P.C.A." I find it hard to speak. I feel muffled, unable to take in in any rational way why I am here in a vacant lot with a crowd peering in at me and Patapouf bloody on the ground.

"Has someone called the police?" I hear Andrew ask.

Yes, that has been done, but in answer to his second question, "Did anyone see whoever fired the shot?" there is no response.

Now a young girl bends down and says in a low voice, "I heard the shot as I was coming along and I saw an old woman running across the street. Wild gray hair, and she seemed to be carrying a rifle."

"Will you be willing to tell the police about this?" Andrew asks in a low voice. All around us I can feel the pressure of people coming in closer, whispering to each other, and it flashes through my mind, suddenly alert, that the attacker being a woman makes sense. It has occurred to me that it could be a woman. A fanatic. It is like being shot in the back.

Time stops. What seems like hours may be at most a half-hour before the S.P.C.A. truck drives up and the police finally make an appearance. "Andrew," I whisper to him, "tell them I want her cremated." At least in that interminable half-hour I have come to admit that she is dead. The men are very kind and gentle as they lift the body up. "I want to go with her," I am now sobbing. "It's so lonely for her to go alone."

But Andrew holds me back firmly. "I have to get you home, Harriet. You can't help the dear thing now, and you must wash off the blood." I am standing and recognize the black police officer. He has his notebook out and is busily writing things down. "Sir," Andrew says, "there is a woman here who saw a woman with a gun run across the street after the shot."

"Yes." The young woman comes up to the officer and tells him her story. The crowd is beginning to melt away at last. Several people speak to me to express sympathy and outrage.

One elderly woman says, "I can't believe it, that such a cruel thing could happen here. That old woman is obviously crazy and should be put away—and people like that can get hold of a gun!" She is explosive, but I can't respond. I cling to Andrew's arm and see that he is right. I must get home as fast as possible. Luckily he has his car. I am not sure I can walk, and it is an escape, too, from all the eyes.

"Do you think she shot Patapouf by mistake, that you yourself may have been the target?" Andrew asks me as we sit in the frighteningly empty room, Patapouf's bed in the corner, her water dish with her name on it near the fridge. There is something in me that wants to be alone, in spite of Andrew's support, but thank goodness he did come to the lot. What would I have done without him?

"I don't know. How can I know? But, Andrew, I am ready to believe that the goon who is after me may, after all, be a woman. In an odd way it makes sense."

"Why?" Andrew asks.

"It's women, after all, who are violent against lesbians. This afternoon two fussbudgets turned up from Our Lady of the Sacred Heart and sniffed around like dogs looking for drugs. They would not be violent perhaps, but someone on a different level, a fundamentalist or simply a crazy who has found something and someone to hate. The need to hate runs deep and strong these days. You know that, Andrew, you do know that."

"Yes, I do. So again I marvel at your courage."

"The bad thing is that I have no reason to believe the police will catch this creature."

Andrew looks up now and scrutinizes me. "Harriet, this time something has to be done, if it means hiring a private detective. I am going to talk to Fred about this. We are simply not going to sit by and let you live here in danger."

"But I'm not going to be driven away, Andrew. You are aware of that, I trust?"

"You're not going to run out under fire." He smiles his warm smile and squeezes my hand. "Bully for you."

I feel very tired and want terribly to be alone for a while, but I remember that I have told Joe and Eddie that we would drop in after supper. Could Andrew go alone? That might be just as well. So I suggest he get a bite to eat at the little French restaurant and then go and meet them alone.

"You are anxious to get rid of me, aren't you?" he teases.

"Yes, I guess I am. I'm still in a state of shock."

"May I drop in afterwards just to be sure you're all right?"

"Yes. I'll be in bed by then, but that's all right. It was wonderful that you were there in the vacant lot. Thank you, dear Andrew," and I add, "I hope you like Joe and Eddie. They are in such a nightmarish thing with Eddie having AIDS, but they will like you, I feel sure. And right now they need support and distraction."

The minute I hear the door close downstairs and Andrew's car revving up it is as though I have been holding back an earthquake for hours and now it can explode. It is more like a howl than an outburst of tears and what explodes through me is not only Patapouf but also Vicky, Vicky . . . for in losing the old dog who was our friend and companion for fifteen years, I lose Vicky. As long as Patapouf was with me, Vicky was still here. I feel absolutely abandoned and, for the first time since Vicky's death, possessed by grief and by nothing else. "How can I live without you?" I say aloud to the empty dog dish and the empty dog bed.

I do not know. I can't imagine where to bury the ashes when I go to get them. Here there is no garden, nowhere to plant a lilac, and now I think of Angelica and how good she has been to the old dog and how she loved her. Angelica! It is like a reprieve for a moment even to think of her, but I can't bring myself to call her as it would mean telling the whole brutal story. To what end? And I cannot stop crying. I must not inflict this on anyone until I have somehow got hold of myself, but it is a comfort to think of burying Patapouf in Angelica's beautiful garden. That gives me the courage to drink a glass of milk, get undressed, and get into bed, but I can't put my grief to bed, my mind racing, memories welling up, tears rolling into my ears. How can I call this house home if there is nowhere in its space to bury my dog?

It is Vicky speaking. Furious with me for being the instrument of Patapouf's death, for insisting on opening a bookstore in such a desolate neighborhood, for spending a fortune on a losing proposition from the start. "Oh Vicky!" I long for her arms around me, for her way of knowing what to do always, never hesitating. Vicky was so sure of herself, and I am not. I embark on what she would call a wild venture without really knowing what I am doing. Far worse, I antagonize people by coming out as a lesbian. If I am in trouble, it is my own fault.

When the phone rings I wonder whether I have the courage to answer it, but luckily I do because it is Joe. "I'm in a bad way, Joe," and the tears start streaming down again.

"Andrew told us, of course. It's too terrible, Harriet. It's time something was done."

"I don't mind about that," I stammer between loud embarrassing sobs, "it's Patapouf. And, Joe, it's Vicky. I'm in an undertow of the past. It is as though I am taking in for the first time that I have lost Vicky too."

"Yes, I can see how it is. I can only say, do not hold back on grief. You've been so brave. Maybe now you have to let yourself grieve, Harriet."

"As long as Patapouf was here, Vicky was here too, in some way. I don't know how to handle everything alone."

"Don't even try for a while. Andrew will help, and I'll help."

"But you have enough trouble, Joe."

"I need someone I *can* help. With Eddie it is proving hard. And, by the way, I must thank you for sending us Andrew. He and Eddie are playing chess now. He seems eager to do what he can. He offered to come over and be with Eddie when I have to be away for late hours."

I stop crying. I am pleased that my hunch proved to be good. I am back in my life again in some strange way. "Thanks, Joe, thanks for calling."

"Andrew says to tell you he'll be along in a half-hour and has his sleeping bag with him."

But when I put the receiver down I know I do not want anyone overnight. I have to think things out. I have to be prepared for family and friends to advise me to move the store away, that it is impossible to remain here. For the first time I begin to face what is involved. Can I stay on? Is there some way to put an end to the threats? Am I crazy to insist on a staying power I am beginning to feel slide away? What makes me so determined to stay? But as I ask myself these questions the answers well up, the nucleus of friends the store has brought me and brought together: Nan, Marian Tuckerworth, Martha, Sue Bagley, and dear Fanny and Ruth who take over on Saturdays. Their faces surround me in my bed like guardian angels. Already in a few months the store has come to represent something in the neighborhood. Of course I have to stay!

So by the time Andrew comes by my mood has changed, so fast do things happen in the psyche. "How was it over there?" I ask him, sitting up in bed. "Just sit on the bed and we'll talk, then I must really get some sleep."

"I intend to spend the night," he says, patting my feet under the covers.

"No one will do anything tonight. Whoever it is has had her fun. Andrew, I want to be alone."

"You sound very much in command," he grants, and continues, "I liked Joe a lot, and Eddie too, but Joe is someone you can lean on. He talked about you in a very admiring and wise way. And I'm sure you know you can call him at any time. That is a comfort to me. I don't want to leave you, Harriet. I'm going to be anxious about you. Can't I stay? I can sleep downstairs in the store and you won't even know I'm here."

"All right. Who am I to turn down a dear brother and his concern? The fact is that without Patapouf it has ceased to feel like home here. She has taken Vicky with her. Oh, it's so strange and awful!"

"I envy those two men," says Andrew, "and I envied you and Vicky. You are right, Harriet. At this point I need to be in touch with some exemplary lives. I hope I can help with Eddie."

There is a moment's silence between us, then Andrew looks up and asks me whether it is all right for him to use the phone downstairs. He wants to call Fred.

"As long as I don't have to bother with telling it all. Go ahead and call Angelica too. You'll find her number in the small phone book on my desk. Ask her, will you, if I can bury Patapouf's ashes in her garden. I'd be sure to cry if I talked to her."

"Of course. I'll go right down," says Andrew. He looks at me, hesitating for an instant, before coming over to hug me hard. It is a singular blessing to be hugged as I slip down in the bed and close my eyes. All I need now is to be allowed to forget.

As soon as I'm alone, however, I am wide awake. Sleep is as far as heaven. Vicky used to say, "Don't meet things head on. Confrontation doesn't help. Meet them sideways." And she was right, but how am I to meet sideways a murderous old woman who has shot my dog? And what is she thinking of doing next? Is she alone or is someone else, a son perhaps, also engaged in this sinister game? I am exasperated, and I see why. It is significant in an odd way to be threatened and attacked because of the kinds of books I offer for sale and even because I am a lesbian and have said so openly, but there is no significance and no point in becoming a martyr to simple madness!

So what can we do? This whole dreary business has gone on long enough and it is clear to me that the police will never try to solve this case. They are not interested, partly because I am a woman, partly because I am new in the neighborhood, and no doubt they think I feel superior. Did someone yesterday suggest a private detective? I must call Jonathan and see what he thinks.

I suppose private detectives are wildly expensive, and if the detective does unearth the culprit, what then? My head is whirling and I feel rather sick. I keep listening for Patapouf's deep breathing, then realize that I'll never hear that again. It is an interminable night, but I must have finally gone to sleep because I am startled by Andrew's gentle knock on the door and see that it is after eight.

"Oh, sorry, did I wake you?"

I pull on my wrapper before opening the door but I must look disheveled. "I guess I finally went to sleep. What an awful night."

"Let me make us a cup of coffee and then I'll be off to work."

We sit at the table and I find some coffee cake in the fridge and pour glasses of orange juice; all this in a daze.

"Fred will be over later on. He is convinced that we must get a private detective on to this and not delay."

"That is exactly what I decided in the night. I have not been kept from what I planned to do here, but too much energy gets wasted in anxiety." I sound businesslike and balanced, I am glad to hear. "Fred did not talk about my moving the store, did he?"

"Well," Andrew grins at me, "he did at first but I told him you would never be forced out, and that was that."

"Thanks, Andrew."

"Angelica Lamb, on the other hand, was rather violent on the subject. She can't understand why you stick it out, but of course," Andrew says, his tone changing to a gentle one, "she will be happy to have Patapouf's ashes buried in her garden, wherever you choose. She wants to take you out to lunch today."

"I don't want this day," I say, "not in any shape or form. It's a getting-used-to-loss day and that is all." I realize suddenly that Joan doesn't even know about Patapouf and she will be here shortly. "Oh Andrew, thanks for everything."

231

When he is gone I get dressed. Everything today seems an immense effort. When shall I ever be able to resume a normal life? That is what I long for, quiet days of talk about books with customers, people I know now as friends dropping by.

21

I have never seen Joan angry but now, when I tell her about
Patapouf, her face flushes and she is so angry that she can't say
anything. Then she slams the telephone book on the floor and
curses. Then she comes over to my desk and hugs me hard.

"Harriet, I've had enough of this. We are going to get who-
ever it is. Why aren't the police here now if they didn't come
last night?" she asks, picking up the phone.

But I beg her not to make the call. "Fred and Jonathan are
coming over. They'll be here any minute, but thanks anyway.
What a support you are, Joan! Your anger," and I stop to take it
in. "The strange thing is that I have not felt anger this time, just
woe. I feel like a sandbag with all the sand poured out, useless
and beyond anger."

"It's the shock," Joan assures me.

I can't bring myself to tell her that it is grief, that it is Vicky. I
do not feel anger in myself, but anger in Vicky. I feel she is
furious with me, that all I have done is a bitter mistake. I feel
tears splash down on my hands and rub them off.

"Do cry," Joan says, "it's all right."

Fortunately I have time to blow my nose and pull myself together as Jonathan and Fred push open the door. Fred kisses me on the cheek. I suggest that we all four sit down around the table and offer them coffee.

"No thanks," says Jonathan.

There is a slight pause while Fred exchanges a look with Jonathan. "Harriet, Jonathan agrees with me that the time has come to clear this whole dirty mess up and get hold of the goons, as you call them."

"All right, but how are we to do that? The police washed their hands of the whole business weeks ago." My tone is testy but I can't help it. I resent needing help. Is it always men who deal with violence?

Jonathan coughs his nervous cough. "It may be time to call in a private investigator."

"Won't it be frightfully expensive? We're operating on a wing and a prayer already, as you well know."

"The alternative appears to be that you leave this area and find a more tolerant neighborhood," says Jonathan.

"I won't run away." I turn to Fred. "You know I can't do that. I can't let all the people down who come to the store and find a refuge here. I can't break down what I have been slowly building up."

"Very well. Then what about getting a sleuth in on it? Andrew told me someone had seen an old woman running across the street just after the shot, and she had a rifle. So there is at least a clue."

"Are there any women private detectives? I would prefer a woman."

"I'll see what we can turn up," Jonathan says agreeably. Though he usually manages to irritate me, he means well, I have to admit.

"I can't help wondering what this madwoman is feeling now. Is she gloating? Or filled with remorse? And is she afraid?"

"You have a vivid imagination, Harriet."

"No, I really don't, but this is such a strange and horrible thing. I want to get to the root of it. I want to *know* what goes on in that woman's psyche."

"You're so like Vicky when you say that," Fred says, quite amused apparently, "tough and resilient."

"Maybe I am at moments but I am never sure of myself, and Vicky always was, or seemed to be. Oh, if she were only here she would fight for me!" The words spring out but I see at once it is a mistake. Here are two men who have come to help me and fight for me and all I do is wail for Vicky. "I'm sorry," I say quickly, "that was a childish remark."

"It's natural enough," Fred says, reaching over to take my hand and hold it for a moment in a strong clasp.

"If everything stands still now until we get hold of a detective, maybe I had better catch up with my desk. I guess I need to be alone and resume my life here as best I can." It is not perhaps what I ought to have said, but it is at least the truth. "Thank you for coming so promptly. I am a lucky woman to have your help."

It is agreed that I shall have an interview with a detective, if found, by tomorrow morning. Life is proceeding as it does in small rushes, eddies, and a slow inexorable coursing onward through the human landscape.

I sit down at my desk after they have gone filled with a sense of relief. What helps is the usual, to take up the routine bills and pay them and ponder a way to reduce the deficit. Some kind of reception or party around the Thanksgiving weekend might be a good idea. I forget everything for a half-hour and no one comes into the store. It feels like a reprieve. In one way it is a very different atmosphere from the great gathering after the *Globe* interview with its air of triumph and congratulation, as if I had won a battle—and I suppose in a way I had. That seems now eons ago. My education was just beginning.

What has happened to Patapouf, so innocent and loving, is by comparison a secret. No one can be expected to imagine that her death has brought Vicky's death back in a new way. No one can imagine how desolate I am, how hard it seems to behave in a normal way, how almost impossible to keep going, to appear to be in control.

"I guess I'm not as independent as I thought I was," I say to Joan. "Andrew was a real help, staying the night."

"I think you are amazing," Joan says. "You are so strong."

"Not at the moment, dear Joan. I'm in a muddle about everything."

"Very British of you." Joan often makes me laugh when no one else can and her remark sets me off.

"They muddle through, one is told. I just sit in the middle of the muddle helplessly laughing."

The kaleidoscope of the morning takes another turn and settles into another pattern as the door is pushed open by Nan. She comes right over to me sitting at my desk and says, "It isn't true is it?" as she looks under it to be sure Patapouf is not there snoozing as usual. "It can't be true that Patapouf is dead!"

"They shot her on our evening walk, shot her in that waste place down the street. She went fast. I held her in my arms. Blood everywhere." This I say quite calmly. I am telling it, not reliving it.

But I can see that Nan is very upset. Trying not to cry, she says fiercely but with a break in her voice, "Those criminals have to be stopped. What about the police? Oh, Harriet, it's so cruel, so unfair. What sort of world is this anyway?"

"The lawyer who runs my affairs," I tell her, "and my older brother decided the police were hopeless. They think a private detective is the only hope. If they can find one, I am to interview him or her tomorrow. I hope it will be a woman."

"Why a woman? What difference does that make?"

"Well, someone who was there saw an old woman run away, holding a rifle."

"Oh."

"I have an idea in this case a woman might get further, be able to penetrate the community better . . . I don't know."

"You are so brave," Nan says.

"No. I'm numb right now. I can assure you I wasn't brave yesterday."

"But today you are brave," Nan insists. "Come and sit down at the table. I feel quite weak in the knees."

Sitting at the table makes for intimacy, and that feels good, but it also brings back all the inner turmoil of the last twenty-four hours.

"What is happening, Nan, is very strange. The death of Patapouf—or rather the life of Patapouf before she died—was keeping me alive and keeping mourning away. Now it is almost as though Vicky were the one who was shot in the field. I can't talk about it," I say, blowing my nose on a Kleenex.

There is a silence. Nan always knows when not to push. "You have not had time to mourn," she says quietly. "I am going to leave you in peace but could you come over and have supper with us? We've talked about it for so long. Perhaps this is the time." But as she sees me hesitate she says, "Maybe tomorrow."

I think about the children, the expected response to their interests, about meeting Nan's husband. For a second I think I simply cannot do it. I want to creep into a corner alone. What comes out is, "I feel so old, Nan."

THE EDUCATION OF HARRIET HATFIELD

"Anyone would, after what you have been through these past months. But the children, of course, are totally innocent about age. Somehow or other I have noticed that children take you as being their own age. That is a genius you have."

"Really?" It is an encouraging thought, true or not. "All right, I'll come tomorrow. It's a help to know I can be my childish self." That childish self is warmed by Nan's hug before she leaves.

"Come about six-thirty when we can have a drink and the children are fed. I'll call Phil and tell him to be home early. He will be so pleased to meet you at last. You have become a legend in our family."

I am sitting here thinking that life is like a tapestry that is always being woven with new patterns and colors, and it never stops, nor can we hold it back. So it is no surprise when the phone rings and it is Angelica, who weaves herself in and out of the pattern, and has done so for years. "I'm coming to take you out for lunch," she announces without preliminary.

"All right, but it has to be early as I have to be back at the store by half-past one."

"Two," I hear Joan's voice. "Take your time."

"I'll be there at noon." She has sounded quite calm but her voice breaks as she says, "I still don't believe . . . the dear dog . . ."

"Please, Angelica, I can't talk now," and I hang up rather rudely. At the moment I do not want to hear her grief, which I know is real. I want to get on with my work . . . with my life. I am clinging to it desperately as to a raft in a rough ocean. "I am not drowning," I hear myself say aloud.

"No, you appear to be staying afloat," Joan says and laughs.

"Good God, am I talking aloud now? What am I coming to?" I get up and walk up and down for a minute, suddenly very glad Joan is there and we can talk. "Joan, what I need is to think about the store. That is my lifesaver."

"What's your idea of a compelling undertaking?"

"I have two ideas about windows. One is that we really must do one on AIDS."

"Yes, but I suggest we keep it on hold for a while. Let things die down a bit."

"Maybe. The other is self-indulgent but I want to do it: a kind of memorial window for Patapouf, books about what animals do for people."

"That," Joan says in her most definite tone, "is a splendid idea. It has occurred to you, no doubt, that the murder of an old dog will move a lot more people than that piece in the *Globe* did."

"No." I am shocked by the very idea which seems implicit in Joan's remark. "I am not about to exploit Patapouf's death for publicity purposes!"

"Don't be cross, Harriet. I was not thinking of a newspaper story, God forbid, but that people who were on the other side may well come over to your side when this gets out around the neighborhood."

Perhaps she is right and, if so, it will be very interesting to see. In an instant we have an inkling, for the door is pushed open by a rather seedy old man carrying a copy of the *Chronicle.* He peers at Joan and then at me and decides evidently that I am the woman he is after, for he raps the paper with his hand and asks, "Are you the woman whose dog was shot yesterday?"

"Yes, I am."

"Those punks should be shot at dawn. It's a dirty thing to do. I came to apologize for this neighborhood, which is running downhill so fast it's amazing anyone stays here, and quite beyond me, if I may say so, that you chose to open a bookstore here and expose yourself as you are doing."

"Sit down, won't you?" The man has penetrating, dark eyes under tufted eyebrows and has not smiled since he came in. I like this man.

"Oh, I can't stay. I just wanted you to know someone is on your side."

"You say 'punks' but someone saw who shot Patapouf, and she says it was a woman with a rifle. I don't suppose you have any idea who that might be?"

"No, I don't. God knows there are enough crazies around here." He does not want to get involved and is anxious now to leave.

"I appreciate your coming very much. My name, as I expect you know, is Harriet Hatfield."

"Mine is Shawn Fleming. Everyone knows me around here. I used to run a secondhand furniture store, so if you need anything let me know. And a good morning to you, Miss Hatfield—or," he catches himself, "is it Mrs.?"

"No, Miss."

Now he smiles for the first time. "You escaped prison, did you, just like me. I wasn't about to be tied down for life to someone who can't make as good a cup of coffee as I do."

"Do you like living alone?" I really wish this curious creature would stay and talk some more.

"Well, I don't, you see. I have a black cat called Timothy. That's why I got so mad when I read about your dog. Why, if Timothy died I don't know what I would do."

He is at the door and now slips away. Joan and I agree it is amazing that someone has come out of the blue like that to express condolences.

"I told you," Joan says triumphantly, but we have no time to discuss Mr. Fleming because it is noon and Angelica is at the door.

22

Angelica wants to take me right away from the neighborhood but agrees on my insistence that we go to the French restaurant nearby since I must be back at two to release Joan. I am afraid of the emotion Angelica brings with her. I dread her tears and mine. A perfect stranger is easier to take at this point and I quickly tell her about Mr. Fleming to ward off the too personal and raw, but Angelica is too full of her own anger and grief to stay away for long from the subject, and over a glass of wine while we wait for our soup, bursts into tears suddenly.

"She was such a gentle soul," she says, "the way she looked at one, such fondness in her old eyes. At least she was old," she says, wiping her eyes, "and had had a very good life."

"I can't talk about it," I say.

"But what is going to happen now? What are you going to do now?"

"Jonathan is getting a private detective, so until he finds one—and I want a woman if possible—"

"Are there women detectives?" Angelica interrupts.

"I don't know."

"Why can't the police handle it? After all, that's what they're for!"

"One would suppose so, but I have been harassed for months, Angelica, as you know, and they are simply not interested or have been bought off long ago."

"You are cynical."

"Maybe. The brouhaha over the *Globe* article taught me something at least—and that is that the police are not out to defend homosexuals."

"Oh." Angelica ponders this.

"Besides, there must be more than an old woman involved. How would one old woman steal a cord of wood all by herself?"

"I keep forgetting how much you have had to take of threats and actual attacks. It is appalling."

"I am sick and tired of it! There is so much I want to do with the store. We are just beginning to make a go of it, and more and more young people are discovering that we exist. It is frustrating, I must say, to have to spend so much energy on anxiety and grief." But even as I say this I feel grief swallowing me again. "Oh, Angelica, poor Patapouf has somehow opened the door into all I need still to mourn about Vicky. That is the real thing that has happened." I push the soup away, feeling suddenly sick. "She would feel it is my fault—that I killed our dog," I say, as cold as ice.

"Try to be sensible, Harriet. I know you are under frightful stress and if all this has brought you to mourning, more than a year after Vicky's death, perhaps that is a good thing. You held back the mourning, but sooner or later it has to be experienced or it becomes a wall between you and your life. I have wondered sometimes how you could launch yourself into a wholly new life as rapidly as you did—extraordinary of you. Such strength, Harriet, strength and imagination!" This is the Angelica of the deep steadfast caring, and I cannot meet her eyes, I

242

am so close to tears. Still it is true, and I sense it is true now, that sometimes things can be said in a public place that could never be uttered in a silent room.

"I don't understand how I was able to do it, but you see, what I am finding out is that as long as I had Patapouf, I somehow still had Vicky, and now I am alone. I could not know till now how hard that would be." And I have to add, "I feel she is angry with me, disapproving of all I have done. Oh dear, I sound quite crazy."

"No, not crazy, but I think grief makes one a child again, terribly lonely. That is how I felt when my sister died. It is as though loss after middle age takes us very deep down, back perhaps into early childhood or even infancy. It takes with it a whole past, a kind of deprivation one cannot even believe for months."

"Yes," I say. It is, beyond words, comforting to hear all this from Angelica.

"When will you come and find a place in my garden for the ashes?" Angelica asks, as the bill comes and we get ourselves together.

"I'll call when I can fetch them, and we'll decide on a day."

So that is decided and when, after our walk back, we see how many people are gathered in the store, we say goodbye on the street. "I don't know how you meet all this, day after day," Angelica says, peering in.

"It's rarely a crowd," I murmur. "Oh dear . . ."

"Force et confiance!" she calls as she gets into her car. That is something we used to say years and years ago. In fact it was a phrase of Vicky's which she had read in a biography of Eleonora Duse. Fortified by it, I push open the door.

Joan comes over from her desk to explain in a whisper, "It's Patapouf."

I recognize the three Lesley girls as they hurry over, then

243

stand, blushing with embarrassment, not knowing what to say.
"It's because . . . your dog . . . we heard about it. We just want to
say . . ." They all speak together.

Then one says, "She was such a dear dog. We can't stand it."

"We want to kill the person who shot her," says another.

Sue Bagley has been listening of course, as usual. "A lot of
good that would do," she says, then turns to me. "I told you it is a
bad neighborhood. I knew from the start you couldn't make a
go of it." This is so typical of Bagley, who is a genius at putting
people down, that I almost laugh.

"But I am making a go of it," I say gently, "and I have no
intention whatever of leaving."

"You don't?" Sue Bagley is amazed. "I thought this brutal act
would be the last straw. Your poor dog . . ."

I manage to push myself through the gathering and take ref-
uge by sitting down at my desk where Joan joins me to ask if I
would like her to stay. "It's been like this since you left," she
says.

"No, you go along. It's really rather heartening, isn't it?"

"In a way, but people are so upset they aren't here to pur-
chase."

"It's Patapouf's funeral," I whisper.

"What can we do?" someone asks quite loudly after Joan
leaves.

"Oh, Martha!" Here she is in her black hat, looking animated
for once. "What can you do?" I glance around at the eager faces.
"Nothing, my friends. It's your coming that is doing something.
It's your support. Thanks." I find it a little hard to be stared at
with so much eager compassion. I have not, after all, let these
people into my private life . . . or have I?

Now I do have an idea. "I hope those of you who live in the
neighborhood will tell me if you hear anything that might give
us a clue. I've about had it now as far as harassment goes."

"Murder," says one of the Lesley girls passionately, "is more than harassment surely."

"Are you here alone at night?" someone I do not remember now asks.

"My brother Andrew insisted on staying last night. He slept in the store in his sleeping bag. But I am all right—except—except," and with awful inevitability I feel the tears rising, "I listen for the dog's breathing and it isn't there," but I catch myself and say, "I must not begin to cry or I'll never stop. Look," I say, shuffling some papers around to save face, "it is awfully kind of you to come, but . . ."

"She needs to be left alone, for God's sake," says Bagley's harsh relentless voice. It is her way of helping of course, but I wish she could do it with a little grace.

"Goodbye, goodbye," the air is full of goodbyes and before I know it, they have all gone like a bevy of birds taking flight and I am alone.

It has been quite a day so far and I wish I could go and lie down somewhere and sleep, but there are three hours to go before I close up shop. Fortunately a young professor from Wellesley comes to ask me for advice about books in women's studies she has not been able to find. She has limp, fair hair tied in a bow, a very broad face with wide-apart gray eyes, wears a very long skirt, high boots, and a dark blue vest over a ruffled white blouse. Her name is Emily Woods.

She and I sit down for a half-hour and share a cup of tea. This visit does more for me than anything. It is my normal life, and what I mean it to be. Besides I find her congenial and eager to talk. She is impressed by the stock and finally dares to ask me whether I am breaking even financially.

"Not quite," I have to answer, "but I expect to within a full year. It takes time to develop a clientele, you know, and I am off the beaten track."

"You certainly are. Why did you choose such a rundown community? Why not Wellesley? There is no longer a good bookstore in town these days."

"Why not Wellesley?" The very idea repels me but I can't say that, of course. "I guess I wanted an environment which contains various kinds of people, not just my kind."

"Brave of you."

"Yes, it has gotten me into a lot of trouble lately."

"What kind of trouble?"

"Well, I am accused of running a pornographic bookshop, and the fact that I came out in an interview as a lesbian has not helped."

"How is that hazard ever to be stopped?" she asks, and it is obvious that she has had an experience, hard to handle in the same way as mine, and for the same reason.

"I don't know. Enlightenment on the subject faces formidable barriers." I risk a direct question. "I gather you have faced trouble of the same kind."

"Yes. It was two years ago actually, but it stays with me. I guess I had never before faced what being a lesbian means, what violence it may elicit."

"What happened?" I ask. "It helps to learn what other women have gone through."

"Well," Emily waits a moment and brushes a strand of hair back from her forehead. Maybe she doesn't want to talk about it, but then she begins and tells it almost as though it were a hair-raising story about someone else.

She was then living in Brookline and was coming home from a gay and lesbian march about discrimination against gays in housing. Her friend was away that weekend so she was alone, walking back from the march along the curb to avoid the crowd. Suddenly a roadster came toward her dangerously near the curb and she felt an arm and hand around her neck and she was being dragged. There were two voices, one saying "Go forward, go back" and "that's the way" and for some seconds she thought they would break her neck. Unconsciously she rubs it with her right hand as she talks. When they let her go she could hardly stand she was so terrified, and they rode away laughing and shouting "Gays stay out of the street."

Emily tells me she was dazed but managed to ask whether anyone had seen what happened and two men offered to be witnesses and wrote down their names and addresses. "All I wanted was to go home," she tells me, "but I felt I must go to the police. It had to be reported. I was in shock and naive enough to think the police would want to know that such things happen."

"But they didn't, I must presume?"

"They didn't even ask me to sit down," she says, "and when I said there were witnesses they asked if they were gay and when I said I thought they were, they simply dismissed the whole story. My neck was hurting a lot and I knew I had better get home. I guess that was the loneliest walk I ever took. I felt dizzy and angry and hurt."

I swallow the bitter taste of her story before I speak. "Six months ago I would have found it hard to believe. Somehow, Emily, we have to find a way to bridge the two worlds and I keep hoping the store may help in doing just that, although at the moment it simply appears to be a target for the worst element." I did not intend to speak of it, but the words come out. "Yesterday the homophobes around here shot my dog while we were on our evening walk."

"You don't mean it?" Emily looks at me, visibly wincing. "Why, for God's sake?"

"Because they are determined to drive me and the store out of this neighborhood."

"Oh dear, it seems so strange and inhuman. What is happening, that there is so much hatred? It hurts, Miss Hatfield. What

247

have you done to deserve it? I wish I could understand," and she adds, "Oh your poor dog," and puts her hands up to her face as if to blot out the cruelty.

"I'll tell you something cheerful at least. Somehow the dog's death has caught people's imagination. I have had a lot of support today and from people who have never come into the store till now. Dear old Patapouf, perhaps she is building a bridge . . ."

"You really are a remarkable person," Emily says.

"No, not really," I am quick to answer, "it has all somehow happened since I lost my friend. I have been catapulted into a position where I have to fight. It's not courage but necessity, as I see it, for I am a very ordinary old party who is lucky enough to be able to afford a wild dream."

"You are paying a high price for it," she says.

"Now we must see what books we can find for that course of yours. Are the students responsive?" I ask. "A lot of young women pile in here lately. That at least is a heartening sign."

Emily thinks a second. "They are curious, fascinated often, but uninvolved. Sometimes I find it hard to deal with girls who really haven't a clue as to what I am talking about."

"And why is that? They must have crushes themselves now and then."

"Oh they are so afraid of those feelings, you see. They never relate all this to themselves, except here and there a lesbian who would never admit that she is one. They are back in the days of *The Well of Loneliness*," and suddenly Emily laughs. "They imagine lesbians dress like men."

I do find four or five books that Emily has asked for and finally it is nearly time to close and she leaves.

When I finally slip into bed I keep busy making lists of books I can summon in my head about animals in relation to human beings, such as Mowat's *Never Cry Wolf,* Carrighar's *Wild Heritage,* Lilly's *Man and Dolphin,* and Maxwell's *Ring of Bright*

Water. There must be something about how good it is for old people to have an animal to care for. I go to sleep dreaming about writing a book about Patapouf for children, well aware that I shall never do it. I am not a writer and must prepare my mind, not for a work of art, but for a detective tomorrow morning. Jonathan calls at nine when I am half asleep to say he has found someone, not a woman, but what looks like a sensitive and efficient youngish man, called Earl Cutler.

So tomorrow is on the way. No way to stop the rush of time like white water over rocks. I am borne along willy-nilly, but at least there was real comfort in Emily, a new friend. I feel sure I shall see her again.

23

I wake expecting Patapouf, and then it is a shock to realize that she is not waiting to be let out, that she is not here and will never be here again. This day of the detective's coming I am slow and a little confused. What will happen exactly? And is it really a good idea?

I wander around getting dressed and drink a cup of coffee without sitting down to a real breakfast. The truth is I am not prepared for this detective who is about to enter my life and pry into its corners.

It is better when I am downstairs in the more formal atmosphere of the store and I am kept busy washing teacups, dusting the shelves, and have just settled in to go over yesterday's mail when I see Jonathan's car draw up and a rather tousled young man in a duffle jacket get out and look up at the store windows with concentrated attention. They come in and Earl is introduced.

"Happy to meet you, Miss Hatfield," he says. "You certainly have a nifty store here."

"Take off your coat," I say, "and we'll sit down and get to business."

Jonathan coughs his usual cough. "I'll just run along and leave you to it," he says. "I'm due at the office."

"Thanks, Jonathan." I follow him to the door and we shake hands.

"You should be out of this mess in a week," he says, smiling. "Earl is a wizard."

"That would be good news if I could believe it," I say, sitting down and giving Earl an appraising look.

He is not what I expected, looks rather like a graduate student, is not at all solemn or, for that matter, businesslike, for the first thing he asks is, "Do you enjoy living in this neighborhood?"

"Very much. I chose it deliberately. You know, Mr. Cutler, until I was sixty, I led a very sheltered, and I suppose one could say privileged life. I wanted to know all kinds of people. I wanted the store to make bridges, to help people understand each other."

"And has it done that?" he asks, a touch of irony audible.

"Yes, in a way it has."

"But I gather you have also made enemies. Perhaps you had better tell me all you can about that, from the beginning to the tragic murder of your dog."

Slowly I put together the whole puzzle for Earl Cutler, from the obscenities on the windows, to the anonymous letters about the books I sell, to the stealing of the firewood, and finally the brutal murder of Patapouf. Laid out like this in about fifteen minutes while Earl has his tape recorder going, I am embarrassed that it is not even worse than it is, and so I ask, "Am I stupid to be upset? Until Patapouf died I thought I could just muddle through. Friends have rallied, you know."

"Miss Hatfield, you have every reason to try to stop this sort of harassment. I hope we can fit the pieces together soon. As I listened to you talking, my first reaction was that there seem to be two different people or groups involved. I must certainly see your friend Joe, who had an encounter with the two men who were writing obscenities on the windows. But then, weeks later, someone says they saw an old woman with a rifle who presumably shot your dog."

I feel I have told him all I know, but as he asks more and more questions I realize how much one forgets—for instance, the ostentatiously nosy women from the church, and how far the church may have fostered the hostility. As far as possible, I have put all this out of my mind as the only healthy way to handle it.

"It is too bad the police retained that second anonymous letter threatening you," he says, looking up from the pad where he seems to be chiefly doodling. After all, we are being recorded on his tape.

"At that time I imagined they would try for an arrest," I say. "More fool I."

We are now approaching the crucial question, and I dread it. "In your own mind, do you lay the attacks on you to the allegedly pornographic nature of the books you sell?"

"I don't know. That is how it all began, with, as I have told you, someone taking *Pure Lust* to the police."

"Yes, I understand, but it seems as though the woman who shot your dog may have been motivated by a more personal hatred or whatever it is, a fanatic of some sort, that she, in fact, may have entered the scene later."

"Homophobia, perhaps. I told you that an article appeared in the *Globe* calling me a lesbian. 'Lesbian Bookseller in Somerville Threatened' was the headline."

"There was at that time a change in the atmosphere around the store?"

"This will surprise you. There was indeed. A great many people charged in the next day to give their support, and I was actually treated like a hero."

"And that, no doubt, only added to some people's wish to harm you," he says with a smile.

During this conversation I am becoming aware of Cutler as someone I can trust. He is after the facts and makes no comment when I provide them. I like that. He is very professional without ever putting me down, or for that matter sympathizing overtly with me, and I am grateful. If someone has to pry into my affairs I am glad that it turns out to be Cutler.

Until now we have talked alone and had time to establish, it seems, a mutual regard. Now Joan comes in and I realize it is ten and we have been talking for an hour. I introduce them and suggest that Joan join us at the table. If customers come in Mr. Cutler and I will go upstairs, but he suggests that we do so now. "It will make my work a lot easier if no one sees me with you. Is there a back door I can leave by?"

"But you will want to talk with Joan, won't you?"

"Mrs. Hampstead, could I call on you at your home, perhaps?"

"Of course," and she jots down her address and phone number and suggests he come at four today.

When we are settled upstairs in the two comfortable armchairs opposite the fireplace, it is my turn to ask questions. For some reason the greater intimacy of the apartment makes me feel self-conscious, as though I am suddenly required to talk about myself and not simply "the situation." "You see, Mr. Cutler, I never intended the bookstore to become a lesbian bookstore. The interview in the *Globe* set that one element in high relief and it has been, I must confess, embarrassing."

"Naturally. No one likes to be labeled and here you are living alone and suddenly in a spotlight you had not even imagined."

"How do you know?" I ask now.

"Well, your lawyer filled me in somewhat, at least as to the loss of your friend of so many years. After such a long rich relationship it must be offensive to be hauled before the world as some sort of monster."

"It has been in some ways excruciating, but I have to admit that it is giving me an education I had missed. It has forced me to be honest about myself. That is a salutary thing. I can identify for the first time with any persecuted minority and"—here I can't help laughing—"I know it is absurd, but I am proud of being in the front line. Because, you see, I am safer than most gay people are. By that I mean I am more or less self-supporting and no one else, except Patapouf, has been intimately involved. So I can dare without fear of hurting."

"You are really admirable," Mr. Cutler says.

"But my dog paid the price," I say, "and now for the first time I want those goons to be caught, and punished." There is a short silence. "How are you going to go about this?" I feel it is my turn now to ask the questions.

"First of all, by getting to know the neighborhood. I'll find a furnished room. I'll have to feel my way, and I'm not good at explaining how, but I expect to have sleuthed out a fair amount of information in a few days. Meanwhile, don't tell anyone that I have been engaged."

"But if you do find out who is involved, then what?"

"If I can find enough witnesses, we could go to court."

"More publicity, more newspaper stories. That is what I dread."

"Expensive. And, considering the neighborhood, you might even lose the case."

This is a sharp blow. It never occurred to me that if it came to court, I could lose. "Is there any alternative?"

"Of course I can't tell yet, Miss Hatfield, but there is always hope that things of this sort can get settled out of court. I can't promise, but that is what we would be aiming at. A threat is a two-edged sword."

"And shooting a dog, an old, good, and quiet animal . . . that must be treated, mustn't it, as a crime?"

"At present we are in a thicket of possibilities and impossibilities."

"Why is there so much hatred and meanness of spirit?" It comes out of me as a cry of despair. I do not want any of this. I hate the whole business. Since Patapouf's death the whole world has gone awry. Nothing is any good any more. I want to go somewhere and bury myself. I want to be left alone.

Mr. Cutler, sensing my distress, leans forward, clasping his hands. "Please do not let yourself get into a panic, Miss Hatfield. It was high time you ceased to handle all this alone. Trust me."

He is so earnest and seems so young that it makes me smile. "Johathan said you are a wizard. So I must trust you, mustn't I?"

"We shall see, Miss Hatfield. And now I am going to leave you in peace. I'll telephone you now and then, but do not expect to see me for a week at least. Wish me luck!" We shake hands, and his hand clasp is reassuring.

24

It is lovely to be getting dressed to go over to Nan's as my after-
noon at the store has been rather a hassle—one of those days
when too many people want attention and there's no time to
make tea for a few real friends, and no good talk. I complain, but
that is ridiculous since I sold a lot of books. Now it is a pleasure to
dress in my red dress, which I hope the children will like, to find
a book for them, and then off I go. It's only a few blocks but it's
near M.I.T., and the river seems like another, rather brilliant
world, especially now at dusk with the tower windows all lit up
and such interesting faces seen on the street as people go home
from work. It is very different from my neighborhood. Here
there are restaurants with huge plate-glass windows, parking
lots filled with expensive cars. Life in a faster lane.

The Blakeleys live in a tower apartment with a small view of
the river. "Oh, isn't it beautiful?" I say, running to the window
before I have been introduced to Phil.

"See," Eve shouts, dancing up and down, "she likes it."

"Harriet, this is Phil," Nan now says. "We are all so excited to
have you here!"

"And for me it's the reward for a harried afternoon at the

store. Thanks, Phil" I say as he takes my coat. Someone is tug-
ging at my dress to lead me into the living room. "What if I told
you I have forgotten your name?" I ask the tugger.

"It's Serena. You remember!"

Now we are in the living room, the children are in a fit of
giggles, and I soon see why. Every chair and the divan has on it a
stuffed animal: a tiger, an elephant with a purple trunk, a teddy
bear in a red sweater, and on the divan a gray seal with a white,
baby seal. "Good heavens! How am I going to sit down on a
tiger?" I ask, "or an elephant?" This is greeted with hoots of
laughter.

"Or a mother seal," says Eve.

"Or a teddy bear," says Serena in an ecstasy of laughter.

"Perhaps the teddy bear would sit on my lap," I suggest.

"He groans when you pick him up," Eve informs me.

It is a relief to be transported like this into the child world
again and I catch Nan's eye and burst into laughter myself. "I
brought you a book. *The Wind in the Willows.* Do you have it?"
I ask Eve.

She takes it from me and studies it for a second. "No."

"Please read it to us," Serena breaks in. "Bear can sit on your
lap."

"But," Phil says, laying a hand gently on Eve's tightly curled
head, "Miss Hatfield has been working all day. Maybe what she
needs is a drink first, and then maybe she would be kind enough
to read." He turns to me with a smile. "What can we offer you?
Scotch, rum, gin and tonic? But please sit down and make your-
self at home. The children do displace a lot of atmosphere."

"But it's really not a madhouse," Nan offers.

"Or a zoo," Serena shouts. "Daddy calls it a zoo."

After deciding on a scotch and soda I pick the bear up and sit
down with him on my lap in the corner of the divan. "I didn't
hear any groan, Eve."

"Oh, you have to turn him upside down for that."

"He wouldn't like it, since we hardly know each other," I say, patting his head and pulling his sweater down. "Good bear," I say to him, "shall we be friends?" With one hand I lift a paw and bend down so he can pat my face.

The two little girls are watching all this intently. Then Eve says to Serena, "She knows about bears, you can tell."

I am taken right out of all the problems and anxieties in this high place above the river, and feel happy and relaxed. Nan is sitting on the arm of Phil's chair. How distinguished they look as a couple—he, small-boned, elegant even in shirt-sleeves; she tall and flowing, a woman people on the street turn to look back at as they pass. "I am so happy to be here," I say and my pleasure must be obvious.

"Well," Phil says, taking Nan's hand for a moment then releasing it, "Nan has talked so much about you and your store, I couldn't believe you were true. Now I see you are."

Serena has climbed up beside me and announces, "She promised to read to us. It isn't fair."

At this Nan laughs. " 'It isn't fair' is Serena's *leitmotif*."

"What does that mean?" Eve asks, frowning.

"It means what she says all the time, every other minute."

"I see that I had better tend to my knitting. You sit beside me, Eve, and we'll all be together." When we are settled in I begin to read. It is all fun but nevertheless I am relieved when the doorbell rings and it is a neighbor come to fetch the little girls, who it seems, have been invited out for supper. Serena runs to me at the last moment and throws her arms around my legs and I lift her up and kiss her. Then we three are alone and can be grown-ups.

I drink my scotch in the welcome silence while Nan disappears into the kitchen. "I won't be long," she says. "You and Phil talk in peace."

"They are adorable," I tell him, "those two little girls of yours. Irresistible, but I don't think I would ever have had the stamina to be with children all day. How does Nan do it?"

"Well," Phil lifts his glass to me, "you did awfully well, Miss Hatfield."

"Do call me Harriet."

"Thanks, I will. To answer your question, Nan does get help, as you no doubt know. There is a day-care center in the building and Eve of course is at school all morning."

"It does seem like a great place to live. That view . . ."

"In a way it is, but we loved our house in Charlestown. There was space. We had a backyard. I'll tell you something," he looks at me intently, "this apartment has never felt like home. The children talk about Charlestown, about having a pet again, not allowed here of course."

There is something he is not saying. I can sense it. "Why did you move? I suppose it is easier for you. You can walk to work."

There is a short silence. Now, as Nan comes back to join us he looks up at her, a little hesitant perhaps, but decides to say it anyway. "It's pretty anti-black over there and we finally had to decide that we had better leave for the children's sake."

Nan comes over and sits beside me. "Harriet, we know all about what you have been going through, but we had small children. We just couldn't afford to tough it out as you are doing."

"Nan says they shot your dog," Phil says, leaning back and looking up at the ceiling. "I don't know how one can take something like that. What's the matter with these people?"

"I'm learning a lot about hatred, Phil. It dries up my mouth."

"But you can't do anything about it? I mean take them, whoever they are, to court?"

"I don't know about blacks, but the police are not about to protect gays, that's for sure."

"It's all based on myth and rumor, isn't it?" Nan says, her hands clasped tightly on her knees, and as I am not quite sure what she means she glances over at me speculatively. "We are so visible, Harriet. Anyone who looks at me is saying to herself or himself, she's black. It may not mean she dislikes blacks but something is registered for good or ill. But how could anyone passing you in the street register anything at all except white, not young, and good-looking. There's no way they would say at once 'lesbian.' "

"So I am not a target for hatred unless someone blabs about me, unless it gets around that I am some sort of leper, to be avoided and if possible be forced out. I see what you are saying, and I guess it is true."

"And it's just as crazy as some people's idea that I am out to rape any white woman I can get hold of." Phil laughs, but it is a harsh laugh. We are in the country of pain.

"I've never had to live with any of this before. I had to be sixty before I could even say the word 'lesbian' and it still doesn't come easy."

"But you wouldn't want to go back to your safe life, would you? Nan says you lived in Chestnut Hill in a house with a big garden, and your friend was a publisher. Or do you sometimes want to cut and run? I wouldn't blame you."

I have to consider Phil's question and my answer does not come until we are sitting down to dinner, roast beef and Yorkshire pudding, real mashed potatoes, and fresh beans. I am suddenly very hungry and realize I have hardly been eating for two days. I must tell Nan so and thank her while Phil pours us each a glass of burgundy. Now I lift my glass and make a toast Vicky often made:

Think where man's glory most begins and ends
And say my glory was I had such friends.

"W. B. Yeats," says Phil. "I read Yeats at the university. He was a feisty old man."

Finally it comes round to Phil's question earlier on. "Phil, to answer your question, I don't want to cut and run. Besides, you can't recapture lost innocence, can you?"

"Only if you move backwards."

"The only trouble is I don't know what I am moving forward into."

We eat and are silent for a moment. The silence, I realize, is one of accord, of tacit acceptance of each other, of freedom to be ourselves whatever that self may turn out to be.

It is Nan who breaks the silence to say, "I feel with you partly, I suppose, because we are not activists where race is concerned. I sometimes feel guilty about this; but then I say to myself that bringing up two children who are able to grow, free from hatred, may be what I am meant to do. I think you have been thrown into this hassle about sexual preference not exactly against your will, but against your temperament. You find yourself in the front line of a war you never chose."

"Or even knew existed." I cannot help smiling. It seems such a grotesque position to find myself in. "It has its humorous side, but I must confess that I am tired of it. I wish I could have some peace to run the store in. Without Joan, you know," I say, turning to Nan, "I really couldn't manage at all. What a help she is." I am dying to tell them about the detective but remember my promise. "I sometimes hope something so bad will happen that the police will be forced to get involved."

Phil exchanges a glance with Nan. "It's interesting," he says, "what we seem to have in common. I expect you know that they do not go out of their way to help blacks. We learned that in Charlestown and it came as something of a shock." He takes a sip of burgundy. "Not bad, this wine. I have to suppose that any minority in this country is somewhat outside the pale when it comes to justice, hence the anger. One way or another we have to handle a lot of anger, don't we?"

"Harriet never seems angry," Nan interposes. "It is rather wonderful."

"You weren't angry when your dog was shot?" Phil presses.

"I was too shocked, too thrown, to be angry. I was in grief, not anger, I guess." Do I sound smug? I know Phil does not quite believe me. He is looking at me very quietly and nods.

"I understand," he says. "It was too terrible in some way."

"But also I think the goons who have been out to get me are crazy people. You can't get angry with mad people."

Phil laughs his bitter laugh. "No, you just want to kill them and be done with it. Is there no one to defend you?" he asks. "I mean literally someone to be there if you are attacked."

"One of my brothers, the younger one, Andrew, is with me a lot and is very supportive. He spent one night in his sleeping bag in the store after Patapouf was shot. By a miracle he was passing by when it happened and took over for me and got me home." I have talked too much about myself, I am thinking. "You are too kind, and I have babbled on. Let's change the subject."

"If only we could," Nan sighs. "If only we could think of people one by one, not as groups. After all, every minority contains the whole range of human qualities and failings. There are plenty of black crooks and lesbian crooks. Not all gay men look for several sexual partners a day. It's the generalizing that is so inflammatory. People tossed together become hazardous waste."

"Hey, that's quite an image," Phil gleams across the table. "Sometimes I think Nan should use some of her brilliance—go back to being a reporter."

At this Nan laughs. "I'd never make it now. I'm so bad at competing."

"We'll see, when the kids are grown-up," Phil says.

I have enjoyed the interplay between these two, the so evident sharing and love, the occasional challenges. I look at my watch. It is nearly nine, and no doubt the children will be coming home any minute and I would rather go now on the high tide of the evening, so I say, "Time I went home, you two. Patapouf . . ." The second the name is uttered I see that I have imagined Patapouf is alive and wanting her evening walk. And suddenly I am weeping, "But she is not there. I forgot . . ."

Nan has come round to my chair and puts her arms around me. "Dear Harriet, we are with you, you know that. The children cried when they heard about the dog. We love you."

I clasp her hand and squeeze it hard, then turn to say to Phil, "Nan is one of the reasons I've got to stick it out. She has been such a joy to meet, to know," and I am able to laugh. "She makes so much sense among all the crazies."

"I married a sensible woman, didn't I?" Phil says, smiling.

"This has been such a treat, an island of peace, somehow. I can't tell you what a blessing it was to come to you just this evening—like touching base." But as I say it I see what I have said and that it is strange and wonderful that touching base means having black friends, friends who understand all about living on some dangerous edge between security and danger.

"We do have quite a lot in common," says Phil. "Nan said we did, but I had to see for myself. We have some white friends, of course, but no one like you."

"No one on the front line, Phil means." He has gone to fetch my coat and Nan slips an arm through mine while we wait. "You know, I forgot all about dessert!"

"Just as well," I say quickly.

Phil insists on seeing me to my car and I promise to call them when I am safely home. "Next time I'll come and get you," Phil says. "I don't like your going home by yourself."

"Thanks, Phil. Thanks for everything." I wave as I back the car out and toot my horn as I take off.

The apartment feels cold and dismal when I let myself in. It was such a good evening with Nan and Phil, but now I am home and alone, terribly alone without my dog. I wonder how I can go on without a companion, without someone to love and to be loved by. Seeing their swift exchange, the way they tease each other, the way they smile at each other has driven home that this will never happen to me again, for Vicky and I teased each other and exchanged a judgment or our enjoyment of a guest with a single glance, and mostly there was the comfort of lying curled around each other in bed, that tender loving sharing of the night. I am lying in bed and it all comes back and I can't shut it out. But at least for the moment the storm of tears is over. I am simply in a state of extreme loneliness and depression.

So it is a good thing that when the phone rings now it turns out to be Earl Cutler, quiet and assured, to tell me he has learned quite a lot this first day and expects to have some real news soon.

"What I can tell you now is that the shooting of your dog has, ironically enough, done you a lot of good. They were talking about it in that bar down the street and people expressed outrage. Besides which, one very red-faced burly man said, 'That's not the way to get that woman to move on. She's a stubborn old thing and she has guts.' A young man who looks like a carpenter or something of the sort asked, 'What harm is she doing? What do people have against her? What can you buy in that store? Crack?' The only answer was, 'Obscene books, and she's a queer herself—brings the wrong kind into this neighborhood.' "

I interrupt Cutler to spare myself the rest. For some reason I don't want to hear these things, to see myself in the eyes of the neighbors as a kind of caricature. In some ways it is worse than a physical act of aggression. "All I long for is a little peace of mind," I say before wishing him luck. I find it hard to get to sleep.

25

It is fortuitous that, because Fanny and Ruth are not available, I am working in the shop this Saturday. Four former members of my class at Smith turn up. I have had no response so far to an ad I put in the Smith alumnae magazine, so this is heartening.

"Tuffy! Anna! Jennifer! and . . ." For a second I can't remember the name of the fourth one as she comes over and hugs me.

"Don't you remember Sandra Hoffman? I lived across the hall."

"Am I glad to see you! Of course I remember!"

"We are hoping you can come out with us for a drink or something," says Tuffy, who looks amazingly as she always did, her red hair tousled.

"Well, I don't close 'till six, so maybe we can settle for a cup of tea right here."

"What an amazing store it is!" Anna has left the group and is pulling books out of the shelves on "herstory." "I had no idea there was so much. Look at this whole row on nineteenth-century black women, Jennifer. Wow!"

"Make yourselves at home while I put the kettle on. I so hoped someone from Smith would show!"

Their enthusiasm is a tonic and I take my time arranging a plate of English cookies because I want them to have a chance to find out what the store is all about. Sandra already has three or four books of poetry in her hands when I come back with the tray. "Do you still write poetry?" I ask her.

"Oh, I don't know. I used to think when the kids left home I'd get back to it but I'm in such a groove of committees and stuff, there's no time." She lays the books down on my desk. "I want to take these home with me. Don't let me forget."

While they browse and exchange finds—Tuffy is delighted to find the Sylvia Beach biography, Anna seizes on O'Brien's Willa Cather—I try to bring them into focus in my memory. I did recognize them by name, but from below the conscious level, since they have changed—except Tuffy. It must be nearly forty years since we have met! And none, not even Sandra across the hall, was among my best friends.

It is wonderful to hear their excited chatter and real response to what the store is and represents. Who before now has appreciated it in just the way they are doing?

"You can have no idea how happy I am to see you," I say when we are finally seated around the table and I am pouring tea. Tuffy, since there are only four chairs, has hauled out Joan's stool. "It could be a dorm," I note. "Never enough chairs."

"What you need is a couch," Tuffy says. "That is the only thing missing."

Anna has been silent and sits leafing through Willa Cather, but she is listening and, looking around as she lifts her head, breaks into a warm smile. I recognize the smile and the very pale blue eyes.

"How shall we ever catch up on everything?" I ask.

"How can we catch up on forty years?" Jennifer says.

"Organize . . ." That is so like the old Tuffy, the most disorgan-

268

ized person I ever knew, who talked always about organizing, that I burst into laughter.

"Let's just tell a little about ourselves, one at a time," says Anna. "You start, Jennifer, and we'll go around the table and end with Harriet, for of course," she turns to me, reaching out a hand, "it's you we want to hear about, Harriet. You're the extraordinary one."

"You're the one who is doing something remarkable," Tuffy adds.

It is absurd to enjoy their praises as I do. After all, they are old friends and we share the bond of Smith, but I have been starved for such praises and the feeling of being included instead of being off on the perimeter.

"I don't have much to show for forty years out in the world," Jennifer says, and I remember how modest she always was, brushing aside all the honors she pulled down. "I did not go into a daring career as a political scientist. I married one instead and did a lot of typing and proofreading for Ben and . . . well, we had four children, two boys and two girls, and I'm a grandmother three times over. That, I have to tell you," she says with a laugh, "is the most thrilling and exhausting thing in my life at present!"

"Hear, hear," murmurs Sandra.

"I bet you a dollar you're holding back on something," I tease. "Jennifer as the happy useful housewife and mother and grandmother just isn't enough. Come on now!"

She is actually blushing. "Well, I'm rather active in the whole abortion business, the right of choice, you know. And just now in the last year I am helping to organize a chapter of Hospice to provide help for babies with AIDS. We live in Watertown—Ben is at Brandeis—and I am finding it a rather bigoted community. We have only a small center now—five beds. The need is simply enormous. One can have no idea until one gets involved. I guess that is my King Charles Head these days, trying to raise money, blood from a stone."

I am stunned to think of all Jennifer manages to do, and we are all silent for a moment before Tuffy breaks the mood. "After a short pause in honor of our friend, it is my turn to exhibit my total failure and lack of anything at all to tell you that could possibly be of interest." But she says this with a toss of her wild red hair and is simply greeted with laughter. "You may remember," she says, her hands clasped on her knees, and she is suddenly in earnest, "that I wanted to be a writer, the new Katherine Mansfield, though I do not have t.b., a big mistake."

"But you do have talent," Anna breaks in. "No doubt about that."

"Do I? It seems so long ago since I believed that." She pauses to push her hair back. "Well, I wrote three novels after I left Smith and one got published by Houghton Mifflin, but they turned down the other two and so did every publisher you ever heard of. I worked in all kinds of stupid jobs, as a typist, for a time as an assistant editor at *Yankee.* I consistently fell in love to no good end except a couple of abortions."

"Oh, Tuffy," Sandra sighs, "how awful."

"I've been in therapy of course and what comes out is lack of self-esteem. And why not, for God's sake? Your work is rejected, you are rejected as a woman—and so how are you still supposed to stand like the Statue of Liberty, torch in hand, singing 'O say can you see' when all that is to be seen is a woman who has failed completely to be anything but a dud?" And as Tuffy always used to when telling bad news, she bursts into laughter. "A soap opera," she laughs, "incarnate."

Anna gets up and puts an arm around Tuffy. "You can't let your talent go, Tuffy. You just have to keep at it."

"But I'm sixty-one, Anna, after all."

"How do you manage, Tuffy? You are so resilient," Jennifer says. "Who but you could laugh at so much misfortune?"

"I've always thought humor could be the saving grace," Tuffy says, "but the *New Yorker* doesn't see it that way. They consistently turn me down like everyone else."

"How do people handle so much rejection?" I wonder aloud. "To me it seems heroic."

"When my pop died I inherited just enough so I can live without a job. So it's not half bad now. And who knows? Maybe it will end with that wonderful title of Mansfield's, 'Not for Nothing Did the Chicken Sing.' "

We can't help laughing, and Tuffy laughs the loudest. Her laughter is a kind of triumph. What a lovable woman and how strange that she did not marry after all. These days I see so much pain everywhere. And now here it is again being overcome. I have tears in my eyes and hope no one notices. I am so afraid a customer will come in and break the spell that I turn quickly to Anna. "Your turn," I say, "and I am dying to hear. It's a piece of luck that no customer has interrupted us so far."

"Especially," Anna says, "because what we really want to know is all about you, Harriet, so I'll be brief." She thinks for a moment, her chin in her hands, and I register once more what a presence she is, how quietly she makes herself felt, and wish I had known her better in college. "I don't know how I do what I am doing these days, it is so complex—a little like opening Pandora's box and after all the devils fly out finding there is another box inside that one, and then another and another. I'm a social worker, working with abused children and the parents or others who abuse them. It's complicated and confusing a lot of the time. We can rarely get an open-and-shut case. What is depressing, of course, is how much child abuse there is—and in all levels

271

of society. I work mostly with small children in nursery schools, children whose parents are middle class, educated, and fairly well-off."

Having said this Anna breaks off and looks round at us. "I could talk about it for hours, but I'll spare you and simply add that my husband is a pediatrician and we have two grown-up sons, one of whom wants to be a psychiatrist, and the other is now at Harvard Business School. My problem appears to be how to detach myself enough from my job. It is devouring and frustrating, a poor combination."

"Yet," I say impulsively, "you seem so serene, so full of some quiet assurance and—yes—power."

"It's a professional disguise," Anna says, but to me that sounds like an evasion.

"It's tantalizing to hear all these things so briefly, isn't it?" I say. "Now it is Sandra's turn."

"Well, I am the perfect example," says Sandra with a smile, "of the intelligent woman who wanted to write poetry but instead has let herself get involved in God knows how many causes, from better housing for the old, to birth control, to cleaning up waste, to helping plant new forests in areas completely deforested in Africa and elsewhere. Sometimes I do feel useful, which I never did as a poet. My husband and I divorced years ago. Luckily we had no children. So there it is. The slogan around my Cambridge friends appears to be 'Let's ask Sandra—she has time.' "

We all recognize this state of affairs and the smile goes round the circle, and is then interrupted by Jennifer, who demands that I at last tell them about myself.

"We know that you lost your publisher friend, Vicky Chilton, and that you opened this bookstore. What an adventure at sixty!" Tuffy breaks in.

Now the attention is focused on me I realize that I do not

have the vaguest idea how much to tell, how much to let go. None of these women apparently ever loved a woman. It doesn't sound as though they were aware of what has been happening and I feel rather like a person on the moon trying to make contact with normal people going about their business on the earth. "I'm really afraid of shocking you," I murmur.

"How could you possibly do that?" Jennifer asks. "This bookstore is clearly an enormously enriching and life-giving place." She hesitates. "Isn't it?"

"Sometimes when I think of all the friends I have made since I opened it, I do think so, and I am kind of proud of the mixture, all sorts of women dropping in and talking with each other—just as I dreamed."

"So what is wrong, then?" asks Anna, giving me one of her penetrating looks, the professional look that requires an honest answer.

"What is wrong is that some half-crazy locals are out to force me out of this neighborhood. Their threats and actions against me and the store have been going on for weeks."

"Aren't you frightened? After all, you are alone here, aren't you?" asks Jennifer.

I sense their real concern. They are involved. They care. "I live upstairs alone and until my dog was murdered I felt quite safe because she would have defended me, although she was old, but she had a very loud, dangerous-sounding bark."

"Did you say your dog was murdered?" Sandra asks, her eyes very wide.

"Apparently, by an old woman with a rifle. I was taking Patapouf on our evening walk."

"It doesn't seem possible," Tuffy murmurs. "I mean, why are they, whoever they are, trying to drive you out?"

"And why do you stay under such circumstances?" Jennifer, who is quite pink with emotion, asks. "It's too dangerous, it

273

seems to me. I mean, after all, it's only a bookstore and you could move to a different neighborhood."

"It's not 'only a bookstore,' " I react quickly, "it's a special bookstore, a feminist bookstore, and so a lot of what I sell is offensive to some people. I have been accused of running an obscene bookstore, for example. People took a sample to the police and complained."

"I am utterly in the dark," Anna says. "You just have to tell us more."

"When the threats began, the *Globe* sent a reporter and the interview was headlined 'Lesbian Bookseller in Somerville Threatened.' " I say this too loudly, I realize, as though I were addressing a crowd. "The whole attack took me by surprise. I lived with Vicky for thirty years. We were lovers, but somehow we never thought of ourselves as lesbians. It was a dirty word to me and, I feel sure, for her. We simply did not face the fact that we had set ourselves on the fringes of society and were lucky enough and rich enough not to pay the price."

I am not embarrassed now. I am glad to be able to tell them all this. It is a new sort of freedom of which I had a taste last night with Nan and Phil. "While you told about your lives I listened with a kind of envy, I suppose. You seem so safe even when you are, like Anna and Jennifer, dealing with dangerous subjects, subjects around which a lot of emotion and irrational fear and prejudice gather."

"The embalmed middle class," Tuffy murmurs.

"It must have been an enormous step you were, in a way, forced to take," Anna says meditatively, "and how anxiety-making at best."

"But shooting your dog!" Jennifer gets up and comes round to lay a hand on my shoulder. "By golly, that you can't take, can you? I mean, something has got to be done."

They are all listening to me intently, but I know I mustn't say anything about the detective, so I evade the subject as best I can. "Something will be done," I assure them. "My brothers, by the way, have been very supportive through all this, especially the younger one, who is gay himself. One good thing that came out of that *Globe* story is that he came over next day to talk about himself. We had never been close, so it seemed an amazing joy to be able to talk freely and be at ease with each other." I turn to them now and ask, looking from one to the other, "I suppose a great many people feel they have to conceal their true selves. I don't have to do that any more and it feels comfortable," I laugh, "when it doesn't feel dangerous."

"At sixty maybe we all have the right to be whatever we feel we are," Anna says. "My husband was very much against my going into therapy with child abusers. The whole subject filled him with such horror and disgust he hated for me to get involved . . ."

"But the point now is," Jennifer breaks in, "what can we do to help Harriet, isn't it?"

"I don't know that there is anything specific," I say quickly. "It's been a huge lift to have you turn up and to be able to talk as we are doing. I do get rather lonely at times, I must confess. I miss Vicky. I miss that kind of companionship. In the store I meet all sorts of people and they pour out their stories and I listen. That is what I dreamed would happen, that I could help make a real center for women. It's amazing the variety of people who come back again and again: nuns, kids from the colleges, old women, but then there is no one to share it all with. I do have an awfully good associate who takes the store in the mornings. I don't know what I would do without her. She bearded the police when the first threatening anonymous letter came. She is a lionheart all right. So you mustn't think of me as in sore need."

"Oh we don't," Tuffy says quickly. "It's we who are in need, not you. Somehow or other you are at the center of life in a way that none of us seem to be."

"That is so strange," I say, leaning my head on my knuckles, thinking it out, "because I have been trying to get accustomed to being on the periphery, on the fringe, where it is quite hard to stay in balance." I look over at Anna. "What has been staggering is to meet such hatred—hatred and fear, I suppose."

"They surely go together," says Sandra, who has been silent, I realize, until now.

"Will there ever be a change?" I ask. "I suppose people need someone to hate and look down on. Is that it? Or . . ." I pause to feel sure I am saying what I mean, "is the homosexual ordeal partly that it threatens almost everyone. If you are black, you are black and it is quite clear that you are, but if you are homosexual you can rather easily live a completely secret life—as my brother Andrew does. And how many people do? How many husbands stop at a bar on the way home, for example?"

"They may have done, but AIDS is changing all that, thank God," says Jennifer.

"How many women, then, feel for another woman a passion they have never experienced with their husband?"

"Many, many more than any of us have any idea exist," Sandra says. "I am one of them and it's wonderful to be able to say so for the first time in my life. How I envy you and Vicky," she turns to me.

"But I now feel we had it a little too easy. We didn't have to fight. No one could put us out of our house. As far as society goes, Vicky's money and her prestige as a publisher protected us." Could I dare say it to these old friends, so far so supportive and dear? "I am glad that I have to take my place among the persecuted. I am proud to be who I am, 'still crazy after all these years,' as Simon sings it."

Almost unbelievable that no one has interrupted our talk so

far. Nearly five now, and someone will be sure to come. I can't help wondering who it will be, but I do hope someone will come to show the store in action, to make it all come alive in the way it is meant to be.

Unfortunately, the first person to push in is Sue Bagley, ever curious. "Such a crowd!" she says, taking my friends in. "It looks like a party."

Of course now I introduce her all around and explain our connection, on both sides. "Sue is a neighbor and a great reader."

"So you all went to Smith," she says, taking off her gloves, "but I bet none of you is anything like Harriet Hatfield here. I sometimes think she is out of her mind."

"Why?" Anna bears down hard. "This is a fine bookstore. I would consider her a public servant of a rather extraordinary kind." This conversation pleases me very much. I have not been defended in such an intelligent way before. My chief defense has been to laugh at myself.

Sue Bagley looks over at me and launches into one of her monologues and there is nothing I can do. But my friends drift off to find books they may want to buy and Sue is left high and dry, though still voluble. "It is this mixture of people," she explains to the air, "so many gay people, such queer old women, so many nuns. You never know what or who you will see when you open the door."

"And I suspect," says Anna, who is sitting down and listening, or pretending to, "that is why you come in—to see what is going on, to be part of such combustion."

"Combustion!" Sue Bagley seizes on the word and repeats it loudly with a guffaw. "This woman is turning the neighborhood upside down. After they shot her dog things began to happen. It's like a small war only people are changing sides." She ends triumphantly, giving me a significant look.

"How do you know, Sue?" for now I am really interested.

"Well, you know, down at the grocery, you wait in line and people talk. I hear things like 'Whoever shot that poor woman's dog is a criminal,' whereas I used to hear, although I never told you, 'Why doesn't that crazy woman take her dirty books somewhere else?' Things like that."

"That's good news." I am amazed to hear it, actually. "And I've always said it would take time . . ."

"Only that poor dog had to be murdered. I have nightmares about it," Sue says. "Things aren't the same now she is not lying there under the desk at your feet."

It is too soon for me to talk about Patapouf's death.

"Harriet, we are going to have to tear ourselves away," Jennifer says.

"Of course. It's nearly six, but I am so glad you came! Somehow I feel I am back in my real country with you. I'm not quite the outsider I was . . ."

"We'll come back. It's been a great day!" Jennifer says.

"But we've got to pay for our books," Anna says, smiling. So they come to the register, settle up, and go off with the pile each has accumulated.

"You made some money," Sue says, after the door has closed behind them.

"The books I have to sell here are not that easy to find in suburbia. This visit gave me back some sense of what the store is about. It did me a lot of good."

"I understand that all right. I should think you'd get sick and tired of all the loonies and queers who pop in and out—that bag lady who sits for hours waiting for the bus . . ."

"Oh Sue, she's a friend! And she bought one of Martha's paintings, you know."

"She did?" Sue is not pleased to hear this, I know. She wants to be the only amateur of art connected with the store. It has taken the wind out of her sails that a poor old woman has managed somehow to buy a painting.

"She is fascinated by those roots," I explain to Sue.

It is time to lock up, and I make it clear by thanking Sue again for telling me about what people are saying, standing at the door.

"I keep my ears open," she replies, and I sense that she would have liked to sit down for a good gossip, but I am not in the mood. I want to think about my Smith friends. Why did I imagine they might be shocked or not cooperative? I suppose because I remember them as they and I were in our twenties when homosexuality was a taboo subject except for some jokes about "pansies" and Bea Lillie's song "There are fairies at the bottom of the garden." However bad things may be now, it was far worse then because we lived in total ignorance. And in any case we had lost sight of each other for thirty years or more. The women I saw this afternoon have changed, just as I have.

I climb the stairs to my flat with unaccustomed peace of mind. "All shall be well" I murmur aloud.

Only when I am sitting smoking a cigarette in the armchair and about to turn on the news, what Sue said just now, of the change of heart about me, floods in and makes me sit up straight with the shock and relief it brings me. Is it truly possible that a reaction as irrational, after all, as the reaction to the bookstore in the first place is turning the tide? The death of my dog? I cannot quite believe it, but it is interesting, to put it mildly.

The phone rings and it is Earl, who suggests that we meet at a motel in Lexington where we can talk. "I have news that will interest you," he says.

"Good heavens. I can't wait. Let's say noon, before the crowd. I just might have something that will interest you," I add.

It occurs to me as I put down the phone that Earl has been on the job for only two days. And he had said it would take him about a week.

26

Earl is late, which I find irritating because I hate waiting in public places and being stared at. When Vicky and I lived together this sort of exposure never happened as we were always together, shielded by each other. Only now since her death am I learning what Joan often talks about, the lack of identity of a person alone, and the vulnerability. "A woman alone is not invited out," she tells me. "No widow or divorcée expects this so it is quite a shock when it happens."

I sit uncomfortably on a straight chair, not daring to smoke until Earl, full of apologies, arrives. He got stuck in traffic on Route 128 after an accident. Finally we are seated at a corner table among the artificial flowers in a huge, almost empty dining room. I am waiting for the curtain to rise. It rises when the waiter brings us two scotches and takes our order. There is a slight pause.

"Miss Hatfield," Earl says, lifting his glass, "I know who shot your dog and I know why she did it. That is the interesting part—why she did it."

"Tell me," I beg, "first, who this old woman is."

"She's a very pent-up grandmother who lives in a three-decker with her married son and his wife and small daughter and her own unmarried daughter. There is little space. It is noisy, crowded, and the atmosphere is full of rage. This is a very angry woman."

"No doubt." I am living myself into her situation, trying to imagine. "How do you know she did it? It seems so strange."

"I know she did it because her son blurted it out in a bar."

"He told you?"

"Well, he gathered I was not from the neighborhood, on my way west, I explained, so he felt safe. And it became clear that his mother, whose name is Rose Donovan, is now very scared, as though you had threatened her—an interesting reversal of roles."

At this point I want the facts, not interpretation, so I say sharply, "I suppose she is afraid of being arrested or taken to court, and it is worse for her because she knows she is guilty."

"Her son, Jerry, wants to have her committed."

"He does?" At once I am on Rose Donovan's side. "She's not crazy, is she? But what angered her so much? Why did she shoot my dog? You haven't told me that."

"You sound quite cross," Earl says. He is as baffled as I am, apparently.

"I'm sorry, but from what you tell me her son is hardly *simpatico*. It might be better for him and his wife and baby to move out than to have his mother committed because she is in the way. Yes, I am cross. Women never get a break."

Earl goes on with his story. "When I asked Jerry, over a third beer, why she shot your dog he mumbled something about the gun first. It had belonged to her husband, his father, and she won't part with it. He is afraid of the gun in the house, and with good reason."

"All he has to do is take it and sell it," I suggest.

At this, Earl, for the first time, relaxes a little and smiles at me as he explains, "He is more afraid of her anger than of the gun, you see. There is such a thing as a holy terror, and she appears to be it."

"But why did she shoot my dog? You still haven't told me."

Unfortunately at this moment food is served and there has to be a short pause with a fill-in of small talk.

"Why did she shoot your dog?" Earl looks at me meditatively. "I can't be brief," he says. "It's complicated."

I light a cigarette. I can't eat. "Make it long if you must, but begin somewhere."

"Rose's son's friends boasted that they were going to drive you out after some woman from the church discovered *Pure Lust* in the store and took it to the police. From then on the gossip about you spread like wildfire. You were running an obscene bookstore and with the *Globe* interview headline they felt more and more justified in harassing you."

"To the point of murdering my dog?" I am not convinced, ugly as it all is to hear.

"Rose Donovan had at last found a rationale for her rage, but I feel sure she didn't imagine shooting your dog at first, and in fact did not enter the scene until verbal attacks against you were the stuff of gossip all over the community."

I feel nauseated. Put bluntly, as Earl does, it is sickening that I have been pilloried and jeered at in bars. "What explains her violence then? What went on in her head? I don't get it."

"Jealousy," he says laconically.

"Jealousy? How can she be jealous of me?"

"Because, don't you see, you have stood your ground, and not been scared off, because you are rich and can do whatever you want to do, because you are a lady."

"Oh stuff and nonsense!"

"I'll try to explain. I know it sounds crazy. In the first place, the young men who began it all by writing obscenities on the store windows and later stealing your firewood boasted that they were going to have you out of there in a few weeks, then some guy who was jogging past attacked them and using karate or something knocked one of them flat with a twist of his wrist."

"Yes, that was Joe. He and his friend Eddie used to stop and clean up for me when they went jogging every morning. I suppose those boys were pretty mad. But I am puzzled. What started them writing obscenities in the first place?"

"The typical antagonism toward a stranger. I don't believe they care a hoot about what books you sell. But later they capitalized on latent antagonism and even fear." Earl stops to light a small cigar and looks at me as though sizing me up. "Miss Hatfield, I got an earful in all those hours I spent in bars and joints. Homophobia seems to be the local obsession."

"So they are out to get me." I swallow what is left of my scotch. "But from what you said earlier, Rose is scared now herself. Shooting my dog was a rather stupid thing to do."

"Yes, it was. But by then she was furious because you had not been scared off and she decided to take things into her own hands. You and what seems to be your immunity to threats and active antagonism made her boil. What the boys could not do, she was jolly well going to show that she could do. What mere men could not achieve, she, an old woman, would achieve."

I could see it all so clearly now that it made me laugh, and then feel as though I were going to cry. "I think I had better have some coffee, Earl. All this is rather a lot to take in."

"I am sorry," he says, signaling the waiter, "but you have to know."

"Of course. In fact you are to be congratulated on managing to dig all this out so fast. Go on."

"The good news is that Rose made a fatal mistake. Somehow or other shooting your dog, an old dog, whom many of the neighbors had seen you walking, changed some minds. Maybe fifty percent of the people who appeared to be rabid about homosexuals were outraged by Rose's violent act. I sometimes wonder whether if you had been shot they would have reacted as passionately. 'An innocent old dog,' I heard one workman say, 'that woman is a monster.' "

"It is all so upside down," I murmur, "so irrational. How does one handle the irrational?"

"That," Earl says with a smile, "remains to be seen."

"How is she to be stopped? I guess what troubles me most is that I have been attacked in so many ways for so long, ostensibly because I am a lesbian and run a bookstore which contains dangerous feminist books, and now it appears that all this is a kind of game. I am not attacked as a righteous cause, but simply as a rich woman who can be baited and perhaps driven away. It makes me sick." I am not smiling and he senses, I hope, that humor on his part would make me furious.

He is very quiet and waits a moment before saying, " 'How is she to be stopped?' you ask. I can't really answer that, you know. My job is to get the facts and after that decisions can be made by you and your lawyer and your brother."

"But what do you think?" I press him.

"If you'll promise to keep it under your hat, I'll tell you what I think. Rose Donovan is being harassed and attacked whenever she goes out and must be close to a nervous breakdown. It is possible that if your lawyer and your brother had a talk with her, she could be persuaded to give up herself, go away somewhere for a while."

"Rose Donovan give up? You're kidding!" For by now I have imagined a Rose Donovan with whom I feel a certain bond. It happened when Earl told me her son wanted to commit her. "I guess it sounds crazy, but in some peculiar way I find myself on her side. I wish I could see her and have a talk with her, make friends . . ."

"There, Miss Hatfield, I'm afraid you are a sentimentalist. You have become, for various reasons, the channel for her anger, an obsessive anger. It's quite possible that if the case goes to court she might be taken under observation. A nice little talk, in which your very way of talking would be an affront, your expensive shoes, your whole upper-class manner, could make matters a lot worse than they are."

I had never been aware of any of these things—upper-class manner? "I guess I can see that I am unforgivable." This whole conversation has been so unexpectedly painful, so baffling, I feel I have stepped on a hornet's nest.

"By the way," I ask, as it whirls up in my mind, "why did those goons not go after Joe after he threw one of them down?"

"Because they're cowards," Earl says coldly.

"Which Rose Donovan is not."

"Right."

"Is there anything else you have to tell me?" I ask. I am now anxious to get home. If only Patapouf were there! I need to take something loved in my arms, I feel so lonely and tired suddenly. And full of tears I must not allow to flow. Patapouf had to die so the hatred could be healed. It seems freshly cruel after all I have just heard.

"It's been hard to say all I have," Earl says, "but if you can bear with me for another minute, I do have something to tell you and perhaps I should have done so in the beginning."

I prepare myself for shock by quite consciously shutting down the capacity to feel. I light a cigarette. "What, then?"

"As you have gathered, I have made it a point to get into conversation with every Tom, Dick, and Harry on the street, in the bars and joints, in lines at the IGA. Now and then your dog came up, and from there, some talk about what kind of woman you are. I was quite amazed at how often what came through was a sort of reluctant affection. People said things like 'Well, she's a fighter all right. She can't be scared off.' Or, once a tough young construction worker said, 'She's doing what she thinks is right, against the odds, you might say. Doggone it, you have to give her that.' "

"It's those people, non-readers I presume, whom I wish I could reach. There's been little substantive talk at the store, Earl. It's mostly people telling me their lives."

This made Earl laugh. "All this and substantive talk too?"

"Oh very well, I'm a dodo."

"You're not a dodo," Earl says, "but just what you are I do not know. One of a kind, that's for sure."

Before we part it is agreed that Earl call Jonathan and arrange a meeting to talk things over. "Maybe better if I am not there," I suggest. "Right now I feel chiefly bewildered and must confess I haven't a clue as to what should or can be done at this point. Though my dog has been murdered I am still a lesbian, Earl. There is still homophobia in this community. Won't it rise again in some other way?"

"No doubt it will, but a small change has taken place in some minds and I call that a victory. By that I mean that some people no longer simply label you. They think of you as Harriet Hatfield, a specific person who is grieving for her dog. The stereotype has, at least in some cases, given way to a real person whom they know."

"You are comforting, Earl. You do not seem at all like a detective."

"I do smoke a pipe, however," he says, taking his out and filling it.

"So you do, but, Earl, I must get home now."

"Of course. Sorry," and he puts the pipe back in his pocket while I signal the waiter to bring us the bill, and when I have paid it, he takes me back to my car and we say goodbye.

My head is buzzing with undigested images and facts, but my

287

chief reaction to Earl's tale is one of irritation and letdown. Once more, I think to myself, the human situation is so much more real than any ideology or preconceived interpretation that it staggers me. Here I have been imagining myself on the frontier against homophobia and it turns out to be chiefly one woman's jealousy because I wear expensive shoes and have an upper-class way of speaking. Damn it all!

I must call Joe and have a talk with him. Even though it has been only three days, it seems ages since we have talked. I do not even know how Eddie is doing. Andrew has not been in to see me, and I need to talk to someone who understands why what is good news upsets and depresses me. The only thing to do at present is laugh at myself because now that catastrophe may have been averted, I feel limp, and somehow disappointed. It is called, I remind myself, falling on your face.

27

In the last two weeks there has been time to live a little, to look around me, to enjoy talking to the people who drop in, to be leading at last a more or less normal life. There has been a respite even from facing decisions to do with Earl's uncovering of the culprits, and no call from Jonathan to tell me what is going on. For a little while I am allowed off the hook.

One day I went to the animal hospital and fetched Patapouf's ashes, such a small light box to contain such a precious life! Now I need to bury her safely in Angelica's garden and presume that can be accomplished soon. That is on my mind but very little else. I have not even called Joe lately, knowing that Andrew is there a great deal and there is little, if anything, I can do.

Then Joan tells me when I come down for my afternoon stint one day that Andrew has called to say he may drop in later this afternoon, and I hope there will be better news.

Before she leaves I ask her, "How are we getting on with a window about people and animals, by the way?"

"Not very well. There are lots of books about pets but rather little on the subject that I would call literature."

"Ah, I'll get back to that list," I murmur. "So long, Joan."

I am jotting down titles, and in a state of objective bliss as I note *Flush,* by Virginia Woolf, the biography of Beatrix Potter, and, with some hesitation, *My Dog Tulip.* I am thinking about Ackerley's book and wondering whether I really want it on the list when Andrew wanders in. I see at once that he is upset. He looks quite white and throws himself down in a chair by the table in a rather dramatic way, which is unlike him, his head leaning on his hand.

Since he says nothing, I say, "It's good to see you, Andrew. How are things with Eddie? I take it you have come from there."

"They're horrible," Andrew says. "He is suddenly much worse." Then with a groan he adds, "Joe says he is lucky that Eddie is already so ill, with a high fever at times, pain everywhere, because the worst is when AIDS takes a year of suffering. I can't see how Eddie can last much longer."

"You are there a lot?"

"I'm there when Joe can't be, which is often most of the day."

"What about your job?"

"I told them I had to have time off. It did not go down very well and the chances are I won't have a job when this is over. Harriet, you understand, don't you?" he lifts his head and looks at me intensely. "I can't leave that boy to die alone, to die such a dreadful death alone."

"Have you been able, you and Joe, to get someone from Hospice?" I am thinking, of course, of Bettina Morgan, that wonderful woman who sang songs to her patient all night to help her die.

"I don't think Joe has been in touch with Hospice, but I'll ask him. At least he is with Eddie all night, and when he is at his office I'm there. It works out."

"You have changed, Andrew." I have been observing him

closely since he walked in distraught and flung himself into the chair.

"Have I?" He pretends to be surprised and then throws that mask away. "Of course I have. I have to be more than I can be. I can't sleep, trying to erase the images of pain, the ugliness of pain. Eddie has open lesions inside his thighs now. He talks about being a leper. He hardly has strength to curse as he did at the beginning. Anger is being tortured out of him."

"Impossible to accept. How do you handle it?"

"I was doing pretty well until today. Today Joe told me their landlord is trying to get them evicted. Their lease has six months to go but the landlord says they are a threat to the community's health. Can you believe the meanness of people?"

"I have reason to."

"Of course you do. I'm sorry, Harriet. I guess all this blots everything else out. Has that woman who shot Patapouf been found? Where does all that stand?"

But he is not really able to listen and I am not in the mood to talk about it. "Surely the landlord can be sued if he breaks the lease?"

"Maybe, but those two guys don't need a legal battle at this point. Joe is on the thin edge of breakdown. He becomes so furious at small things you can imagine his black rage. I am terrified that he'll let go somehow and give the landlord a taste of what karate can achieve. I had literally to hold him down just now when he told me about it." (

"That doesn't sound like Joe," I murmur. "Joe always seems so serene and wise and on top of things."

"He is when it comes to patients. I should say he still is, but where Eddie is concerned he's an open wound himself."

"They've lived together so long and in such amity, it doesn't seem fair."

Andrew lifts his head and there is such pain in his eyes I have to look down while he strikes his clenched fist on the table. "A few casual encounters in a bar, and now all those years of real caring go up in smoke. That is what Joe is facing, and the inability to talk it out with Eddie is eating him up. Can you blame him?"

"Eddie or Joe?"

"Joe, of course. He watches his lover die because of sexual encounters that didn't mean anything at the time. He sees a man committing suicide, one might say, in brief moments of lust. Joe has become bitter inside, but so far he has held the demons down. He's a disciplined person. I do admire him, Harriet."

"But somehow you identify with Eddie—that is what I sense. I may be wrong."

"I suppose I love Eddie. He is like a piece of me. I told you when we first talked about my world that I don't want a permanent relationship, that I prefer to pick someone up for one night." Saying this he gives a short bark which is, I presume, a laugh. "Not possible these days. Too dangerous."

"I have to admit, Andrew, that I don't understand it and never will." I soften this by quickly adding, "But I think I do understand that there has been an earthquake in your orderly surroundings."

"Yes. It was time for an earthquake." He smiles at me at last, coming back to normal, some of the stress melted away for the moment. "I'm learning quite a lot, Harriet. A lot that is painful, as you can imagine."

"Yes, I can. I'm learning a lot, too, these days."

"My remarkable sister." He is smiling at me in an almost fatherly way, as if I were the younger one.

"I have observed that people treat me often as you seem to, as a slightly retarded person who manages somehow to live a normal life. There are liabilities to being an innocent."

My response is not what Andrew expects and he is taken aback. "I didn't mean it that way, for heaven's sake! What's got into you, Harriet?" He studies my face very intently. "I think you are one of the bravest people I ever encountered, and I honor you for it." Now he smiles a mischievous smile. "Fred, of course, does think you are mildly off your rocker."

"All I can say, Andrew, is that most of what I hoped would happen for the bookstore is happening—I mean as a human endeavor. I am still ignorant about a lot of things I should know, still haven't read two-thirds of what I should, but it is all immensely interesting. I am never bored and, as I said just now, I am learning a lot about other people and about myself."

"And what more can one ask?" He is still smiling at me, but then he frowns and settles back in his chair and rubs his forehead. "I'm not as lucky as you are, Harriet, for what I am learning about myself is not very pretty, I must say. Getting to know Eddie and Joe is forcing me to change everything or almost everything about the way I am living and have lived. It's almost gruesome."

"Really? Of course growth is painful. You are being forced to grow, aren't you? It seems like a religious conversion. Forgive me if that sounds stupid. It's what happens when one begins to think aloud. But what's so good is that we can think aloud with each other. Would you ever have imagined that when you put thumbtacks in my chair and knocked down my snowman?"

"It's awesome to think how horrible I was." But both images as we remember them make us burst into laughter.

"Pretty hard to take."

"You used the word 'conversion.' It's not unlike that in a way. I am confronted over there by something I have never imagined possible."

"What? True love?"

"Not exactly. The phrase that haunts me is 'exemplary lives.' On the whole gay men do not lead exemplary lives. There is too much tension about sex. The drive to indulge that side at the expense of every other is too powerful, I suppose. Things like Joe's fidelity are new to me and the responsibility gays have toward each other. Joe is such a compassionate person, Harriet. I watch him with Eddie, the way he takes Eddie in his arms and leans Eddie's head against his shoulder and just stays there for a long time, and sometimes Eddie goes to sleep. Sleep is the best present he can be given now. Sometimes when I am reading aloud he falls asleep and I keep right on for fear he may wake up." Now Andrew's eyes narrow and he leans his chin on his right fist. "When he wakes, all hell breaks loose. Pain is always there, and fear, the fear of dying. Sometimes he cries and I wonder when Joe will ever get home to rescue me. That's how selfish and inadequate I am."

"It sounds to me as though you have become as necessary as some relieving drug. What would they do without you, Andrew?"

"That's what Joe says, but for Eddie I am mostly a receptacle for bitterness and woe. To me he can let off steam and curse when he wants to."

"And that spares Joe. They are lucky to have you and I think you must occasionally put a laurel on your head and admit that. Otherwise you would be a saint. Who wants that?"

"I don't, that's for sure. What I want is the kind of love they have but I don't suppose I'll ever find it." Now he looks up, a bright quick glance at me. "You and Vicky had it, didn't you?"

"Yes, I think we did, but it wasn't perfect, Andrew—no relationship is."

"You must miss her terribly."

"I do." I wonder whether to go in a little more deeply to prevent Andrew from building up an illusion of perfect love.

Why not be honest? "Especially at night, or when I am dying to talk something over, I feel awfully lonely. Now that Patapouf is not here—she was the last link between us—it is worse. But, Andrew, I am more myself, I am more of a whole person now than when I was a kind of appendage to Vicky. She dominated our life and I willingly went along with it. We were happy and peaceful, but we were also shut off from a lot of things. So it is not so much mourning and missing her now as building and moving forward into what feels like my real life."

"I am too old for all that," Andrew says. "I'm an old man, Harriet."

"Nonsense, you're ten years younger than I am!"

But Andrew is not in the mood for teasing. "Do you really believe that in any successful relationship one person dominates?"

"It looks that way. Joe dominates Eddie, partly because Eddie is so much younger. The strange thing is that I think Mother dominated Father."

Andrew chuckles, "At least he let her think that was true."

"It doesn't matter, does it? I mean, if the relationship is life-giving for both parties, who cares who dominates?"

"No doubt that is wisdom, but I don't buy it, Harriet."

"You sound like your old self, Andrew, always putting your sister down."

"Frankly I don't understand how you can say first that Vicky dominated your lives and that seemed perfectly fine, and then say that you are now able to live your real life. It doesn't make sense. What is your real life, anyway?"

Spoken like that, so rationally, I have to admit that it does not make sense, but I can try, for my own sake as well as his, to answer the last question. "I'll try to tell you, Andrew. Maybe my real life has to do with other people, with being available to other people, with stretching to meet lives totally apart from mine. Here in the store there are no walls. Vicky and I lived very happily not caring what was happening beyond our walls, you see. Maybe we did not want to know, did not want to get involved . . ." I must be honest, I tell myself. "At least Vicky did not want life in any disturbing shape to knock at our door."

"She was quite a person," Andrew muses. "She terrified me, of course. I expect she didn't much like having your family around."

"I think she may have been a little jealous. After all, she was an only child, and in a funny way she demanded that I be an only child."

"Curiouser and curiouser."

"One thing I am learning is that people are stranger and more mysterious than one can imagine." I am tempted to tell him about Rose Donovan but feel I had better wait till Fred and Jonathan and possibly another lawyer have met with Earl. Not telling Andrew cramps my style. I hate not telling him, and he no doubt senses some barrier and gets up to go. "I hate to see you go, Andrew. At least give me a hug." The hug is warm and very satisfactory. "Whatever I may say, I do get awfully lonely. So when you come it's always good and nourishing. I guess it's lonely for you, Andrew."

"I don't know why."

"Because they are two and you are one, but you are the needed one. Not easy, I should think."

"It's hell," he says, letting me go. "So long, Harriet. Enjoy your real life."

28

After I'm in bed Earl calls to say there will be a meeting at Jonathan's office to hear and discuss what he has to report—at eleven o'clock tomorrow. I am glad to think that something will be decided, but I wonder what, and how Rose Donovan and her sons can be tamed or removed, at least for a while, from the vicinity. It flashes through my mind that Joe would be a wonderful person to talk with her, but I guess it is too much to lay that on him at the moment. I go to sleep finally, uneasy and undecided.

I decide to be a little late and call Fred to warn him and explain that I've heard the whole strange story from Earl so there's no point in my being on time at the meeting. "He is quite a wizard to have found out all that he has. I am impressed and awfully glad you and Jonathan persuaded me to get a detective."

So when I walk in at a quarter to twelve I find the three men I know and a fourth, a Mr. Firestone, who turns out to be a lawyer Jonathan asked to join us to "give us his wisdom," as Jonathan explains. Firestone is a heavyset, square-faced, owlish man.

"Proud to meet you, Miss Hatfield," he says as we shake hands.

"I don't know why, but I'm glad you are," I say. We are seated in a semicircle around Jonathan's huge desk. "Isn't this an amazing story Earl has unearthed?" I say to Jonathan, and then turn to Fred, who is on my left, and ask him, "Can you believe it?"

"You have stepped on a hornet's nest all right," Fred answers, "but then you have been crazily honest."

"Let's get down to business," Jonathan interrupts. It is not the place for family squabbling.

Mr. Firestone turns to me. "We must, I feel, if possible, keep this whole business out of the courts."

"I wouldn't get a fair trial? Is that it?" I am really furious inside. Here we are back in the maze of homophobia. It makes me sick.

"Well"—Firestone's "well" is a long drawn-out "well"—"I wouldn't say that, but some of the material that would have to come up is inflammatory. Why take a risk?"

"But if we don't go to court, what do we do?" I ask. "I do hope those devilish boys will get their comeuppance."

"It is Rose Donovan who is the real problem," Jonathan says.

"Luckily," Fred interrupts, "from what Earl says, she is terrified now and is getting her punishment from the community. Her neighbors have rejected her because she shot your dog. Who would have believed that Patapouf's death, poor thing, would prove to be such a help?"

"What can we do?" I ask Firestone. He appears to be in command, undaunted by Jonathan's formidable desk. "All I want is to get the whole thing settled so I can go on with my work in peace. We are just about making a go of the bookstore, but there is a lot to be done. This whole mess has been distracting."

"To put it mildly," Firestone says, smiling broadly. "Many women in your place would have moved away."

"Maybe," I answer, "but I think most women would have decided to tough it out as I have. If Rose Donovan were me I feel sure she would do as I am doing, not give in, not be scared off, stick to her guns."

The word "guns" causes a ripple of amusement, but it is brief as Jonathan proposes that Firestone pay a call on Mrs. Donovan and put the fear of God into her. That must include her sending the boys to his office within twenty-four hours. Otherwise, Firestone will make it clear that we have evidence, witnesses, and are prepared to go to court.

"I'm still puzzled," I say, as I try to sort out this plan. It sounds a little too easy, maybe, to work. "Who first bought the so-called obscene book and took it to the police? Either Joan or I would have been aware, I think, that this was no ordinary customer. Something would have given her or him away."

"The police must know," Earl says, "and of course I did not talk to them."

"When Joan and I asked, they were very evasive. We got nowhere. I remember how I felt when we walked back—cross, put down, and treated like a crazy old woman."

"When the wood was stolen," Fred asks, "how did the police behave?"

"As usual, voluminous notes were taken, but nothing whatever was done, as far as I know. By then, of course, Rose Donovan was egging those boys on. I can't help laughing when I realize how infuriated she must have been when the wood was replaced the very next day." I am laughing to think of it. "Whatever has gone wrong I have to admit people have been supportive and kind. That's one reason I want to stay. People have invested in the shop. They feel it is theirs as well as mine. Can you understand?" I ask Firestone.

"I am beginning, perhaps, to understand that your endeavor is rather more complex and more interesting than just an ordinary bookstore." He directs this remark to Fred actually, although it is addressed to me.

"Thanks. But, Mr. Firestone, are we getting near to a solution? Since Patapouf's death there is a less hostile atmosphere in the neighborhood, but is anything going to be settled?"

"Do you mind if I smoke?" Firestone asks, before he answers my question.

"Of course not. I smoke myself."

"Like one of these?" He offers me an elegant cigar case.

"Well, I'm not Amy Lowell, I'm afraid, but thanks just the same."

"I'd like to see what I can do rather quietly behind the scenes if you all feel I can be trusted. I am pretty sure we have them on the run, you know. They may even be glad to be given an out, since they are now the hunted and the despised, and, except for Rose Donovan, they appear to be cowards."

"By the way, Hal," Jonathan says then, "we've got to get hold of that gun. She can't hang around with a gun any longer."

"That," Firestone answers with absolute certainty, "I know the police will act on. Stupid as they have been, they are aware that a loose gun in the hands of someone not quite sane is a threat to them as well as to anyone else."

"What I would like to see," I say suddenly, although it has been on my mind since yesterday, "is Rose Donovan freed from her son and his wife and baby who are making her life hell, from what Earl told me yesterday."

"Well, we are not officials in family services," Jonathan says dryly. "I'm afraid this is one case where your passion to help people is a little out of line."

I am silenced. He is right of course. It is agitating to behave foolishly. Now I add, "When we are more or less in the clear I intend to give a party for the neighborhood, maybe have an accordion there. Don't laugh at me, Fred."

"I'm not laughing. I am simply in a state of astonishment. Your dog is shot, your store is threatened, you have survived many weeks in a state of siege, and you decide to give a party!"

"Vicky would understand." Vicky is my big gun, especially where Jonathan is concerned. But it is not a lie. Vicky loved to do things with panache, to amaze people. And an accordion and a keg of beer would certainly have panache in this neighborhood. It will go very well with the window on animal friends. Perfect.

Jonathan has been doodling on a pad for the last few minutes and is obviously impatient. Now he puts his pencil down and says rather sternly, "Are we all in agreement that Mr. Firestone, with Earl's help, simply goes about the business of some sort of settlement with Mrs. Donovan, out of court?"

Everyone says yes, but I realize, having said so, that I don't really know what we are asking—that they leave us alone? That they pay some reasonable sum that will cover the buying and stacking of the wood? That in fact they give up harassing me in any way? But when I ask Firestone these questions I am told these are legal matters and must be left to him.

"We have to strike now while there is still a lot of anger about Rose shooting your dog. This is the moment to begin to turn things around," he says, "but the culprits are no doubt in a rather different state of mind from the neighborhood in general. They are never going to be sweetness and light, but it may be that we can scare them into behaving themselves. They will have to pay a considerable sum—not only a cord of wood is involved, but the harassment and the killing of your dog. That is what they will have to pay for. That is what this is all about really, isn't it, Miss Hatfield?"

"Yes, I suppose it is," I say doubtfully, because punishing them is not going to change their hatred and contempt and that is what my deepest dream is. "It's a hateful business."

Fred reaches over and puts an arm around my back. "You really have no options, Harriet. Either you sell out and move somewhere else, which is what they want, of course, or they get punished and shut up, don't you see? It's one or the other, win or lose."

"I suppose it is," I say grudgingly. What had seemed so clear and such good news when Earl talked with me now looms like some repulsive monument to hatred and injustice. I dislike having become the hunter rather than the hunted, but there is no question in my mind that I must stick it out, and at least I sense that Firestone will be a powerful man to have on our side. That is a piece of luck.

I can hardly wait to escape back into my real life at the store, and it is almost time to relieve Joan, who will be anxious to hear what has happened.

She is delighted with the news. "A case in Massachusetts—it wouldn't get to court for at least sixteen weeks, you know. You'll be saved all that suspense and publicity as well. It is, I do believe, a sound way of going about this unfortunate mess."

"It's a long time since it all began, isn't it? And in all that time the store has been slowly gathering customers and friends. They have not got us out! I must say, Joan, I am proud of us."

"You have every right to be, but . . ." She hesitates.

"But what?"

"Homophobia is not going to go away."

"I know . . . and I must call Joe. You know the landlord is trying to put them out of their apartment because Eddie has AIDS."

Joan is putting on her coat and getting ready to leave. "Harriet," she says severely, "please don't leap into another neighborhood war."

"But I must. This afternoon I plan to write a letter to the

mayor." I sound calm and determined, but in fact I am ruffled and longing suddenly to talk with Angelica, someone who has known me a long time and will not try to change the original animal or paint out the leopard's spots.

Joan laughs now. "After all this you still take me by surprise. Of course I should have known . . ." She waves quite amicably as she leaves, and now I am happily alone.

I call Angelica at once and ask whether I can come after I close the store and, at last, bury Patapouf's ashes.

"Come for supper, but come as early as you can. It gets dark so early now, but at least we can decide on the right place. I have been looking around and think perhaps under the dogwood tree, but you must decide, dear Harriet."

That settled, I hang up and sit for a while just thinking about Patapouf and crying because it is so unjust that by dying she brought about change. By dying she did what had seemed impossible, softening the hearts that had been so angry and cold. It has been a high price to pay for peace of mind. I miss my dog day and night. It doesn't seem to be a pain that lessens with time because she is so present under my desk, on my bed, barking her deep-throated bark if she thought I might be in danger. She is seldom absent from my consciousness.

Why did this horror happen? Why did Patapouf die? Fred used the phrase "your crazy honesty" and it jabs at me. Why is it crazy to be honest? Because, I suppose he meant, you can bring harm to others, you inevitably involve others. Patapouf, in fact, might be alive if I had not "come out," as they say, in that *Globe* interview. No, I tell myself, it would be crazy . . . what is crazier than false guilt, neurotic guilt? That's what it would be if I persuaded myself that I am responsible for Patapouf's being shot.

"Come to your senses, Harriet!" I admonish myself. Now that Patapouf is no longer there I am often embarrassed to be talking to myself. I used to pretend at least that I was talking to her, and the thump of her tail on the floor when she heard my voice suggested that she thought so too.

All afternoon people come and go. Nan flies in with a piece of apple pie for me; Sue Bagley with the staggering news that Rose Donovan may be leaving town; and for the first time in ages, Bettina Morgan, that wonderful woman who works for Hospice. She buys several books. "I need some nourishment," she says, looking awfully tired. She comes and goes before I have a chance to find out how she is doing with the dying boy, before I have time to talk with her about Eddie. A little girl, very shy, brings me a carefully handwritten note which says "I am very sorry about your dog. Jennifer."

"That is such a kind letter, Jennifer. Thank you."

She is blushing to the roots of her carefully plaited hair. "My dog's name is Buster," she informs me as her mother, who has followed her in, drags her away saying, as they leave, "Jennifer wanted to write you. It was her own idea."

After they have gone I look at my watch and it is time at last to lock up. I shan't even bother to change but charge off to Angelica's through the traffic. The small square box that contains all that is left of Patapouf lies on the seat beside me.

But it is not only Patapouf who is behind this need to see Angelica, it is the need for someone who has known me for a long time, for the friend who has become, especially in these last months, like family. I have been rather lonely these past days, more so than ever since Vicky's death and I do not quite know why.

29

Angelica is waiting for me in the dusk. The garden looks very romantic and my eye goes at once to the dogwood she mentioned. It stands against a high brick wall. For a moment, letting the whirl of traffic fall away, I stand and drink in the autumn smell of earth and leaves.

"Welcome, darling Harriet," Angelica says. Then, as her eye catches the box in my hands, she adds, "and Patapouf who will abide with me."

"Oh Angelica." It overtakes me suddenly, the grief, the sense of the ending of so much, "I am disintegrating so fast I don't know what to do with myself."

"Doesn't sound like you," she says. "You are simply dead tired, and no wonder. What you need is a drink. We can bury the dear thing later."

"No, we must do it now," I say. "I feel I can't face it later. Besides, it is so peaceful now in the half light."

"Do you like this spot under the dogwood? You see, I put a stake to mark the place I thought would be right."

"That's fine," I say. "Give me the trowel."

I kneel down, find the earth good and damp so it is easy to dig a fairly deep hole, while Angelica gives me advice or, what I most appreciate, watches over me like the guardian angel she is and has been for so long.

"Take your time, Harriet. You're out of breath."

"I'm all right. It's nearly done. I long to know she is safely in the earth." But when I open the box Angelica sits down beside me, apologizing for not being able to kneel.

"It's a little awkward," she says, "but I couldn't bear to be standing so far away up in the air." For some reason this statement makes me laugh. "It's not funny," she says, somewhat taken aback.

"I know," but I am bursting at the seams with laughter, a wild gust of laughter like a seizure. And at that moment a slight breath of wind blows some of the ashes out of my hand as I turn the box upside down to let them fall. I am not laughing as I fill in the hole. It seems much harder and sadder than digging it was. Neither of us says anything. What is there to say?

I get up clumsily. Angelica lets me help her up and then hugs me hard. "Come in, come in."

Before we open the front door, I turn back and whisper, "Goodbye, Patapouf." It is permissible to cry at that so final moment, and I do.

"Here's a Kleenex," Angelica says, pulling one out of her pocket. "You sit down by the fire. I expect the chill out there has got into your bones. I'll fetch us a drink."

When she comes back and we are settled I look across at her, how smooth and seamless her face still is, not a line to be seen. It makes me happy to see old age in its beauty, which is, after all, rather rare. "You know, Angelica, you are so beautiful, it is a lesson in something, but I don't know what."

"Laziness and Ivory soap," she says, laughing gently.

"I feel very old," I say by way of explanation. "It's not how I look—people tell me I look fine—it's that something has gone

out of me in these last months. I have come to the end of some-
thing I can't define."

"It's partly of course that your job, the whole complex of the
bookstore in that neighborhood, is frightfully and continuously
demanding. I don't know how you have survived. Perhaps you
should see a doctor, have a general checkup."

"The strange thing is that I was in good fighting shape—noth-
ing like anger to get the adrenaline to flow—until things got
settled."

"Are they settled?"

"Of course, you don't know! I had to keep it a secret but Fred
and Jonathan persuaded me to hire a detective. In less than a
week he found out who shot Patapouf and why, and who the
goons are who wrote obscenities on the windows. So we are all
set."

"To go to court?" Angelica says, obviously distressed.

"Oh no, the lawyer who is advising us is against going to court
and thinks he can calm things down and settle out of court."

"All this has been going on, and you didn't tell me!"

"I couldn't, Angelica, I couldn't tell anyone."

"Well," she says, a little disgruntled, "who shot Patapouf?"

"An old woman called Rose Donovan, and I am rather at sea
about why she did it. The detective says she became furious
because after all the harassment she and two boys, her son and a
friend of his, perpetrated, I held out and was not frightened off.
She went berserk with what amounts to jealousy. She hates me
because I wear expensive shoes!"

"Do you?" Angelica asks. "I've never noticed."

I'm embarrassed to admit it but I do. "Vicky loved expensive
shoes, and I guess I followed suit."

"But surely Rose Donovan must have been full of fear and
hatred of the bookstore itself and all you stand for. Jealousy does
not sound right to me."

"I've thought a lot about it, Angelica, and I believe Earl—that is the detective—got to the truth. It all began with hatred of a newcomer who seemed a threat because of the kinds of books she sells and the kind of people the store caters to. They thought it would be easy to drive this old lesbian out, but when they couldn't, and when after the firewood was stolen the cellar was full by the end of the next day, I guess they were frustrated and exasperated. Apparently Rose Donovan inherited the rifle from her husband. It is a fetish."

"Why haven't the police taken it away from her long ago? She's a menace."

"After Earl told me about it, and about the strange, angry household in a three-decker where Rose lives with her son and his wife and baby—I know you will laugh at me, Angelica—but all I could think of was how we might get the children out. Rose seems to be worn out and in a perpetual state of fury!"

"I'm not laughing because it is so like you to be anxious about someone who has done you so much harm. That is your way, Harriet, and it does make me smile."

"If only I could somehow get to meet her and have a talk, you know?"

This time Angelica does laugh. "You may be irresistible in some instances, Harriet, but I fear in this one you might find yourself hopelessly at sea!"

I know she is right, but Rose Donovan is becoming an obsession. "Angelica, I feel at sixes and sevens and that is the truth. If only Sue Bagley is right. She came in this afternoon to tell me she heard Rose may be moving out."

Angelica sighs. "It's just too bad that your first months with the bookstore have had to be like this. Have you ever thought of moving to a different neighborhood?"

"Never." Her question makes me feel badgered and cross. "It's been two months of revelation. In some ways it has been exactly as I imagined—all sorts of people discovering the store, all kinds of women discovering each other, and even Fred and Andrew turning into real brothers. I never thought of that as a possibility."

"That is the positive side," Angelica says, but other things are on her mind and I can guess what they are.

"As for the threats and attacks, I must admit that there have been times when I felt pretty low in my mind."

"But not frightened?"

"Oh yes, frightened, but, Angelica, the frightening, upsetting things are really part of the whole experience. I am learning a lot about myself, you know. I am being stretched as a human being every day. What is the word? I come on it everywhere these days—'self-actualization.'"

"Oh, one of those words," Angelica says lightly. "What it means God only knows."

"I think I do know," I answer. "I mean I am living it now, this year, in this time, in this place. I have changed. Have you noticed?"

She looks at me quizzically. "I can't say I have really. Except," she ponders this, "except that you seem surer of yourself, I suppose. It quite amazes me how you handle the store and everything else. I couldn't possibly do what you do."

"I'm carried along on a kind of excitement. I never know what is going to happen next."

"I would hate that," Angelica says. "I like my steady routine. Besides, it must be exhausting. How do you ever get to sleep with so much buzzing around in your head?"

"It's much harder without Patapouf."

"You must get another dog. I'd like to give you one."

"Dear heart," I say quickly, to prevent any such idea from being acted upon, "I don't want another dog. Patapouf was my dog. Vicky was my love. And that is that." We sit in silence for a

309

moment, the good silence when two people can think their own thoughts, and mine are of Angelica herself. "Of course you have been the saving grace, Angelica. I'll never forget that cake you had made for the opening, the way you are always there when I need help."

"But you seem to forget that I do not approve of everything you have done, Harriet. I am not always as supportive as I would like to be, I'm afraid."

"That is where that word comes in. I know what upsets you is what you think of as my exposure as a lesbian. You hate the word, as I used to, don't you?"

"The word itself seems to me an invasion of privacy."

"Yes, I would have agreed with you a few months ago, but when the *Globe* interview came out, and I had to face what and who I am, I felt free as I never have before. I felt 'I can be my real self' and even more than that, I felt connected in a wholly new way with all minorities—with blacks, for instance. Nan has become a real friend, and when I was invited there to dinner we talked a lot about what it does to a person to be conspicuous and possibly unwanted, disliked not for oneself, but for the color of one's hair, if you remember your Housman. That would never have happened if I had been in Nan's and her husband's eyes simply a white lady who could not possibly understand what it is to be forever an outsider. Although I have only known them for a short while, I feel that Joe and Eddie have become real friends of mine. All that is a whole new story you do not know, Angelica. But Andrew came to me after the *Globe* interview and hugged me and talked about himself as homosexual. We have never been friends, that brother and I, until now."

"You are saying, and I hear you, Harriet, that you are somehow leading a new life. Your own. I find that moving. Thanks for telling me all this. Thanks for being my friend and trusting me with it."

310

"The surprising thing," I say, taking a last swallow of my scotch, "is that what must look to you like an intrusion of disaster, a time-consuming, energy-depleting irrelevance, all this trouble and harrassment, has not taken me away from the central purpose of the bookstore. That is what talking with you so peacefully, and even burying Patapouf's ashes, has made me see this evening."

"Explain that, if you can," Angelica says. "I am totally at sea, and," she adds, "awfully hungry suddenly."

I look at my watch. "Good heavens, it is nearly eight. Let me help you put things on the table and then I'll try to explain."

"It's Alice's night out so we'll have dinner on trays by the fire. She left a casserole, and it's in the oven. Come and help me open the wine."

The trays are set and the salads all prepared in the refrigerator so there is little to do. Angelica puts another log on the fire, and as it falls on the red core of the burning logs, it shoots out sparks, and we watch it for a moment before settling in to our supper.

"So why has all this brouhaha not obtruded into your vision of what you want to do with Hatfield's bookstore for women? I am dying to know."

"Quite simply, it has been an education I never got at Smith. I have been shocked into consciousness and at a little over sixty. That is surely all to the good?"

"I suppose it is—at high cost, however." She looks across at me and meets my eyes. "But consciousness of what?" she asks.

"I guess the kind of loneliness and isolation anyone who deviates from the norm goes through. I am part of a minority, and I never took that in while Vicky was alive, so I understand a lot I never understood 'til now. Some of it is painful."

"A lot of it is painful, I should think."

"Yes, but not all. The attacks, the threats have brought me

311

real friends. By the way, Joan is wonderful. Suggesting her is another thing I must thank you for."

"I had an idea she would be a help. She is so cool and efficient."

"Yes, that's the surface, and she is very good for me because she teases me about my more extreme fantasies and acts, but she went to the police with me, you know, after that first anonymous letter. I think of her as a partner rather than an employee and must consider making that legal. I couldn't possibly manage without her now."

It occurs to me that I have not yet told Angelica about the Smith alumnae who turned up the other day and what a lift they gave me, and so I do. "I didn't have to make a bridge, you see. We are the same sort of people—at least in most ways. We had so much fun. I felt lonely after they left."

"You see," Angelica pounces, smiling across at me, "there's no substitute for old friends."

I do not answer, for I see that it is both true and untrue, and I don't want to explain. It has been such a good exchange this time.

I have not seen Joe for days and, as I look across the table at him, buttering a croissant, for he has come for breakfast, my breath is caught by the exhaustion so clearly written on his face. What can I say to this man whose lover is dying and who spends his days helping people who come to him for psychiatric counseling?

"It's been such a difficult autumn for you," he says. "I wish I could have been of some help."

"Oh Joe, you have enough on your mind—and what could you have done anyway? You and Eddie were the first people who came to help—washing obscenities off the windows. I'll never forget that!"

For the first time Joe smiles. "Eddie loved it when I knocked that astonished oaf down with a flick of my wrist! We did have a good laugh." That remembered laughter has pain in it and it shows in the way Joe gulps down half a cup of coffee.

"Andrew tells me Eddie is worse."

"It's torture," Joe says. He lights a cigarette. "But I didn't come here to talk about it. It's no good anyway. Talking just makes it worse. I came here to celebrate what I hope is the end of the torment you have lived through—and," he pauses and pours himself more coffee from the pot on the table, "to tell you about Andrew." This is said so gravely that for a moment I wonder what Andrew has done wrong.

"Is there something wrong? I know he is with Eddie a lot. Maybe that is not a good idea."

"No, no," Joe says intensely. "You have misunderstood."

"Andrew is changing."

"All I can say is he is learning about love, and he is, as far as Eddie is concerned and I am concerned, teaching us something about it by his presence in our lives—what is left of them."

"He really was a rather selfish person, wasn't he?" I venture. "When we first talked after I came out and he rushed over here to embrace me and welcome me into his world, I found him lovable. It was an epiphany for each of us."

"Yes, he talks about that."

"But then when I went to his place for dinner and everything was so elegant, I felt bewildered. He talked about not wanting a lasting love affair; he talked about the excitement of brief encounters. I suppose I should have understood better than I did. I'm afraid I already thought of you and Eddie as living exemplary lives together. Andrew did not fit into that image."

Joe has been listening intently but at the phrase "exemplary lives" he laughs a bitter laugh. "If Eddie had not gone in for casual encounters he would not be dying, Harriet."

"Oh." As usual I have rushed in where angels fear to tread. "That is hard."

"Killing!"

"What changed Andrew then? How did it happen?"

This time it is Joe who is silent, puffs at his cigarette, looks over at me, then says, with half-closed eyes, "What Andrew is learning, I think, is something about intimacy without sex, something about tenderness without passion. The words look easy, but what he is actually doing is amazing. Eddie is sometimes very difficult. He is too weak now to indulge in a tantrum, so he turns his face to the wall."

"And how does Andrew handle that?"

"By never going away. By always being there, present. I can't do it. I have to get away a lot. My patients are sometimes simply an excuse not to be there."

"But you and Eddie were so close, and have been for so many years, it is harder for you, much harder."

"God knows I see enough about guilt where the family of the dying are concerned. Who can do enough?" Again he looks at me intently. "Your brother Andrew does enough. I wanted you to know." Now Joe smiles and reaches across the table rather unexpectedly, to take my hand and hold it hard for a long moment. "That kind of grace appears to run in your family, Harriet. And I did come to be in touch with you, you know, to tell you what admiration ripples out from all you have withstood during these months of tension and anxiety."

"What else could I have done?"

"I'll tell you one thing you could have done and that is to have cried more and laughed less. People who come into your store go out refreshed and it is partly because you often laugh at some outrageous thing—that is refreshing."

"I'm an ordinary woman and I guess I laugh to break the tension. Did you know, by the way, that rumor has it that Rose Donovan, the woman who shot Patapouf, is leaving town?"

"Well, that is good news for a change!" Slowly, as we talk, Joe is letting go a little, relaxing a little, and that is good to see. Now he gives me his full attention, almost, I think, as though I were a patient. "How does it feel, Harriet, to be free at last? Not to wake at night wondering if some mouse in the wall is someone trying to break in?"

Because I feel that his interest is real, I have to be honest. "I'll never feel safe, Joe. I'll always be afraid."

Clearly he is surprised. It is not what he expected to hear. "Why, Harriet, dear Harriet, why?" and he adds quickly, "I think you are safe now. I think you have won."

"Not while your landlord is trying to put you and Eddie out, for God's sake! Not as long as people snoop around my store and look at me like some peculiar animal!" And now I do laugh aloud because what I am saying is so painful. "It is laughable to think how innocent I was, how pleased with myself to come out as I did in the *Globe* interview, and how little I could imagine what that will cost me for the rest of my life. It's worth it, Joe—I think it is, but . . ."

"You have opened a door that cannot be closed," Joe says quietly. "You call yourself an ordinary woman, but ordinary women do not do that."

It is my turn to pause and think for a moment. "What I have to hold fast to and never forget when things get tough again, as they are bound to sooner or later, is what immense human riches have come to me through that open door. The store is proving to be a true dream."

"What's a true dream?" Joe asks, smiling.

"One that can stand reality, that can be acted out, I suppose. I sometimes wonder of course what Vicky would think about it. After all, it's her money that has made it possible. I like to imagine that she would be surprised and proud, but that no doubt is wishful thinking. Many of the people I have come to treasure she would have disliked or looked down on."

"From what you have told us about your friend, I have the sense that she loved power and also that power was linked up for her with class. You do not love power. I wonder why? Eddie and I have talked about it."

"Yes, I'm delighted when I can hand power over to someone

else, and thus be free to do what I want. Power in a curious way restricts, closes the door on a lot, as you might say, Joe," and since he does not answer, "don't you agree?"

"I guess I am thinking that you do have power, Harriet—for one thing you have money—but you don't want to recognize it. Nothing wrong with that!"

"Yes, money—I forget about the money," and it feels like a shadow crossing my face. "Vicky empowered me, made it possible for me to do what I wanted to do and had it in me to do."

"But you could have chosen to go on expensive round-the-world cruises, after all. You could have bought a villa in Florence and entertained the famous." He is laughing at me. "But you empowered yourself to open a bookstore, so . . ."

"So you are letting me off the hook?"

It is a moment of vulnerability for both of us and because it is we smile at each other, then laugh. In the middle of that laughter I know that Joe is close to tears. "You took your life into your own hands and were honest. But we never did and now that it is known around that Eddie has AIDS, we have come out in spite of ourselves, forced out, as it were. I hate it."

"But Joe, I did not make any big decision. It just happened, you remember, because the interviewer recognized a news angle and used it! I am really not holier than thou, so don't give me credit for some heroic act I never made."

"The landlord is going to court on the grounds that we did not tell him we are gay and that now his premises are being poisoned."

"That is disgusting," I say passionately.

"It's a pretty lousy world, isn't it? Sometimes I envy Eddie who will soon be out of it."

"You know, Joe, the strangest thing for me to witness in all this is that there has been a significant change in the atmosphere around me and the store since Patapouf was shot. It fascinates me to think that there is a residue of compassion around that suddenly comes into view where an animal is concerned, as though the only pure thing left in this corrupt, hate-filled world is the love of animals."

Joe, I can see, is glad to have the subject changed and shows immediate interest. "The *Zeitgeist* affected by a dog's death! Amazing." He thinks it over. "Yet I can understand it. This is something they can wholly understand. Homosexuality is something they can't understand at all—hugely troubling, causing fear and hatred. It was easy to love Patapouf."

"It seems so cruel that it took her death to arouse some sympathy for me. People sometimes stop to tell me how sorry they are for what happened, and a little girl brought me a painfully written note of condolence. The trouble is that these people will never come to the bookstore and will never read anything that might trouble their minds. The store is an island in the middle of a rough sea."

As I speak, the image comes to me of how I felt about Martha's paintings when she brought them to hang in the store. For me there was something nightmarish about the network of roots under the earth around each tree. It hit me somewhere below the conscious level. Now I suddenly understand why I felt so strongly and explain the whole thing to Joe. "I think I understand now," I tell him, "why I was so upset by that image. I think it is because the roots are what the tree lives on; they cannot be changed. They are there until the tree dies, inherited roots of fear. The homosexual apparently attacks those roots."

Joe takes this in thoughtfully. "Yes, I see what you mean. But after all," he adds, "we are really not attacking the roots, are we? We are quite content to let the trees alone, to flourish each in its own way and form, as long as we are left alone to flourish in our way."

318

"Oh well, like so many metaphors, if you run it into the ground—no pun intended—it suddenly doesn't quite work. People do change. Andrew has, after all, but trees do not. Now I feel confused, as usual."

"We might as well play with images that don't quite work, Harriet, as long as we survive. You are the living proof of that." He is laughing with me now, and it is a good, relieving laugh. Joe himself is startled by it. "When I came in here I would not have thought I could laugh, Harriet. You are a magician."

"Mostly bewildered, as you well know, mostly in the dark, Joe. I wish I could help with Eddie."

"I am the one who needs your help. Invite me for breakfast again, will you?" He is standing, ready to leave, and comes round the table to shake hands, holds my hand hard in his, and then takes me into his arms for a warm hug. "Thank you, dear woman, for being here."

Perhaps, I am thinking, after the door closes behind him, that is all we can do for each other, be available, be here, the door open. That is what Joe does for his patients and what Andrew does for Eddie. In my own awkward way, it is what I do here in the bookstore.

I am startled now by a sharp knock at the door. "It's me." I hear Joe's voice and open it at once. "Halfway to my office I had to come back."

"Sit down, what's on your mind?"

Joe puts his head in his hands and after a moment there is a harsh sob, as harsh as his laughter had been when he first came in for breakfast and talked about Eddie's casual pickups, but when he lifts his head he is himself again.

"Harriet, I had to come back because I realized how unfair to Eddie I was just now—blaming him for getting AIDS as though he had done it on purpose."

"It didn't sound like that to me. Is it possible to come to terms with the plague? You are bitter, but how normal that seems. Why should this happen? How can it happen?"

"I said it happened to Eddie because he went in for brief encounters."

"Yes, you did say you resented that. Why wouldn't you?"

"He is much younger than I am and at that time his needs were different. I accepted that. The trouble is, Harriet, that now I can't accept it." He slaps a fist into his other hand. "I am jealous now as I was not then. And it makes me sick."

"I don't have any answers, Joe."

"I came back to try to tell you what I have again managed to deny. Eddie is the love of my life. Seeing him suffer, being unable to prevent this horrible death, I guess it makes me a little crazy. I guess I came back to tell you I know that, to ask you to pay no attention when I go right off the beam. There is no one except you to whom I can talk at all. Just remember the love when pain obscures it, will you?"

I hesitate to ask, but feel I must. "It would be so easy to run over for a brief visit. Would Eddie like to see me?"

Joe is visibly uncomfortable as he answers. "No. It sounds strange for he admires you, but he doesn't want to be seen. The only visitor, if he can be called merely that, is Andrew. I'm sorry, Harriet." He looks at his watch. "I've got to run. A patient is waiting for me right now, a fellow whose friend died of AIDS two weeks ago."

And this time no goodbye and no hug. He has rushed out, and I hear the car accelerate and roar off.

This is the way my life is these days and the way it will be. One major problem appears to be settled—Rose is leaving town—and then another problem breaks over my head like a huge wave. But it's all right, I say to myself. It's the way things are. It's the real world and I am fully alive in it.